MW01054580

A *the new* rk

cookbook

Fresh and Simple Cuisine from the Pacific Northwest

Chronicle Books • San Francisco

Copyright © 1990 by Jimella Lucas and Nanci Main. All rights reserved. No part of this book may be reproduced in any form without written permission from the publisher.

Printed in the United States of America.

Library of Congress Cataloging in Publication Data
Main, Nanci.
    The new Ark cookbook / Nanci Main & Jimella Lucas.
        p.   cm.
    ISBN 0-87701-698-4
    1. Cookery, American—Pacific Northwest style.   2. Ark Restaurant
(Nahcotta, Wash.)   I. Lucas, Jimella.   II. Title.
TX715.2.P32M35   1990
641.59795—dc20   90-1482
                                                                      CIP

Editing: Carey Charlesworth
Book and cover design: Brenda Rae Eno
Composition: Words & Deeds

Distributed in Canada by Raincoast Books, 112 East Third Avenue,
Vancouver, B.C. V5T 1C8

10 9 8 7 6 5 4 3 2 1

Chronicle Books
275 Fifth Street
San Francisco, California 94103

A wordy dedication
to our wonderful staff,
supportive community,
and clientele.

There's a way of life, traditional in the Northwest, characterized by a fullness of spirit. The people who have come to The Ark express that spirit with particular grace. No matter what form that expression takes, it characterizes them all.

Though some have gone on, we dedicate this book to them all. To them we say, "we salute you and carry you within our hearts."

Table of Contents

Oysters à la Ark

Pan-Fried Oysters with Seasoned Breadcrumbs	64
Oysters Scentiva	66
Oysters Scalloped with Tarragon	68
Oysters Baked in Garlic Cream Sauce with Goat Cheese & Pesto	70
Oysters Baked with Pecans	72
Oysters Baked with Garlic Pine Nut Butter	73
Oysters Baked with Ginger Cranberry Port Sauce	75
Just Oysters	77

Seafood Entrées from the Ark Kitchen

Prawns & Scallops Sautéed with Peaches & Basil	82
Steamed Petrale Sole with Seafood Mousse	83
Sautéed Sturgeon with Wild Mushrooms	85
Salmon with Champagne Chambord Sauce	87
Salmon with Blackberry Hollandaise	88
Scotch Salmon	90
Salmon for Louise	92
Salmon with Tomato-Orange Salsa & Ginger Crème Fraîche	94
Salmon & Seafood Cakes	95
Seafood Frittata	97

More Ark Entrées

Chicken Stuffed with Mushrooms & Spinach	102
Lamb Chops with Green Peppercorn Madeira Sauce	104
Lamb Loin with Apple-Date Stuffing	106
North End Prime Rib of Beef	108
Sweetbreads with Garlic Madeira Sauce	110

Foreword

I have always been fascinated with the quality and the abundance of food in the Northwest. The vegetables and fish are superior and lend themselves so well to fine cooking. The recipes in this book are well researched and easy to follow.

I have personally known Jimella Lucas for many years and have had the opportunity to observe her cooking talents. The Ark restaurant is the result of her efforts as well as those of her dedicated partner, Nanci Main. I compliment them both on their culinary accomplishments.

Pierre Franey

Acknowledgments

For providing crystal for the food photography, we would like to thank Ted and Carol Zell and Zell Bros. Jewelers of Portland, Oregon. For providing accessories and flowers, we thank Peggy Fuller, The Gray Whale Gallery and Gifts of Long Beach, Washington, and Pickety Patch in Seattle.

About the Contributors

Joel Levin, photographer, works from his Capitol Hill studio in Seattle, Washington. He provided both scenic and food photographs for *The New Ark Cookbook*, as well as the back-cover portrait of the chefs.

Elisabeth McPherson of Vancouver, Washington, and Long Beach, Washington, has vacationed on the Long Beach Peninsula since she was a child. A writer and retired teacher and language consultant, she has written historical and regional vignettes for both *The Ark: Cuisine of the Pacific Northwest* and *Bay and Ocean: Ark Restaurant Cuisine*, as well as this new book.

Invitation to the Cook

About six years ago, we started traveling about the country doing cooking classes and special menu presentations. As a native Northwesterner, it never occurred to me that getting salmon, crab, oysters, berries, wild mushrooms, edible wild greens, and a variety of flowers for taste and visual delight would be a problem. It was. We no longer leave town without them.

Having been raised in Northwest farmlands, with majestic orchards of fruits and nuts and plentiful fields of vegetables and berries, I have many memories centering on food: I remember warming my forehead on winter mornings against the cow's belly as I milked her, carrying a pail of steaming milk to the house, then simply pouring the cream over a bowl of rolled oats. And the sweetness of the butter we churned is still unchallenged.

I recall, too, sitting on the cool earth in the middle of a tomato patch in August surrounded by the sharp, acid smell of the plant, rubbing the dried mud off its fruit with my T-shirt for the first bite of the shiny red jewel—its succulent texture, the perfect balance of salt and sugar. I remember spring's sweetness in the Bing cherries followed by the apricots, peaches, and pears.

The pride I felt in harvesting my own little garden and my connectedness with this source of bounty—the Northwest—has grown through the years and has defined the quality that we maintain at The Ark Restaurant. These feelings have expanded past that little plot of land. They now include other products of our backyard: the sweet Pacific oyster, the savory Dungeness crab, the mighty king/Chinook salmon, the Willapa Bay and Columbia River sturgeon, the delectable razor clam, the hard-shell clam, and the wild mushrooms, the patches of wild blackberries.

These last few years have been a time of significant growth, both personally and professionally. We have drawn on this growth in preparing recipes for this book. We have developed an ever-deepening connection with the origins and preparation of the product as well as with the people who contribute all along the way. From the earth to the plate, this new Ark cookbook reflects our growth. We have an abundance here that requires, if we want it to endure, our concern, our attention, and our respect.

Consider this an invitation to let our use of local bounty spur your own search for the best fruits of your corner of the earth.

JIMELLA LUCAS
Nahcotta, Washington
1989

What You Need to Know about Ingredients

At The Ark, where all the recipes in this book were developed and tested, a great deal of experimentation is underlaid by a few sturdy assumptions about ingredients. For the recipes in this book in particular, here are some notes on topics that may come up as you cook.

All ingredients called for, such as chives, parsley, oysters, and lemon juice, are meant to be fresh, unless specified otherwise or (especially when unavailable in other forms, like mace or pickling spices) the measurements clearly indicate dry or packaged forms.

Salt and pepper are often called for "to taste," even though they may be added before the recipe can be tasted in final form. This reflects the need to season many dishes during rather than at the end of cooking and also the tendencies of cooks both to know how much they themselves like and to ignore what anyone else tells them. In general, it's better to undersalt rather than oversalt, as well as to add any salt you use when indicated rather than at other points.

All pepper called for is black, unless otherwise specified. Its flavor always is finer when you grind it fresh, as is specified here where its flavor is especially noticeable.

If an onion or bell pepper is called for and no size is given, size isn't critical to the recipe. (If it is to you, you've begun to make it your own recipe.)

Like amounts of salt, quality of olive oil is a variable that cooks determine according to their own lights. Since olive oil is used in these recipes for the flavor it imparts, use a high-quality virgin oil; where extra virgin is called for, the flavor really stands out in the recipe, so choose accordingly.

About toasting nuts: Distribute nuts evenly on a baking sheet and place in a 425° F oven for 8 to 12 minutes. Check the nuts frequently, agitating and turning them to prevent burning. Trust your nose: The nuts are ready when their fragrance is released, but don't let them burn. (Nuts such as filberts should have skins removed after toasting; rub them between folded layers of a dry towel.)

About toasting wheat germ: Spread wheat germ evenly on a baking sheet and place in a 300° F oven. Check the wheat germ regularly, running a fork through it to prevent burning. Toast for 8 to 12 minutes.

About roasting peppers: Place a whole pepper on an open grill, or extend it by utensil over a gas burner flame. (If these are unavailable, place the pepper in a broiler.) Roast till the skin blisters and blackens evenly. Remove the pepper from the heat and place it in a brown paper bag. Close the bag and let the pepper sweat for 5 to 10 minutes. Then remove its skin, and seed it.

The dishes described in the chapter on oysters could be appetizers or entrées. The notes on numbers of servings cite the chefs' preference in course, if any. The number of oysters to serve per person in all cases depends on the size of the shellfish and the appetites of those you're serving, as well as what you're serving in addition. For an entrée, allow at least six per person.

"Zest" means only the outermost, colored part of citrus fruit. It's to be freshly peeled or grated from the fruit.

To clarify butter, melt it in a pitcher. Let it settle; remove any scum floating on top. Pour off the remaining oil; it will tolerate the high temperatures needed to sauté. Discard the white solids that have settled to the bottom.

To prepare crème fraîche, mix 2 c heavy cream with 2 T buttermilk; cover and let it sit overnight in a warm place. In 12 to 24 hours, it will set to a thick sauce.

Ark Appetizers
& Accompaniments

It Can Be a Touch Damp...

Some days the fog is so heavy you can't see the breakers from the dunes. Some days it's "beach weather"—the air is saturated with water that never seems to fall. Some days the rain drives in from the southwest hard enough to push between the eaves and the walls. Roofers in the area are given to saying, "Oh, you can't fix that leak. It's just the weather." And some years, maybe once in ten, it actually snows.

In between there are brilliant days, with the sky so clear that the sun drops like a great orange ball straight into the sea, and people who watch carefully can see the green flash as the sun slides below the horizon.

Sure, it rains a lot. Average rainfall on the Peninsula is a bit more than fifty inches a year, but that's nothing to the rain forests on the Olympic Peninsula, a hundred miles to the north, where water pours down at the rate of nearly two hundred inches a year.

The weather, as they say, is unpredictable. The television experts are as likely as not to be right— right about half the time, or for about half the day. Rain at nine o'clock, sun at ten, and a drizzle again at noon. The clouds seem to chase across the sky faster than in most places, endlessly fascinating to watch. And as Stewart Holbrook, one of the Far West Corner's greatest admirers, once said, "there are some people who like less glaring sunshine ... who enjoy periods of lowering skies and vagrant mists which lend a touch of mystery to the landscape."

Scallop Cocktail

Yvonne Rothert, former food editor at *The Oregonian*, became a fan of Chefs Main and Lucas long before they opened The Ark Restaurant. She writes, "What has continued to impress me over the years has been the feeling of excitement they have been able to maintain about their work and about their 'product,' as Jimella calls it. This enthusiasm is both obvious and contagious to their clientele—and the 'product' is always dependably delicious, bringing diners back again and again for meals based on fresh ingredients prepared in innovative ways.

"Food buff, bread lover, and dessert freak that I am, I always have found satisfaction—make that delight—at The Ark."

That kind of excitement and sense of experimentation results in such recipes as this one for Scallop Cocktail.

fish stock (note)
bay scallops
peaches
celery
jalapeño pepper
toasted walnuts
chives
strawberry
 vinegar
lemon juice
lime juice
salt
pepper
crème fraîche
 (note)

Bring **4 c fish stock** to a boil; submerge **1 lb fresh bay scallops** for 3 to 5 minutes (*note*). Drain, and set aside.

Peel and dice **1 peach**; reserve some peeled slices from another for garnish.

Toss together drained scallops, the peeled and diced peach, **1 rib celery, finely diced, 1 seeded and finely diced jalapeño pepper, ⅓ c toasted and coarsely chopped walnuts, ½ t minced chives in 3 T strawberry vinegar, 2 T lemon juice, 4 T lime juice,** and **salt** and **freshly ground pepper** to taste.

Top each serving with **1 T crème fraîche** and reserved peach slices.

NOTES AND TIPS:

For the Ark fish stock recipe, see p. 187.

For the Ark crème fraîche recipe, see p. 13.

Be very careful to avoid overcooking scallops. Using a basket or a colander allows you to remove the scallops quickly from the poaching liquid.

Serves: 8 to 12

Tucked among the tall beach grasses that cover the dunes, the summer visitor can find wild strawberry blossoms, the tiny blue and white beach lupine, and most elusive of all, the round yellow heads of sand verbena, with its distinctive scent of lemon, spice, and salty sand.

Smoked Salmon Rosettes on Dill Croutons

Sid and Bette Snyder of Long Beach, Washington, have long been fans of Chefs Main and Lucas. The family's parties in Olympia during Sid Snyder's tenure in the State Legislature annually included a dinner catered by The Ark, which featured such specialities as this smoked salmon appetizer.

cream cheese

Mascarpone
  cheese

garlic cloves

chives

parsley

Dijon mustard

lemon juice

Tabasco

toasted pine
  nuts (note)

smoked salmon

dill bread (note)

dill butter
  (note)

Mix well **8 oz cream cheese, 3 oz Mascarpone, 1 t minced garlic, ½ t minced chives, ½ t chopped parsley, 1 t Dijon mustard, 1 T fresh lemon juice,** and **⅛ t Tabasco.**

Stir in **½ c toasted, chopped pine nuts.** Set aside.

Make the rosettes. Cut thin slices of about **½ lb smoked salmon** into 24 1-inch-wide strips. Lay out the strips of salmon; with a blunt knife, spread a thin layer of the cheese mixture over each. Roll one end of each strip tightly to form a "bud." Hold it firmly, then wrap the rest of the slice around the bud (tight at the bottom and open at the top) to form the petals of the rosette. (If strips are short, you may need more than one.)

Repeat with remaining slices. Cover, refrigerate.

Slice **dill bread** ¼ inch thick; cut slices into rounds with a cookie cutter. Spread with **dill butter.** Place on baking sheets. Bake in a 300° F oven till crisp and lightly browned.

When croutons have cooled, top each with a rosette. Serve at room temperature.

NOTES AND TIPS:

For how to toast pine nuts, see p. 12.

For an Ark dill bread recipe, see p. 39.

For Ark dill butter, see p. 177.

Oven Temperature: 300° F

Yield: 24 appetizers. This is rich and salty; it's safe to plan 2 per person.

Knappton, on the road between Naselle and the river, was once the site of a flourishing cement factory and a sawmill. When the sawmill burned in 1942, the settlement disappeared. Now nothing is left but rotten pilings—and stories told by old-timers.

Salmon Rosettes with Pine Nut Duxelles & Lemon Dill Sauce

This recipe is prepared in three easy steps. Prepare the duxelles and Lemon Dill Sauce beforehand: They are not complicated or difficult, but the salmon cooks so briefly they need to be ready before it's begun. If you also form the rosettes ahead, they'll hold their shape better. Final preparation then becomes a simple matter of assembly.

Step 1: Prepare the Lemon Dill Sauce

fish stock (note)
lemon juice
orange juice
white wine
salt
pepper
cornstarch
fresh dill

In a stock pot, reduce by one-quarter **3 c fish stock**, ⅓ **c lemon juice**, ⅓ **c orange juice**, ¼ **c white wine**, and **salt** and **pepper to taste**.

Mix **2 T cornstarch** in ½ c fish stock. Stir this into the reduced mixture.

Pass the sauce through a fine sieve. Add **2 T minced fresh dill** and set aside.

Yield: 3 ½ cups sauce

Step 2: Prepare the Pine Nut Duxelles

mushrooms
clarified butter (note)
garlic
toasted pine nuts (note)
cognac
powdered sugar
cream cheese
salt
pepper

This is Chef Lucas' version of a classic French food made generally popular with the development of the food processor. It's a wonderful treat: try the duxelles with other dishes as well.

In a food processor, blend **2 c chopped mushrooms** till superfine.

Heat **6 T clarified butter** in a sauté pan. Add the mushrooms and **1 T minced garlic**. Cook till juices are gone. Add ¾ **c toasted pine nuts**.

With this mixture still in the pan, deglaze with ⅓ **c cognac**. Add **2 T powdered sugar**; reduce for 2 to 3 minutes.

Add **3 oz cream cheese** and **salt** and **pepper to taste**; remove from heat. Mix the cream cheese in thoroughly. Let duxelles cool before using.

Yield: 3 c duxelles

Step 3: Assemble the Salmon Rosettes

duxelles
salmon
white wine
Lemon Dill Sauce
fresh dill
dill flowers

For each serving, spread **duxelles** on **2 thin (preferably a bit thicker than lox) slices of salmon**. Roll the salmon slices into rosettes; secure each with a wooden toothpick at the bottom (*note*).

Place rosettes in a small casserole with **3 T white wine**, and bake at 450° F for 5 to 6 minutes.

On each plate, pour ¼ c **Lemon Dill Sauce**. Place 2 rosettes on sauce, and garnish with **fresh dill** and **dill flowers**.

Oven Temperature: 450° F

NOTES AND TIPS:

For the Ark fish stock recipe, see p. 187.

For how to clarify butter, see p. 13.

For how to toast pine nuts, see p. 12.

For more details on the salmon rosette method, see p. 20.

Extra duxelles may be frozen for future use.

Yield: Sauce is sufficient for 14 servings; duxelles, for about 50 rosettes (25 servings).

Caponata

Chef Lucas says that this is "a recipe of my heritage that undergoes some minute changes to fit the bill for The Ark's Garlic Festival." Serve it as an appetizer.

eggplant
olive oil
onion
garlic
tomatoes
tomato paste
salt
sugar
red wine
 vinegar
capers
celery
pepper
olives (note)

Wash, peel, and cube **4 eggplants**. (You'll have approximately 3 qt of raw cubes.) Salt the cubes, and after one hour, drain them. Wipe them dry; deep fry in **olive oil**. Drain on paper towels.

Sauté **1 sliced onion** and **1 T minced garlic** in ½ c **olive oil**.

Stir in ½ **c chopped fresh tomatoes** and **3 oz tomato paste**. Season with **salt** to taste. Cook for 10 minutes over moderate heat.

Add **4 t sugar, 1 ½ c red wine vinegar, 2 to 3 T capers, ½ bunch celery, chopped, pepper to taste**, and the eggplant. Simmer for 15 minutes.

Add ½ **c chopped olives**. Let cool to room temperature, and refrigerate.

Serve chilled.

Serves: 6 to 8

NOTES AND TIPS:

Chef Lucas suggests: "Use Sicilian green or Greek black olives, or both. The Italian ones don't have garlic!"

If properly refrigerated, the caponata will keep for up to a month.

Khachapuri

Chef Main brought home this recipe for Khachapuri ("ha'-cha-poor'-ee") from her trip to the Soviet Union. "My three-week sojourn in the Soviet Union as a culinary diplomat taught me much about the Soviet people and Soviet food. Khachapuri is a cross between cheese bread and pizza. I watched it being made in Moscow and in that wonderful region of Georgia.

"We ate it warm from the ovens, and as Americans and Soviets made appreciative sounds I realized, as I did hundreds of times over on my 'peace table' journey, that we are, after all, very much the same.

"This is my interpretation of the recipe using available cheeses. My special request is that when you serve it, think of peace between our two countries."

Step 1: Make the Dough

butter
eggs
buttermilk
all-purpose
flour
cardamom
baking soda

Melt ¼ c **butter.** Stir it with **2 eggs** into **1 c buttermilk.**

Combine **3 ½ c flour** and **½ t cardamom.** Add this to the liquid mixture slowly, stirring just till it makes a dough that doesn't stick to your hands.

On a floured surface, roll out the dough, dusting the rolling pin often; make a rectangle about 18 x 12 inches.

Sprinkle ¼ t **baking soda** over the dough. Fold it in thirds, covering the baking soda, and turn the rectangle 90°. Roll it out to 18 x 12 inches and again sprinkle ¼ t **baking soda** over dough. Fold into rectangle.

Wrap and chill the dough for an hour.

Step 2: Make the Filling

Feta cheese
Gruyère cheese
Mozzarella
 cheese
egg
Tabasco
parsley

Coarsely grate about **4 oz Feta,** about ½ c (*note*); **4 oz Gruyère,** about ½ c; and **8 oz Mozzarella,** about 1 c, into a large bowl. Reserve ½ c cheese mixture for the top.

Break an egg and work it into the cheese with your hand. Add a **dash of Tabasco** and a **sprinkle of fresh parsley**.

Step 3: Assemble the Dish

dough
filling
egg
water

Lightly grease a 9 x 13 inch baking pan.

Divide the dough and reserve one-quarter of the dough. Roll out the large part of dough to fit into the baking pan, pushing dough an inch or so up the sides.

Spread all but the reserved filling mixture evenly over dough in pan.

Roll remaining dough into a rectangle to fit over top of dough in pan. Pinch to seal. Brush top with egg wash made from **1 egg beaten** with **1 t water**.

Sprinkle with the reserved cheese mixture.

Bake at 375° F for 45 minutes.

NOTES AND TIPS:

If the cheese is too salty, grate a boiled potato or two along with it. Feta tends to be on the salty side, depending on how it's made. Kasseri cheese can be used as an alternative. It adds the sharp bite that the filling needs. Basically, use one cheese that is sharp and another that melts.

Oven Temperature: 375° F

Yield: 10 to 12 servings

The Ilwaco Heritage Museum in the southernmost community on the Peninsula contains Indian artifacts, exhibits showing how local industries developed, relics of shipwrecks, a glimpse of the changing life of the area, and most fascinating of all, a working model of the old narrow gauge railroad that ran up the Peninsula in the first part of this century.

ark appetizers and accompaniments

Pan-Fried Lobster Mushrooms

Lobster mushrooms have a firm and meaty texture. They have that subtle richness of earth flavor that allows them to complement perfectly garlic's boldness and cognac's tangy tones.

eggs
buttermilk
Madeira
lobster
 mushrooms
all-purpose
 flour
seasoned
 breadcrumbs
 (note)
butter
garlic
lemon juice
cognac
chicken stock
 (note)
parsley

Make an egg wash, by mixing **3 beaten eggs** with ½ c **buttermilk** and ¼ c **Madeira**.

Brush clean and cut in ¼-inch slices **1 lb lobster mushrooms**.

Dust slices in **flour**; shake off excess. Place mushroom slices in egg wash; let rest 2 to 3 minutes. Coat generously with **seasoned breadcrumbs** by patting the crumbs on firmly.

Heat **6 T butter** in a large sauté skillet and add the mushroom slices; brown and turn. Add ¼ t **minced garlic** and **1 T fresh lemon juice**.

Without removing ingredients from the pan, deglaze it with **3 T cognac**. Add ¼ c **chicken stock**, and reduce the liquid by half. Remove the mushrooms in their liquid to a serving platter. Garnish with **lemon wedges** and **parsley**.

NOTES AND TIPS:

For the Ark chicken stock recipe, see p. 186.

For the Ark seasoned breadcrumb recipe, see p. 64.

Serves: 4 as appetizer

Spicy Cole Slaw

Spicy cole slaw is a perfect side dish with steamed clams, sturgeon, fish and chips, and other white fish. Or try it with a fried oyster sandwich.

Napa cabbage
(note)
butter
toasted sesame
oil
fresh ginger
root
garlic
red pepper
flakes
sake
rice wine
vinegar
brown sugar
Dijon mustard
mayonnaise

Shred **1 small head cabbage** into a mixing bowl.

Over low heat, combine **2 T butter** and **4 T toasted sesame oil** in a sauté pan. Stir in **1 ½ T freshly grated ginger root, 1 T minced garlic,** and **⅛ t red pepper flakes**. In a few minutes, when flavors have had a chance to mature, turn up the heat and stir in **½ c rice wine vinegar**. When it has begun to reduce, finish with **2 T sake**; let it cook only about 1 more minute, or till the alcohol cooks off.

Pour mixture over cabbage.

Mix together **2 T brown sugar, 1 oz Dijon mustard,** and **1 c mayonnaise,** and toss well with cabbage mixture.

Before serving, allow slaw to sit for 2 to 3 hours at cool room temperature.

NOTES AND TIPS:

Other cabbages work well also.

Yield: 8 to 12 servings

Poinsettia Salad with Ginger Lime Crème Fraîche

This recipe goes back years to Chef Lucas' days as an apprentice at the Waverly Country Club in Portland, when she fed 150 "sassy" ladies an early version of the Poinsettia. Since then this salad has evolved into part of the traditional Ark Thanksgiving dinner menu.

Step 1: Make the Ginger Lime Crème Fraîche

lime juice
fresh ginger root
crème fraîche
  (note)

Add **3 to 4 T lime juice** and **1 t grated fresh ginger root** to **2 c crème fraîche**.

Step 2: Compose the Poinsettia Salad

Texas pink
  grapefruit
pomegranates
Bibb lettuce
fresh mint
  sprigs

Skin and remove membrane from **4 large grapefruit**; cut the sections in wedges lengthwise. Clean the yellow pulp from **2 medium pomegranates**; set aside the seeds.

Arrange **Bibb lettuce leaves** on a plate; shred more of the lettuce and make a little mound in the center. Arrange the grapefruit sections around the mound; sprinkle the pomegranate seeds over the mound so they trickle down its sides.

Drizzle Ginger Lime Crème Fraîche over the fruit, but don't cover it completely.

Garnish the plate with several sprigs of **mint leaves** around the seeds. Serve.

NOTES AND TIPS:

For the Ark crème fraîche recipe, see p. 13.

Serves: 6

Scallop Tortilla Soup

Chef Lucas comments: "This soup was inspired in San Diego as I was being entertained in the gracious home of Martha and John Culbertson during a Northwest presentation for a 'Gala Gourmet Event' to benefit the March of Dimes. Martha served a Tortilla Soup that was simply elegant. It stayed in my mind and taste buds so clearly that I finally produced this variation. The Culbertsons are involved in making wine and produce one of California's leading champagnes as well."

olive oil	Clean and roast (*note*) in **3 to 4 T olive oil** the fresh peppers: **3 Pablano peppers, 2 Seranos,** and **1 Anaheim.**
Pablano peppers	
Serano peppers	
Anaheim peppers	In a food processor, finely chop **4 tomatoes, 1 small onion, 4 cloves garlic,** and the **roasted peppers.** Transfer to a saucepan.
tomatoes	
onion	Add **6 T corn oil;** cook to thicken the mixture. Add **4 qt chicken stock** and **3 T tomato paste.** Cook 20 to 25 minutes.
garlic	
corn oil	
cilantro	Add **3 T chopped cilantro** before removing from heat.
chicken stock (note)	
tomato paste	In a second saucepan, bring to a boil **1 qt water, the juice of 1 lemon** plus **its rind,** and **1 c white wine.** Poach in this **1 lb sea scallops,** 3 to 4 minutes.
water	
lemon	
white wine	
sea scallops (note)	While the stock mixture reheats (if necessary), cut **tortillas** in thin strips; fry them in oil, and dry on paper towels.
corn tortillas	To assemble the soup, cut the sea scallops in halves or quarters. Divide the scallops and tortillas among serving bowls. Ladle in the stock mixture and garnish the tops with **crème fraîche,** thin slices of **avocado,** and sprinklings of chopped **cinnamon sticks.**
crème fraîche (note)	
avocado	
cinnamon sticks	

NOTES AND TIPS:

When you prepare the chicken stock (see p. 186 for the Ark recipe), add a bunch of cilantro and a couple of sticks of cinnamon, which heighten and complement the flavors of the soup. Since the soup is a clear one, also cool the stock and thoroughly skim the fat. Then return the stock to the pot and heat to the boiling point, for use.

For the Ark crème fraîche recipe, see p. 13.

For how to roast peppers, see p. 13.

You can use the smaller bay scallops and you needn't halve them. Poach them half as long or less.

Serves: 8 to 10

Ark Bakery Treats

The Great River of the West

There were rumors of a mighty river in the west for years before any white man found it. Not until May 1792, when the American Capt. Robert Gray managed to cross the treacherous bar and bring his ship, *The Columbia*, into the river, were European-Americans sure that it actually existed. In October of the same year, the British Lt. William Broughton, commanding a ship in Capt. George Vancouver's fleet, got even farther up the river. The Columbia, or the "Oregan," as the natives of the region called it, had a new place in Western history.

The great river that cut its way through the Cascade Mountains thousands of years ago has always held a fascination for Americans, even those who have never seen it. Nearly one hundred seventy years ago a young New Englander, three thousand miles to the east, wrote about "the continuous woods where rolls the Oregon and hears no sound save its own dashings."

Things have changed since 1821. The great river has a new name, the Columbia. The woods are no longer continuous. Cities line the river banks, and between them, bald strips of bare mountain are more frequent than the second-growth timber planted here and there. The river no longer rolls free from its source 750 miles high in the British Columbia mountains. Since the 1930s its dashings have been tamed by the numerous hydroelectric dams, from the Grand Coulee to Bonneville, that furnish power to the Pacific Northwest and beyond.

Where once it was crossed only by the mythical Bridge of the Gods—the great stone arch that, legend tells us, tumbled into the river to save an eloping Indian maiden from pursuit—it is now spanned by numerous bridges carrying railroad trains and automobiles.

Below Bonneville, for more than a hundred miles, the Columbia is a tidal river. Even so, its swift current carries more water per second than any other river in North America. It's still "the great river of the West."

Northwest Ale Bread

The Pacific Northwest is home to a burgeoning microbrewery industry. From ales to stouts, the beers of Washington and Oregon are palate pleasers.

Ballard Bitter
Ale (note)
farina cereal
(note)
butter
salt
molasses
honey
yeast
water
all-purpose
flour
toasted wheat
germ (note)
rolled oats
whole wheat
flour
hazelnuts
egg
sesame seeds
(optional)
poppy seeds
(optional)

In a 2-quart saucepan, bring **2 cups flat ale** to steaming. Stir in ½ c **farina**, ¼ c **butter**, **1 t salt**, ¼ c **molasses**, and ¼ c **honey**. Set aside to cool.

Dissolve **2 cakes (1 oz) fresh** or **2 T dry yeast** in ½ c **warm water** (at 90° F). Stir in ¼ c **all-purpose flour** to make a sponge. After 10 minutes it should become foamy (*note*).

Put beer mixture in a large mixing bowl. Stir in yeast. Add ½ c **lightly toasted wheat germ**, ½ c **rolled oats**, **2 c whole wheat flour**, ½ c **finely chopped hazelnuts**, and **1 c all-purpose flour**. Beat till smooth.

Add **3 to 3 ¼ c all-purpose flour** gradually to make a stiff dough.

Knead dough till smooth and satiny (about 15 minutes). Place it in a greased bowl, turning dough to coat completely.

Proof dough in a draft-free spot about 1 hour, or till doubled.

Punch dough down and divide in half. Shape into round balls and place on a greased baking sheet sprinkled with cornmeal, or form into 2 loaves and put in greased bread pans.

Cover and let double.

Using a sharp floured knife, make four ½-inch slashes across loaves. Gently brush them with an egg wash of **1 egg** beaten with **1 t water**. Sprinkle with **sesame seeds** and **poppy seeds**.

Bake at 350° F for 35 to 40 minutes, till loaves are browned and a tap with fingers brings a hollow sound.

NOTES AND TIPS :

Substitute any favorite medium ale for the Ballard Bitters.

Substitute cornmeal for farina, if desired.

For how to toast wheat germ, see p. 12.

If your yeast does not foam, it is not active. Best to try again with new yeast.

As with any whole-grained bread, keep Northwest Ale Bread well wrapped to prevent dryness.

To freeze loaves, wrap in foil.

Oven Temperature: 350° F

Yield: 2 loaves

Dill Bread

Not only is this an excellent bread, the recipe produces distinctive dinner rolls as well. Often the tantalizing smell of baking dill bread greets Ark diners walking in the front door. All yearnings are satisfied when dill rolls arrive at the table wrapped in a napkin, nestled in a basket.

yeast
water
all-purpose flour
milk
butter
sugar
salt
Tabasco
garlic
Dijon mustard
eggs
fresh dill

Dissolve **1 cake (½ oz) fresh** or **1 T dry yeast** in ½ c **warm water** (90° F). Stir in ¼ c **flour** and set aside in a warm, draft-free spot for 10 minutes. The yeast sponge will "work" and become foamy.

Meanwhile, bring ⅔ c **milk** just to a boil, remove from heat, and stir in ¼ c **butter**, ⅓ c **sugar**, ¾ t **salt**, a **dash of Tabasco**, **2 t minced garlic**, and **1 T Dijon mustard**. Stir to combine; set aside till it becomes lukewarm.

Combine the proofed sponge with **2 eggs**, lightly beaten. Stir in the lukewarm milk mixture, and gradually add **5 c flour** and **3 T finely chopped fresh dill**.

Knead the dough till smooth, add flour if still sticky, and place in a large, greased bowl, turning dough to coat. Cover and set aside in a draft-free spot to rise till doubled in bulk (about 1 hour).

After the first rising, punch down the dough, turn it out onto a lightly floured board, and shape into two loaves. Place the loaves in greased baking pans and allow to rise for 30 minutes or till doubled in size.

Brush the loaves with an egg wash made of **1 egg** beaten with **1 t water**. Bake for 30 minutes in a preheated 350° F oven, till the bread is golden brown. Wait 5 minutes, then remove from pans. Cool on a rack.

NOTES AND TIPS:

For a different loaf, make the rolls and then fit 9 into each greased loaf pan. Fit 2 rows of 3 side by side on the bottom of the pan and the remaining 3 rolls down the center on top.

Oven Temperature: 350° F

Yield: 2 loaves or 18 dinner rolls

One of the earliest "towns" in Pacific County, Pacific City, was from the beginning mostly a mirage. In about 1850, a man named White platted and sold lots near present-day Ilwaco in what he claimed was "a metropolis designed to rival San Francisco." By 1852, seventy-five disillusioned people occupied his fake city. When that same year the government took over the land for a military reservation, the settlers were forced to move.

Brioche

You probably won't have any leftovers if you follow this brioche recipe and serve the brioches warm with butter, but if you plan ahead and make extra, follow Chef Main's suggestion. "This makes the ultimate French toast. We serve it with real maple syrup and whipped butter at Sunday brunch."

sugar *yeast* *milk*	Place **6 T sugar** and **3 cakes (1 ½ oz) fresh** or **3 T dry yeast** in **1 c warm milk** (90° F). Whip to dissolve.
salt *eggs*	Mix in **¾ t salt** and **3 beaten eggs**. Add **¼ lb softened butter** and **5 c flour**.
butter *all-purpose flour*	Knead for 10 minutes with an electric mixer (or 15 minutes by hand: *note*), till dough is shiny, satiny, and smooth. Add flour if necessary.
water	Place dough in a greased bowl, turn dough to coat, and cover with plastic wrap. Let rise in a warm place till doubled, 1 to 1 ½ hours.

Divide dough into 15 to 18 equal rolls. Place in well-greased muffin tins or fluted brioche pans (*note*). Alternatively, divide dough in half, shape the loaves as for bread loaves, and put in loaf pans.

Proof the rolls for 30 minutes or till not quite doubled in size. After 15 minutes, brush with an egg wash made of **1 egg** and **1 t water** (*note*).

Bake at 400° F for 20 to 30 minutes. When brioches begin to brown, brush quickly with the same egg wash.

NOTES AND TIPS:

When kneading, lift dough high and throw it vigorously onto the work table. This helps develop the dough and produces its smooth and satiny texture.

For classic brioche *à tète*, see directions p. 45.

Take care that no egg wash drips down inside pans, since it will cause rolls to stick.

Oven Temperature: 400° F

Yield: 15 to 18 brioches or 2 loaves brioche

Szechwan Brioche

An insight into Chef Main's culinary creative process:

"I'm thinking of fun ways to combine garlic and so I start an inventory of foods and flavors I particularly love. I start combining not only the flavors but also the possibilities of ethnic sources.

"I love the excitement of Szechwan food: a physical sensation, as well as a taste zap, and I regard brioche as the most sensual dough of all.

"I think of the butter and the texture. Then I think of how rich and spicy elements could mix. They could move in a taste progression: from sweet to crunch to butter to hot. Plus it could be pretty with red, green, and copper.

"The sensual pleasures of the dough, now developed, go from the beginning to the end. When I walk into the bakery, I can put my nose in the air and follow the flavor waves as it proofs and bakes. Punching this dough on the first proof gives an incredible aroma; it fills the room with scents even before it begins to bake.

"There are still many people not really familiar with brioche: lots of folks hesitate even to pronounce it. But I have a great time just talking to them about the ingredients, rolling my eyes, getting them excited over a brand new discovery in their mouths.

"At the 1988 Garlic Festival Dinner, I made this bread into the shape of foot-high garlic bulbs with green onion tops for the fronds (*note*). When the breads were presented to the diners, there erupted a standing ovation from 160 garlic lovers."

There is a warning accompanying this recipe: Don't rub your eyes! The red peppers may affect any sensitive body parts they touch.

sugar	Combine ⅓ **c sugar**, ¾ **t salt,** and **1 c milk** in a
salt	saucepan. Place over low heat; stir to dissolve
milk	sugar and salt. Remove from heat; transfer to a
	bowl. Let cool to 90° F.

yeast

eggs

fresh ginger
  root (note)

garlic

toasted sesame
  oil

red pepper
  flakes

butter

peanuts

green onions

all-purpose
  flour

Stir in **2 cakes (1 oz) fresh yeast** or **2 T dry** till dissolved.

In a separate bowl, mix **3 beaten eggs, 1 T minced fresh ginger root, 2 T minced garlic, 3 T toasted sesame oil**, and **2 t red pepper flakes**.

Add egg mixture and ¼ **lb well-softened butter** to milk mixture.

Add ¾ c **chopped peanuts** and ½ c **finely chopped green onions**.

Beating continuously, slowly add **5 c all-purpose flour**.

Either using a dough hook or beating vigorously, knead about 10 minutes, till dough is developed: It will be smooth and elastic with a shiny skin. Add flour if needed.

Place dough in a greased bowl, turn dough to coat, and cover with plastic wrap. Let rise in a warm place 1 to 1 ½ hours, till doubled.

Punch dough; divide in half. Cover and chill (*note*) till it can be shaped comfortably. The amount of butter in this dough can make it slippery to handle if the weather is warm or it has been in a bit too much heat.

Form dough into standard loaves, or make classic brioche *à tête* (*note*).

Place dough in well-greased loaf pans or fluted brioche pans. (You can substitute muffin tins for the latter.) This will yield 2 brioche loaves or about 8 small brioches. Cover; let dough rise till not quite doubled, about 30 to 45 minutes.

Brush gently with an egg wash of **1 egg beaten**

with **1 t water** (be careful not to drip wash inside pans).

Bake at 350° F for 35 to 45 minutes (*note*). When bread begins to brown, remove. Quickly brush on egg wash once again (*note*). Return to oven for 5 minutes. When brioche is done, a tap produces a hollow sound.

NOTES AND TIPS:

You need *fresh* ginger root; powdered ginger gives inferior flavor in this recipe.

To make garlic bulbs, divide dough in half. Divide each half into 5 equal parts. Roll each part into a 12-inch "log," tapered on one end and rounded on the other like an elongated pear. Lay 5 of these next to each other on a cooking-parchment-lined baking sheet and pinch the large part of the pears together to form the bottom of one bulb. Two-thirds of the way up, pinch the 5 pears together to form the neck of the bulb. Repeat with the other half of dough. Proof and bake. The bulbs will have flat backs and have the garlic shape in front. Just before serving, cut about 6 long green onion tops and fit 3 into the top of each bulb, using a paring knife to poke them in. Let your guests pull the bread apart with their best tools—their hands.

You can freeze the punched, unshaped dough, wrapped in foil, rather than chill it. Then unwrap but cover it and thaw it slowly in the cooler; allow for long proofing.

The classic brioche *à tête* has the little topknot

atop the muffin-shaped bun. To produce this, first flour your hands and pinch off a quarter of one of the halves of the dough; roll it into 8 pear-shaped balls. Then roll the remaining dough into 8 larger balls. Poke your finger into the center of each and make a deep indentation; insert a pear-shaped ball, smaller end down.

If the topknot browns too rapidly, cover it loosely with foil.

The second brushing with egg wash gives brioche crust its characteristic deep gold finish. Work quickly and glaze with a light touch so the egg doesn't cook on the crust and take away the shine you are trying to achieve.

Oven Temperature: 350° F

Yield: 2 1 ½ lb loaves or 8 brioches *à tête*

Tsunami Muffins

In April of 1989, as a part of its Centennial celebration, the State of Washington sponsored a 505-mile road race from the eastern border to the Coast. Running the race were more than a hundred teams from around the world. Each team had ten runners; each runner was required to run between 5 and 10 miles per day. Margo Maier, a baker at The Ark, ran—in fact, she was cocaptain on the team named the Long Beach Tsunami.

Since the race ended at Cape Disappointment, just a few miles from The Ark, the Tsunami was, in a way, the home team. Naturally, as the race drew nearer the excitement of the runners intensified, Margo's included. Her liveliness stirred enthusiasm in Chef Main, who turned her own esprit into creativity. As a result the Tsunami was powered to a second-place finish by Tsunami muffins. Happily, a five-hundred-mile race is not a requirement for eating these luscious muffins.

bran	Soak **1 c bran** in a mixture of **1 c buttermilk, ⅓ c pineapple juice, 1 t finely grated orange zest,** and **⅔ c honey** for 15 minutes.
buttermilk	
pineapple juice	
finely grated orange zest	Stir in **1 egg, 3 T melted butter,** and **1 t vanilla.**
Tupelo honey (note)	Chop in ½-inch pieces **1 ripe medium-sized banana.** Peel, core, and chop an **apple** till you have ½ c. Chop **1 c walnuts, ⅓ c dried apricots,** and **½ c dates.** Combine these chopped fruits and nuts with **½ c coconut, ½ c raisins,** and **¼ c cransins or fresh cranberries.**
egg	
butter	
vanilla	
banana	Combine **2 c flour, 4 ½ t baking powder, 1 t salt, 1 t cinnamon,** and **½ t nutmeg.**
apple	
walnuts	Toss the fruit and nut mixture in the dry ingredients till coated.
apricots	
dates	Stir the dry mixture into the liquid ingredients just till combined.
coconut	

raisins

cransins/
  cranberries
  (note)
all-purpose
  flour
baking powder
salt
cinnamon
nutmeg

Fill lined muffin cups three-quarters full.

Bake 20 minutes at 400° F.

NOTES AND TIPS:

Tupelo is the Mercedes of honey. It comes from the Everglades, where the bees buzz in places people cannot go. It is the most floral of honeys—one of Chef Main's friends says it tastes the way you imagine perfume would taste. If you're lucky enough to find it, use it for special occasions and special purposes—like Tsunami muffins.

An offshoot from the local cranberry industry, cransins are dried cranberries that look like reddish raisins but carry the wonderful cranberry flavor.

Oven Temperature: 400° F

Yield: 24 muffins

Cranberry Sticky Buns

Candy Glenn of Seaview, Washington, claims that she and husband Frank "haven't missed a family birthday or anniversary at The Ark since Nanci and Jimella have had the restaurant."

The Glenns operate one of the Long Beach Peninsula's cranberry farms, growing those rich red berries that Chef Main enjoys building recipes around.

Step 1: Make the Sweet Dough

yeast
milk
sugar

Soften **2 cakes (1 oz) fresh** or **2 T dry yeast** in ⅔ c **warm milk** (90° F). Add **4 T sugar** and stir to dissolve.

salt
eggs
butter
flour
mace

Once the yeast has bloomed, stir in ½ **t salt, 2 eggs, 6 T softened butter, 3 ½ c flour,** and **1 t mace.** Knead for 10 minutes, lifting the dough high and throwing it vigorously onto the work table to develop its smooth, satiny texture. (Just think of something you want to get out of your system, and beat it out on the dough.) Add flour as needed.

Place the dough in a greased bowl, turn dough to coat, and cover with plastic wrap. Let rise in a draft-free spot till doubled.

Step 2: Make the Filling and Topping

walnuts
pecans

Combine **1 c chopped walnuts** and **1 c chopped pecans.** Reserve half.

sugar
cinnamon
nutmeg
cranberries
butter

Mix together ½ **c sugar, 2 t cinnamon,** ¼ t **nutmeg,** ½ **c coarsely chopped cranberries,** and 1 c of the walnut-pecan mix.

Spread ¾ **c softened butter** in a 9 x 13 inch baking pan.

brown sugar
vanilla
grated lemon
  zest

Combine ½ c **brown sugar, 1 t vanilla,** and ½ t **grated lemon zest.** Sprinkle evenly over butter.

Step 3: Make the Buns

Roll the dough into a rectangle 12 x 18 inches. Brush rectangle with **2 T melted butter.** Sprinkle the filling evenly over the dough, leaving a 1-inch border at the top of the rectangle. Roll it up jelly roll style, pinching at each end.

Cut the roll into 12 even pieces (cut roll in half, then cut each half into 6 even pieces) like pin-wheels. Lay the pinwheel circles in the pan with the nicest side facing down, 4 across and 3 down, equidistant from each other (*note*). Cover and proof till almost doubled. (Dough will feel slightly spongy when pressed.)

Bake at 350° F for 30 to 35 minutes, till tops are light brown and sugar is bubbling up between rolls.

Remove pan from oven, wait 5 minutes, and invert onto a baking sheet (*note*).

NOTES AND TIPS:

When you have arranged the buns for proofing, the pan can be wrapped in foil and frozen or put in the refrigerator to retard the rising time. When you defrost, allow extra time for the chill to leave the dough.

Be sure to wear heavy mitts when removing the buns from the oven—the hot sugar can give a nasty burn.

Oven Temperature: 350° F
Yield: 12 buns

Native cranberries were a staple of the Peninsula Indians' diet, and they made part of Lewis and Clark's Thanksgiving dinner in 1805. The climate of the area proved ideal for cultivation of the cranberry, the necessary bogs already in place, and in about 1890 cranberry vines were imported from Cape Cod and commercial growing began. At the turn of the century, Indians harvested the berries by hand. Nobody had to send for them; when it was time for the harvest, the Indians simply showed up. Now there are about 465 acres of operating cranberry bogs on the Peninsula, producing twelve thousand pounds of fruit an acre.

Apple Cranberry Bread with Lemon Brandy Spread

Chef Main's Swedish heritage comes forcefully through whenever she gets her hands on cardamom. It adds that special something to this honey-colored loaf with a mosaic of cranberries, apples, and walnuts.

Step 1: Make the Bread

butter

sugar

eggs

vanilla

almond extract

all-purpose

 flour

baking soda

salt

cardamom

orange juice

apple

walnuts

cranberries

Cream ½ c **softened butter** till whitened. Add **1 c sugar** gradually. Add **2 eggs**, one at a time, scraping bowl after each addition. Add **1 t vanilla** and ½ **t almond extract**.

Sift together **2 c flour, 1 t baking soda,** ½ **t salt**, and **1 t cardamom**.

Add the dry ingredients to the creamed mixture alternately with ⅓ **c orange juice**.

Fold in **1 c peeled, cored, and coarsely chopped apple,** ½ **c coarsely chopped walnuts,** and ½ **c chopped cranberries**.

Spread the batter into a 9 x 5 inch loaf pan that you've lightly greased and lined on the bottom and long sides with cooking parchment to facilitate removal of the loaf after baking. Gently tap the pan on a counter to remove air pockets.

Bake 50 to 60 minutes at 350° F, till a toothpick comes out clean.

Cool 10 minutes in the pan, then remove from pan to finish cooling.

Step 2: Make the Spread

cream cheese

powdered sugar

Whip **8 oz softened cream cheese,** using an electric mixer. Add **2 T powdered sugar, 1 T grated lemon zest, 1 T lemon juice,** and **1 T**

grated lemon
zest
lemon juice
brandy

brandy, scraping the bowl while mixing.

To serve, slice Apple Cranberry Bread. Using a pastry bag with a star tip, pipe cheese diagonally across each slice. Garnish with a walnut half.

NOTES AND TIPS:

"This is an excellent holiday bread. It freezes well and goes well with coffee—the Swedish transfusion, as it's known in my family," according to Chef Main.

Oven Temperature: 350° F

Yield: 1 loaf

Since 1923, the Washington State University Extension Station at the north end of the town of Long Beach has conducted research on several improved varieties of cranberries. In their forty acres of test bogs, university researchers have experimented with fertilizer, discovered that frost can be defeated by overhead sprinkling, and introduced beehives for better pollination.

Comfort Cookies

These cookies are moist, chewy, crunchy, chocolaty—all qualities that give comfort to a cookie *aficionado.*

baking soda *baking powder* *salt*	Sift together **1 t baking soda, 1 t baking powder, 1 t salt, 2 c flour, ½ t nutmeg, 1 t cinnamon,** and **1 t mace.**
all-purpose * flour* *nutmeg*	Cream **1 c butter** till whitened; gradually add **1 c sugar** and **1 c brown sugar.** Beat till no longer grainy.
cinnamon *mace*	Add to the creamed ingredients **2 t vanilla,** and **2 eggs** one at a time.
butter *sugar*	Add the dry-ingredients mixture in three stages. Add **3 c old-fashioned rolled oats** (*note*).
brown sugar *vanilla* *eggs* *rolled oats*	Mix in **1 c peeled, cored, and diced apples, 3 c chopped walnuts,** and **1 c chocolate chips.** Fold in **½ c coarsely chopped cranberries.** Chill the dough.
apples *walnuts*	Shape dough into walnut-sized balls; on a baking sheet, flatten them with your hand.
chocolate chips *cranberries*	Bake at 350° F for 15 minutes.
	These cookies will be soft while warm—let them rest a bit on the baking sheet and then transfer to a rack.

NOTES AND TIPS:

Be sure to use old-fashioned oats; quick-cooking oats just won't work.

Oven Temperature: 350° F

Yield: 2 ½ dozen cookies

Italian Pocket Cookies

"My Italian partner," says Chef Main, "has the unsettling habit of reaching into her uniform jacket pocket at unpredictable intervals and pulling out a cookie that she has stashed for backup. Reflecting upon the discomfort a melted chocolate chip or crumbly oatmeal cookie could cause in a warm pocket, I decided to create a traveling cookie that would suit her needs—an all-occasion cookie that would travel in style from bakery to kitchen to office. A variation of biscotti, the Italian pocket cookie fits the bill."

butter
sugar
eggs
vanilla
almond extract
all-purpose
  flour
baking powder
salt
whole blanched
  almonds
whole candied
  cherries

Preheat oven to 350° F.

Using an electric mixer, cream **1 c softened butter** at medium speed till it whitens. Beat in **1 ¾ c sugar** slowly. Add **3 room-temperature eggs**, one at a time, scraping the bowl after each addition. Add **2 t vanilla** and **2 t almond extract**.

Sift together **4 c flour, 1 t baking powder**, and ¼ t **salt**. Add the flour mixture to the creamed mixture gradually, scraping down the sides of the bowl as necessary. The dough should be stiff; add extra flour if necessary.

Beat in, at low speed, **1 c whole blanched almonds** and **1 c whole candied cherries**. Beat just enough for the dough to turn a light pink and the cherries to break up a bit.

Line an 18 x 12 inch baking sheet with cooking parchment. Form the dough into a log 12 inches long and about 2 ½ inches high. Bake at 350° F for about 40 minutes, till log is a light golden brown and a toothpick inserted in the center comes out clean. (The log will have spread out to about 8 inches wide and 14 inches long.) Remove and cool.

Slice the log crosswise into 1-inch-wide strips.

(There will be approximately 14.) Slice the strips in half crosswise, doubling the number of cookies. Lay these on a baking sheet and toast each side lightly at 350° F for 3 to 5 minutes. Store in an airtight container.

NOTES AND TIPS:

Coffee, wine, and Italian chefs are complemented by this confection.

Oven Temperature: 350° F

Yield: 28 cookies

Molasses Ginger Cookies

This recipe is a favorite of Chef Main's from her mother, Margaret Main. The chef says, "I've added fresh ginger to give the feel as well as the taste of the spices as they interplay. These cookies stay moist and chewy and are always ready for that all-American cookie sidekick—an ice-cold glass of milk."

butter
sugar
dark molasses
eggs
fresh ginger
  root
all-purpose
  flour
baking soda
cinnamon
dry ground
  ginger
cloves
salt

Over low heat in a heavy-bottomed saucepan, melt **1 ½ c butter, 2 c sugar**, and **½ c dark molasses**. Bring the heat up to medium. Using a whisk, stir till ingredients form a thick, caramel-colored syrup. Cool to lukewarm in a mixing bowl, stirring occasionally.

Mix in **2 eggs**, incorporating each completely. Add **2 T minced fresh ginger root**.

Sift together **4 c all-purpose flour, 1 t baking soda, 1 T cinnamon, 1 t ginger, 2 t cloves**, and **1 t salt**. Add this to the liquid ingredients. Make sure batter is fully mixed. Chill it.

Roll chilled batter into balls the size of walnuts. Roll each in sugar and place on a cooking-parchment-lined baking sheet. Flatten cookies slightly with the palm of your hand.

Bake at 350° F for 10 to 12 minutes.

Oven Temperature: 350° F

Yield: 2 dozen cookies

Shortbread Nut Cookies

So, it's been a rough day and your grandma's nowhere in sight. Bake up a batch of these shortbread nut cookies, stack a plate high with some just cooled from the oven, and pour yourself a big glass of cold milk. Then imagine that you're sitting on the lap of that gray-haired granny from all the picture books. You're leaning into her welcoming arms, head nestled against the crinkle of a starched linen apron, being rocked to sleep on a winter afternoon.

butter	Cream ¾ **c butter** till it whitens. Gradually add
sugar	**1 c sugar** and ¼ c **brown sugar**. Add **1 c peanut**
brown sugar	**butter,** ½ t **vanilla,** and **2 eggs,** one at a time,
peanut butter	scraping the sides of the bowl as necessary.
vanilla	Mix in **2 ½ c all-purpose flour,** ¾ t **baking soda,**
eggs	and ¼ t **salt.** Stir this into the butter mixture till
all-purpose	combined.
flour	Stir in ½ c **chopped walnuts,** ½ c **chopped**
baking soda	**hazelnuts,** and ½ c **chopped pecans.** Shape the
salt	dough into a log, and chill it.
walnuts	Cut the chilled log into slices. Place them on a
hazelnuts	cooking-parchment-lined baking sheet.
pecans	Bake at 350° F for 8 to 10 minutes. Remove and
	cool till firm. Store in airtight container.

Oven Temperature: 350° F

Yield: 1 ½ dozen cookies

Sourdough Pumpkin Spice Cookies

"Little Old Nahcotta" has come a long way since its early days as terminus for the rail line from Megler. No longer do the steamers head out for South Bend across the bay, but folks still travel quite a way to sit down to a dinner at The Ark. And many Ark fans finish their stay with a stop by the bakery for "just a few" cookies for the drive home.

butter
brown sugar
vanilla
egg
sourdough
 starter
pumpkin purée
all-purpose
 flour
baking powder
salt
cinnamon
nutmeg
ginger
walnuts
chocolate chips

Cream ¼ c **softened butter** and ½ c **brown sugar** till light. Add **1 t vanilla, 1 egg, ½ c sourdough starter** (*note*), and **½ c pumpkin purée.**

Sift together **1 c flour, 2 t baking powder, ½ t salt, 2 t cinnamon, ½ t nutmeg,** and ¼ t **ginger.**

Gradually add dry ingredients to butter mixture, scraping bowl twice.

Stir in **1 c coarsely chopped walnuts** and ¾ c **chocolate chips.**

Drop the dough by tablespoonfuls on a cooking-parchment-lined baking sheet. Flatten them slightly. Bake 10 to 12 minutes at 350° F.

Store in an airtight container.

NOTES AND TIPS:

Do not use canned pumpkin pie filling. Use canned pumpkin, or fresh pumpkin that you have cooked and drained.

Chef Main says "I have a hundred-year-old starter that I use in the restaurant. Only trusted bakers such as Margo and Peggy are allowed to handle it. If you are not lucky enough to have

your own venerable starter, you can make a new
one overnight."
To make a sourdough starter, use a wooden
spoon to stir **1 T dry yeast** in ½ **c warm water**
(90°) till it dissolves. In a glass or pottery bowl,
stir **2 c all-purpose flour** into **1 ½ c water** with a
whisk. Add the yeast. Cover with plastic wrap.
Let it work in a warm, draft-free place (about 85°
F) overnight. (Many people use the heat from
their oven pilot light as a good place to develop a
starter.) Now it's ready to use.
Store your starter, still covered, in a refrigerator,
with holes punched in the plastic wrap that will
allow the gases to escape.

Keeping the starter takes a bit of attention. Once a
week, add equal parts of flour and water and let it
sit out, covered, overnight. Stir it occasionally
when it is in the refrigerator, and don't worry
about any clear liquid that appears. Just stir it
back in. If the starter seems to become less active,
stir in a little dry yeast. Always avoid metal
touching your starter because it will affect the
taste and purity.

Oven Temperature: 350° F

Yield: 2 ½ dozen cookies

Oysters à la Ark

A Climax Forest

Diners at The Ark can look out the eastern
windows to Long Island, an uninhabited six miles
of land in the southern half of Willapa Bay.

The area, named for its length, has no land access
from the mainland. Hikers, birdwatchers, and
hunters who want to try their skill with bow and
arrow in season must provide their own water
borne transportation. At one time the scene of a
heavy oyster harvest, the island's major
commercial activity in recent years has been
logging.

Much of the timber has been cut, but one of the
island's most interesting features has escaped the
chain saw. Long Island is home to a unique stand
of old-growth red cedars, now protected by
federal law. The 274-acre grove is one of the last
remaining reproducing climax forests that
appeared during a dramatic climate change on
the West Coast four thousand years ago. The
cedars that stand in the grove are huge, from 5 to
11 feet in diameter and more than 160 feet tall.

The climax forest is worth a visit, but visiting it is
not easy. The visitor must find a boat, make the
mile-long trip across the bay, and hike two and a
half miles along the main road, keeping a careful
eye out for the logging trucks that may be sharing
the road. Visitors are on their own. There are no
telephones, no first aid stations, no grocery stores,
and there's no way to call for help.

But it's worth the trouble and risk. Where else can
you see a living climax forest?

Pan-Fried Oysters with Seasoned Breadcrumbs

Nanci Main and Jimella Lucas own their restaurant in every sense of the word, and since they love the area and its richness, The Ark reflects the location adamantly, even vehemently. This little spit of land, stuck out into the ocean right where the Columbia joins it, scintillates with wild berries and mushrooms. Salmon at The Ark do not come from the market; they come from the people who catch them. The herbs come to Chef Lucas' hand from the garden outside the restaurant's window. Radiccio? From the garden. Crab? From the ocean nearby. Berries? From the woman who outwits the local bears to pick them. And oysters, of course, from the people who grow them in the Willapa Bay.

seasoned breadcrumbs (note)	Set out **1 recipe of seasoned breadcrumbs** on a baking sheet. Mix an egg wash of **4 beaten eggs** and **1 c milk**. Set aside.
oysters eggs milk flour olive oil clarified butter (note)	Gently rinse **1 pt to 1 qt oysters** with cold water, to remove nectar. Drain in a colander for about 5 minutes. From this point, prepare the oysters 6 at a time.
	Heat ½ **c olive oil** and ⅓ **c clarified butter** in a skillet till hot, but not smoking.
	Lightly dust **6 oysters** in **flour**, then put them into the egg wash. Remove them with a slotted spoon or skimmer. Let the excess wash drain off, then add the oysters to the seasoned breadcrumbs and coat generously.
	Pan-fry oysters 4 to 5 minutes, turning at least once; do not overcook.

NOTES AND TIPS:

To prepare seasoned breadcrumbs, combine 3 to 4 c bread chunks from a day-old baguette and ½ c

parsley in a food processor. Mix till coarse.
Remove to a bowl, and toss with 2 T minced
garlic and a pinch of cayenne.

For how to clarify butter, see p. 13.

Chef Lucas can't say it too strongly: "To overcook
the oyster is a *cardinal* sin."

Serves: As entrée, 1 pt serves at least 3 diners.

*Lewis and
Clark left St. Louis in
May 1804, on their
famous Western journey
with a party of twenty-
seven men. On November
7, 1805, they recorded in
their Journals: "Great
joy in camp we are in
view of the Ocian, this
great Pacific Octean
which we been so long
anxious to See, and the
roreing or noise made by
the waves brakeing on
the rockey Shores (as I
suppose) may be heard
distinctly."*

Oysters Scentiva

Where else would you find an oyster named like this? Perhaps only at an Ark Garlic Festival Dinner, as in 1988, second course.

oysters	Shuck **12 extra small Pacific oysters**; set aside. Save the shells.
red onion	
zucchini	Chop enough **red onion** to make about **2 T.**
carrot	Julienne enough **zucchini and carrots to make about 2 T of each.** Steam each separately; cool in an ice water bath.
lemon	
garlic	
anchovy fillets	Mix the vegetables. Add **2 T lemon juice** and **½ t minced garlic**; toss. Set aside to marinate.
butter	
rock salt	Purée in a food processor (adding the ingredients in this order) **3 T minced garlic, 2 anchovy fillets,** and the **juice of ½ lemon.** With the processor running, slowly add **½ lb softened butter.** Remove and fold with a spatula just to ensure even consistency.
garlic béchamel	
sauce (note)	
seasoned	
breadcrumbs	
(note)	
Parmesan	Spread a layer of **rock salt** in a baking dish (*note*), and press the shells partway into it.
cheese	

Place a nugget of garlic-anchovy butter in each shell. Distribute the julienne-cut vegetables, and place an oyster in each shell. Top each with **1 T garlic béchamel** and a sprinkle of both **seasoned breadcrumbs** and grated **Parmesan cheese.**

Bake for 8 to 10 minutes (*note*) at 425° F.

NOTES AND TIPS:

The butter for these oysters can be used for a variety of dishes. Try it on toast to make garlic-anchovy toast. Use it as a topping for vegetables—such as spinach or broccoli or baked potatoes.

For the Ark garlic béchamel recipe, see p. 178.

For the Ark seasoned breadcrumbs recipe, see p. 64.

The rock salt does three things: it looks good in contrast, it sets the oysters firmly, and it conducts the heat more thoroughly.

Cooking time for this dish may vary, because the cream sauce acts as protection for the oysters. To brown the sauce and heat the oysters properly may take as long as 15 minutes. They're done when the sauce is browned.

Oven Temperature: 425° F

Serves: 3 to 4 as appetizer; 2 as entrée

Oysters Scalloped with Tarragon

A snapshot of the oyster shells piled two stories high at the west end of the restaurant parking lot has become one of the comfortable cliches associated with a visit to The Ark. The size of the pile depends on the time of year, since the shells aren't just dumped and abandoned there but stored for bagging and a return to the bay for each year's new seeding. In their first stages of development the microscopic oysters must attach to something in order to grow; what better medium (called cultch) than old oyster shells.

oysters	Shuck and drain **12 oysters**, and put them aside.
butter	Sauté, in ¼ c **clarified butter**, ¾ c **sliced mushrooms, 1 t minced garlic**, and **1 t minced shallot**. Add **1 good shot Tabasco, 1 T fresh French tarragon** (*note*), and **salt and pepper to taste.** Add ¼ t **flour;** work this in well.
mushrooms	
(note)	
garlic	
shallot	
Tabasco	Quickly add the **12 drained oysters** and the **white and green ends of 2 green onions, chopped.**
fresh French	
tarragon	
salt	Without removing the oysters from the pan, deglaze it with **3 T sherry.** Add ⅓ c **heavy cream** and remove from heat.
pepper	
flour	With a slotted spoon, remove the pan's contents to a casserole dish, then cover with the sauce from the pan. Sprinkle with ¾ c **freshly shredded Kasseri cheese.** Sprinkle generously with **seasoned breadcrumbs.**
green onions	
sherry	
heavy cream	
Kasseri cheese	
(note)	
seasoned	Bake in a 450° F oven for 10 to 12 minutes, till bubbling around the edges and golden brown.
breadcrumbs	
(note)	

NOTES AND TIPS:

Wild mushrooms are wonderful here, but domestic button mushrooms do just fine.

Sharp cheddar cheese will do, also.

For the Ark seasoned breadcrumb recipe, see p. 64.

To substitute dry tarragon, use 1 t.

Oven Temperature: 450° F

Serves: 2 as entrée

Perhaps the loveliest remnant of a town that appeared and vanished from the southwestern Washington Coast was built in Diamond City, on Long Island. For more than twenty years, beginning in 1867, oyster-gathering families lived where Indians had camped for generations. When the native oysters grew scarce, in the eighties, the settlers made themselves scarce too. Now the only remaining record of the town on the island is a large white house on Sandridge Road, on the mainland, moved by barge.

Oysters Baked in Garlic Cream Sauce with Goat Cheese & Pesto

The Garlic Festival, for which this recipe manifestly qualifies, has become an Ark tradition. So have some of the dinner guests: Martha J. Logan of Portland is one such. "My friends and I had followed Nanci and Jimella's cooking career since staying at the Shelburne, and I looked forward to my first Garlic Festival after their acquisition of The Ark. The live music, street dancing, crafts, competitions, and food booths sounded like a lot of fun, topped off by feasting far into the evening.

"Because I had to work that particular Saturday, I ended up missing the afternoon festivities but was under the (mistaken) impression that the costume contest, which appealed to me, would take place during dinner. So that was how the queue ended up with seventy-five people in silk dresses or suits, and me—dressed as a pig (the *pièce de résistance* being the baby-bottle nipples pinned down the front of my oversized pink T-shirt). Tourists asked to take my picture. Nanci spotted me from inside and mouthed an exclamation, causing various heads to pop up at all the kitchen windows. I smiled weakly from behind my large rubber nose.

"I'm happy to relate though that, once inside, employees dressed as giant heads of garlic put me at ease, and in later years I spotted Lady Godiva and belly dancers there, so to future guests of The Ark— wear what you will, as long as it's large."

oysters rock salt clarified butter (note)	Shuck **24 to 36 Pacific oysters**. Set them in shells on a layer of **rock salt** in a baking pan, and set the pan aside.
garlic shallots flour	In a saucepan with **¼ to ⅓ c clarified butter**, cook **3 to 4 T minced garlic** and **1 T minced shallots** till tender. Add **4 T flour** and continue cooking 2 to 3 minutes, stirring frequently.
milk salt pepper	Add **1 ½ c milk**; reduce heat (*note*). Add a **pinch of salt,** and **pepper** to taste. Cook 5 to 6 minutes, or till sauce reaches a medium thickness. Remove from heat.

*mild goat
cheese
pesto
Parmesan
cheese*

Whisk in **4 oz mild goat cheese**. Set aside.

Lightly lace each oyster with **brandy** (*note*). Place 1 to 1 ½ T of garlic sauce over each oyster and ⅛ **t pesto** in the center. Sprinkle with freshly grated **Parmesan cheese**.

Bake for 8 to 10 minutes at 425° F.

NOTES AND TIPS:

For how to clarify butter, see p. 13.

Be especially watchful when adding milk: do not allow to boil or scorch.

The brandy is optional.

Oven Temperature: 425° F

Serves: 10 to 12 as appetizer

Oysters Baked with Pecans

Oysters abound in the waters of Willapa Bay, and The Ark Restaurant has always meant oysters—long before it was taken over by Chefs Main and Lucas. But now, with the national availability of seafood, a dish like this one is possible even for those who don't have the time for a trip to the southwest coast of Washington.

Pacific oysters (note)
rock salt
brandy
heavy cream
Parmesan cheese
Gruyère cheese
toasted pecans (note)
Dijon mustard
salt
pepper

Shuck **24 oysters**. Embed their bottom shells in a layer of **rock salt** in a baking pan; return oysters to shells and lace each with a little **brandy**.

Mix well in a small bowl **2 c whipped heavy cream, ½ c freshly grated Parmesan, and ½ c freshly grated Gruyère.**

Fold in **½ c finely chopped toasted pecans** and **2 T Dijon mustard;** add **salt and pepper to taste.**

Top each oyster with the mixture.

Bake in a 375° F oven for 10 minutes, or till browned.

NOTES AND TIPS:

Pacific oysters are small, so adjust the quantity if you plan to substitute another kind.

For how to toast nuts, see p. 12.

Oven Temperature: 375° F

Serves: 6 as appetizer; 4 as entrée

Oysters Baked with Garlic Pine Nut Butter

Bivalve specialist Rich Bohn of Hollywood, Maryland, spent two years in Nahcotta at the oyster research station there. "My favorite memories of The Ark are tied together by a common thread—Table 16. Ever since the carved wooden booths were placed near the fireplace, I've claimed one as my own. The view of Willapa Bay is without parallel: waves breaking against the rock jetty, blue herons talking through the marsh grass, the old-growth forests of Long Island in the distance. The light of the salmon boats, navigating their gillnets through the channels in the dark. I'll never forget any of them. The privacy of the booth has been the site of many celebrations; I fondly remember birthdays, anniversaries, and the rekindling of old friendships. Being perched near the kitchen door, I could usually expect Nanci or Jimella to drop by, and it was only a few steps to the bar for an after-dinner coffee. I have, on occasion, even delayed my dinner to wait until the booth became available. It was always worth the wait."

shallots
garlic
toasted pine
  nuts (note)
parsley
chives
lemon
brandy
pepper
butter
oysters
rock salt

In a blender or food processor, blend **3 shallots, 6 cloves garlic, ½ c toasted pine nuts, ¼ c coarsely chopped parsley, ¼ c coarsely chopped chives, the juice of 1 lemon, 2 T brandy,** and **2 t freshly ground pepper.** Add **1 ½ c softened butter,** slowly. Be careful to achieve a smooth compound butter that still shows tiny bits of the ingredients.

Preheat oven to 375° F.

Shuck **36 oysters**, retaining bottom shells and juices. Place oysters, on their bottom shells, on a bed of **rock salt** in a baking pan or shallow, ovenproof serving dishes.

Distribute the compound butter over oysters.

Heat in oven till butter has melted and oysters have firmed up a bit, 10 to 12 minutes. Garnish with toasted pine nuts.

NOTES AND TIPS:

For how to toast pine nuts, see p. 12.

Oven Temperature: 375° F

Serves: 10 to 12 as appetizer; 6 as entrée

Visitors to the Lewis and Clark Interpretive Center can admire the glittering prisms of the magnificent Fresnel lantern that served first in France, then at the Cape Disappointment lighthouse, and finally at North Head, till it was displaced by a modern automatic light.

Oysters Baked with Ginger Cranberry Port Sauce

Once again, Chef Lucas draws on the local bounty to create a new entrée. "With that connectedness to the origin, there's a simplicity that helps you address the sensual basics of preparation and presentation, the composition of things: the flavors, the colors, the textures, and the visual identity. Dazzle the eyes and develop the hunger." And next thing, a dish like Oysters Baked with Ginger Cranberry Port Sauce.

oysters	Wash and shuck **24 extra small Pacific oysters.** Rinse them and set them aside. Save the shells.
butter	
fresh ginger root	Mix **¼ lb softened butter** with **2 T ground fresh ginger root,** and set aside.
cranberries	Cook **2 c whole cranberries,** **½ c port,** the **juice of**
port (note)	**½ lemon, ¼ t raspberry vinegar,** and **2 T brown**
lemon	**sugar** over high heat till the mixture reduces by half.
raspberry vinegar	
brown sugar	In a food processor, purée the cranberry mixture. Pass it through a fine sieve.
rock salt	Lay enough **rock salt** on an ovenproof platter to
toasted walnuts	stabilize 24 oyster shells.

Put a nugget (⅛ to ¼ t) of ginger butter on each oyster shell. Place an oyster in each shell.

Spoon about 1 T cranberry port sauce over each oyster.

Bake at 450° F for no more than 8 to 10 minutes, and garnish with toasted walnuts (*note*).

NOTES AND TIPS:

Chef Lucas uses Ficklin port.

If oysters are especially small, reduce cooking time.

Occasionally Chef Lucas adds finely chopped toasted walnuts to the oysters right before putting them in the oven, instead of as garnish.

Oven Temperature: 450° F

Serves: 4 as entrée

Just Oysters

This recipe from Chef Lucas asks you to be the chef and create your own oyster specialty.

oysters
other things

Chef Lucas tells you how to do it.

"Well, here we go again.

"More oysters, and why not?

"We certainly have an edge on them in my neighborhood. To a person who loves them or a person open enough to get past their texture, oysters have their own personality. Whether you're sitting in the mudflats cracking them open with a pocketknife or enjoying the salty sea smell in a gorgeous market display, oysters incite a hunger in your eyes long before your stomach gets the message. To develop hunger in the eyes is an important element in creativity that fits perfectly with what I'm going to suggest next.

"The oyster goddess has just stopped by with 2 dozen still-dripping-bay-water oysters in the shell. Naturally their perfection dazzles your eyes. As you look around the kitchen, come up with 3 ripe tomatoes, 4 green onions, a bunch of cilantro, 3 jalapeño peppers, 3 limes, 2 lemons, a small seeded (of course) cucumber, 3 cloves of garlic, extra virgin olive oil, and some ground cumin.

"How would you prepare these ingredients to complement the oysters? That's your job. What would you name the presentation? Let us know."

Notes

Seafood Entrées from the Ark Kitchen

Whale Watching

Perched on a high promontory—North Head is a good place—patient observers can see gray whales moving south in the winter and returning in the spring. Beginning in December and lasting till early February, the whales head for their breeding grounds off the Mexican shore. Then in March and April they return to their home in the Arctic. Adult males and immature young are the first to go north in the spring; females with calves are still passing the Peninsula in May.

Early morning on a calm overcast day provides the best watching time. A bright, sunny day produces too much glare, and wind makes too many whitecaps. Successful watchers first spot a blow, the water or vapor a whale throws up in the air as it breathes. Where there is one blow, there will be others, perhaps from the same whale, more likely from other whales traveling with it. During the migration, a whale usually has a regular pattern, five or six short shallow dives before a deeper, longer one that lasts from three to ten minutes. Watchers who concentrate on the turbulent eddies left after a whale has dived are usually rewarded by finding a blow or two in that same area.

It's unusual to see whales leaping clear out of the water, but the heads and backs will show, often in groups of several whales together. Even a glimpse of these great mammals spouting, however, can provide a thrill unavailable to those who know them only in books and pictures.

Prawns & Scallops Sautéed with Peaches & Basil

Anna Johnson Ward first heard of The Ark from local watercolorist Charles Mulvey. From her home in San Diego, she had traveled to the Northwest for a class with Mulvey, and thus she made her way to the restaurant. "I ate my first chanterelles there. Now when I'm going to be there I call ahead to make sure my favorite things are available."

This dish gives Ms. Ward another new way to enjoy her chanterelles.

prawns *scallops* *all-purpose* *flour* *clarified butter* *(note)* *chanterelle* *mushrooms* *garlic* *shallot* *basil* *Dijon mustard* *lemon* *peach vinegar* *(note)* *peaches* *fish stock (note)* *heavy cream* *anisette*	Dust **3 prawns** and **3 to 4 scallops** lightly in flour. Sauté the prawns lightly in **¼ c clarified butter**. Then add the scallops with **½ c sliced chanterelles, ½ t minced garlic, ½ t minced shallot,** and **1 T chopped fresh basil,** and cook about 2 minutes more. Add **1 t Dijon mustard, the juice of ½ lemon, 1 T peach vinegar, 4 narrow wedges of fresh peaches (preferably Yakimas), 3 T fish stock, and ¼ c heavy cream**. Add **2 T anisette**. Reduce, cooking for about 2 minutes more, since the scallops should cook for no more than 4 minutes.

NOTES AND TIPS :

For how to clarify butter, see p. 13.

If peach vinegar is unavailable, you may substitute ½ T peach brandy and ½ T cider vinegar.

For the Ark fish stock recipe, see p. 187.

Serves: 1

Steamed Petrale Sole with Seafood Mousse

When you explore the Peninsula, where you can't get more than a mile away from the Pacific, you walk to the tune of the ocean, a tune that accompanies you no matter where you walk. Notice the strange hue in the air here caused by the foliage—more blue in the green than anywhere else. Feel the air near the relentlessly pounding ocean—the air that many find so healing, so comforting.

And complete your day at The Ark, tasting the rich bounty of that ocean.

rockfish or lingcod (note)
salmon
bay or sea scallops
garlic
shallot
heavy cream
salt
white pepper
eggs
petrale sole
Roasted Garlic–Prawn Sauce

Mix together no more than **2 c rockfish (or lingcod) pieces, salmon pieces, and bay or quartered sea scallops**. Set aside.

In a food processor, pulse **1 t minced garlic** and **½ t minced shallot**. With the machine running, add the seafood, a little at a time. Add **¾ c heavy cream** to the mix, and turn off machine. Add **salt and white pepper to taste**.

With machine running once again, add **2 eggs**, one at a time.

Remove mousse mixture from processor bowl and let stand in refrigerator 1 to 2 hours.

Select **4 5-oz fillets of petrale sole**. Place 1 to 2 T of the seafood mousse in the center of each fillet and fold the fillet around it.

Steam for 8 to 10 minutes.

Serve topped with Roasted Garlic–Prawn Sauce (*note*).

NOTES AND TIPS:

Chef Lucas uses rockfish or lingcod in the mousse, depending on availability.

For Roasted Garlic–Prawn Sauce, see p. 179.

Seafood Mousse may also be used as a stuffing for salmon fillets or wrapped in blanched spinach leaves and steamed.

Bake the extra Seafood Mousse in a terrine for about 10 minutes at 375° F and serve as an appetizer.

Serves: 4, with extra mousse

Sautéed Sturgeon with Wild Mushrooms

The coastal regions of the Pacific Northwest abound in wild mushrooms, among them chanterelles, wild turkey mushrooms, lobster mushrooms, those called King Bolete, and running hedgehogs. As with seafood "catch of the day," mushrooms don't pop up to order. The chefs must wait and see what's available and respond with a dish that highlights the particular features of each day's harvest. Sautéed Sturgeon with Wild Mushrooms is one such delicacy.

sturgeon
all-purpose flour
clarified butter (note)
wild mushrooms (note)
garlic
shallot
Dijon mustard
Tabasco
lemon juice
salt
pepper
brandy
fish stock (note)
heavy cream
Madeira

Dust **2 6-oz fillets of sturgeon** lightly with **flour**. In a large sauté pan, heat **¼ to ⅓ c clarified butter** to medium hot. Pan-fry the first side till light brown; turn over.

Add **½ c sliced wild mushrooms, 1 t minced garlic, 1 t minced shallot, 1 t Dijon mustard, 1 dash Tabasco, 2 to 3 T lemon juice**, and **salt and pepper to taste**. Cook till garlic loses its sting and fish is nearing done.

With the fillets still in the pan, deglaze with a **round of brandy** (*note*). Add **2 to 3 T fish stock** and ⅓ c **heavy cream**. Reduce briefly, then add **2 to 3 T of Madeira** and reduce by about one-half.

Check the texture of the fillet and consistency, flavor, and color of sauce. Serve when the fish is slightly springy to the touch and the sauce has a rich brown color.

NOTES AND TIPS:

For how to clarify butter, see p. 13.

Chef Lucas prefers chanterelle mushrooms, but any wild mushrooms will do just fine.

For the Ark fish stock recipe, see p. 187.

A "round" is a quick pour around the pan's outside perimeter, away from and back to the handle—about ¼ c.

Serves: 2

At the Lewis and Clark Interpretive Center, perched high on the cliff where a coastal defense post once stood, visitors can travel the eight thousand miles of that famous Western journey. Moving down the curving ramps, one can see huge photographs of the country the explorers passed through, explained by actual extracts from the journals. Kids are reassured by the originality of Lewis and Clark's spelling and charmed by the tiny figures of the explorers on the lower level, including Sacajawea with her papoose, her French interpreter husband, and the black man York. The figures can be made to speak by pushing a button.

Salmon with Champagne Chambord Sauce

It's a cool, clear autumn evening and the calendar promises a full moon. Go early for your dinner reservation and spend a little time in the lounge before your table is ready. Order champagne and Willapa Bay oysters on the half-shell—and watch the moon rise crisp and bright over the hills beyond the bay. Toast its silver gleam on the water as the tide rises to cover the grass and oyster beds.

And when you're ready for dinner, order Salmon with Champagne Chambord Sauce.

salmon
all-purpose flour
clarified butter (note)
shallot
fresh ginger root
raspberry vinegar
lime juice
champagne
fish stock (note)
heavy cream
Chambord (note)
raspberries
Candied Lime Zest (note)

Dust **1 5-oz salmon fillet** lightly in **flour**. Shake to remove any excess flour.

In a sauté pan, heat **4 T clarified butter** and add fillet. When you turn it, add ½ **t minced shallot** and ½ **t minced ginger.**

With the fillet still in the pan, deglaze with **2 T raspberry vinegar, 3 T lime juice,** and ½ c **champagne.**

Add **2 T fish stock** and ¼ c **heavy cream**. Reduce till thickened.

Finish with **2 to 3 T Chambord,** cooking only until alcohol evaporates, just a minute or two.

Garnish with whole **fresh raspberries** and **Candied Lime Zest** (*note*).

NOTES AND TIPS:

For how to clarify butter, see p. 13.

For the Ark fish stock recipe, see p. 187.

Chambord is a raspberry liquor.

For Candied Lime Zest recipe, see p. 185.

Serves: 1

Salmon with Blackberry Hollandaise

"I've got to meet these two ladies," is what David Apple—the self-proclaimed "crazy weatherman" from Portland—thought when he heard they were going to be at his TV studio. "I'm an amateur chef and we had the rapport of food people. It was instant love." A few months later he had a chance to visit the restaurant and the Long Beach Peninsula. "What an inspiration, discovering a whole area. And two of the most charming people in the world."

For most, it's still the food that attracts people to The Ark's way with the Northwest's particular bounty; dishes such as this, which combines local fruits and seafood.

blackberries
Dijon mustard
garlic
shallot
lemons
Madeira
hollandaise
* sauce (note)*
fresh mint
white wine
fresh mint sprig
fish stock (note)
salmon fillets
mint or borage
* flowers*

In a small saucepan, bring to a boil and reduce by about one-fourth **2 c blackberries, 1 t Dijon mustard, ½ t minced garlic, ½ t minced shallot,** the **juice of 1 lemon,** and **3 T Madeira**. Stir often to keep from scorching. Purée in a food processor; pass through a fine sieve.

Set aside one-quarter of the reduction for garnish. Fold the remaining reduction into a **4-egg hollandaise**.

In a fresh saucepan (*note*), add a quartered **lemon** and a **mint sprig** to **2 c white wine** and **3 c fish stock**, and bring to a boil; reduce to a simmer. Using a spatula, carefully place **4 6-oz salmon fillets** in the saucepan. Poach for 8 to 10 minutes. Remove fillets with the spatula so that they retain their shape.

On each plate, spoon some Blackberry Hollandaise in the center, then drizzle a thin circular line of reserved purée. Lightly draw the back of a spoon across it, making a scallop effect toward the outside of the plate. Place a salmon fillet in the circle and garnish with mint flowers or borage flowers and 3 to 5 whole blackberries.

NOTES AND TIPS:

For the Ark hollandaise recipe, see p. 182.

If you have a fish poacher, use it in place of the saucepan.

For the Ark fish stock recipe, see p. 187.

Serves: 4

On the Long Beach Peninsula, this narrow spit of land bordered by the ocean and the bay, flowering shrubs abound, from the ever-present Scotch broom to the imported gorse, whose seeds can survive for more than twenty-five years. There's the deep pink blossom of the salmonberry, the paler pink of the wild rose, the tiny white clusters of salal, the big flattish nosegays of the blue elder, the white plumes of ocean spray, and the rich pink plumes of hardhack that smell like peaches.

Scotch Salmon

Even if you don't have fresh spring-run Chinook for this dish, you'll find yourself sold on this preparation for salmon. A regular menu item at The Ark for one season, it became one of Chef Lucas' most popular salmon dishes and might well become your favorite too.

salmon
clarified butter
  (note)
salt
white pepper
garlic
shallot
Dijon mustard
brown sugar
raspberry
  vinegar
Scotch
orange juice
heavy cream
Drambuie
crème fraîche
  (note)
Candied
  Orange Zest
  (note)

Dust a **6- to 7-oz salmon fillet** lightly in flour. In a sauté pan, heat **2 T clarified butter** and brown the fillet slightly on one side. Add **salt and white pepper to taste**. Turn fillet over.

Add **½ t minced garlic, ½ t minced shallot, ¼ t Dijon mustard,** and **¼ t brown sugar.**

After the ingredients cook for a few seconds, add **1 T raspberry vinegar**. By now, the second side of the fillet will have browned slightly.

With the fillet still in the pan, deglaze it with a **round of scotch—about ¼ c** (*note*). Add **¼ c orange juice**. Move pan in a circular motion so ingredients marry.

Reduce sauce till it begins to thicken. Finish with **¼ c heavy cream** and a **round of Drambuie— about 3 T.**

Garnish with crème fraîche and **Candied Orange Zest.**

NOTES AND TIPS:

For how to clarify butter, see p. 13.

For crème fraîche recipe, see p. 13.

For Candied Orange Zest recipe, see p. 185.

A round is a quick pour around the outside perimeter of the pan, starting and finishing at the handle.

Serves: 1

Perhaps the most spectacular of the local flora is the white devil's club, a perennial herb that often grows more than six feet tall, with deeply cut leaves more than a foot wide. More properly known as cow parsnip, devil's club gets its common name from the big, bent fistlike bulge that precedes its flowering. And unlike many plants that bloom and disintegrate, devil's club turns brown and stays erect, still standing when its seed produces next year's plant.

Salmon for Louise

At The Ark, occasions or guests often inspire new recipes. This recipe came from the visit of the mother of one of The Ark's friends. Chef Lucas recalls: "This was a special presentation, for a dear woman who came to dinner wearing a smile radiant with sweetness and excitement."

salmon
all-purpose
flour
clarified butter
(note)
garlic
shallot
red Christy
peppers (note)
cilantro
chanterelle
mushrooms
dry sherry
fish stock (note)
cream
Madeira
crème fraîche
(note)
cilantro

Dust **2 6-oz fillets of salmon** with **flour**. Shake off excess flour.

In a sauté pan, heat ¼ c **clarified butter**. Add fillets, and brown on one side; turn. Add **½ t minced garlic, ½ t minced shallot, 2 T julienne-cut roasted sweet red Christy peppers, 1 t chopped cilantro, and ½ cup sliced chanterelle mushrooms.**

With fillets still in the pan, deglaze with ¼ c **dry sherry**.

Add ¼ c **fish stock**. Reduce over high heat for 2 to 3 minutes. Add ¼ c **cream**.

Reduce till sauce thickens, taking care that salmon does not overcook.

Remove salmon to heated serving plate.

To the sauce still in the pan, add **2 to 3 T Madeira**. Cook only a minute more, long enough to evaporate the alcohol.

Lace salmon with sauce; garnish with a dollop of **crème fraîche** and a sprig of **cilantro**.

NOTES AND TIPS:

For how to clarify butter, see p. 13.

Christy peppers are similar to Anaheims in size and taste, so if you can't find the Christy peppers, you can substitute Anaheims. For how to roast them, see p. 13.

For the Ark fish stock recipe, see p. 187.

For the Ark crème fraîche recipe, see p. 13.

Serves: 2

The roadsides on the Long Beach Peninsula are lined with fireweed, that tall magenta weed that is first to spring up after a burn or a clear-cutting, and with the even taller spikes of foxglove, ranging from white to pink to deep red. On the paths to the lighthouses, the white blooms of wild cucumber climb higher than a man's head.

Salmon with Tomato-Orange Salsa & Ginger Crème Fraîche

Ted and Carol Zell met Chefs Main and Lucas at their first restaurant, in Seaview, Washington; the chefs were working on their first cookbook. "We went in to lunch and Nanci came out in her whites, looking for volunteers to return later and help test some of their new recipes. So we did—we'd only just met and we were in the kitchen with Nanci and Jimella, just like we were old friends." Now the Zells keep a beach house in neighboring Ocean Park. And whether it's fish and chips in the bar or Salmon with Tomato-Orange Salsa in the dining room, a meal at The Ark has become part of the ritual of the Zells' frequent visits.

salmon
orange juice
lime juice
fresh ginger
  root
garlic
olive oil
crème fraîche
  (note)
Yakima
  Beefsteak
  Tomato-
  Orange Salsa
  with Ginger
  (note)
fresh cilantro
orange
  segments

Marinate **4 salmon fillets** for at least 2 hours in **1 c orange juice, ½ c lime juice, 1 T freshly shredded ginger root, 1 T minced garlic,** and **4 T olive oil.**

Mix together **1 T freshly shredded ginger root, 3 to 4 T lime juice,** and **1 c crème fraîche.**

Broil salmon to the doneness you prefer. Transfer the fillets to plates and spoon **salsa** over them. Top each with a dollop of ginger crème fraîche.

Garnish with **fresh cilantro** and **orange segments.**

NOTES AND TIPS:

For the Ark crème fraîche recipe, see p. 13.

For salsa recipe, see p. 175.

Serves: 4

Salmon & Seafood Cakes

Brunch will never be the same when once you've served these cakes. Topped with corn relish and crème fraîche and served with fresh orange juice, your richest coffee, or your favorite champagne, they redefine this genuinely American meal.

salmon
scallops
rockfish or
  halibut
celery
onion
green pepper
garlic
butter
Tabasco
all-purpose
  flour
eggs
half and half
salt
white pepper
cayenne
corn relish
  (note)
crème fraîche
  (note)
fresh basil

Cut all the seafood into small pieces to make **1 c salmon, ½ c scallops,** and **½ c rockfish** or **halibut.** In a food processor pulse till the mixture is coarse. Set aside.

Chop roughly, then grind to a fine texture in the food processor **3 ribs of celery, 1 medium onion, 1 large green pepper,** and **1 T garlic.** Sauté in ½ c **butter** with **6 dashes Tabasco,** till tender.

Place **1 c flour** in bowl, making a well in the center. Crack **6 eggs** into another bowl and whisk well. Add them slowly to the flour, stirring simultaneously. Add **1 ½ c half and half,** then fold in the seafood and vegetable mixtures, plus **salt** and **white pepper to taste.** Add as much as ½ c **more half and half** to even out texture of batter.

Oil a griddle with **butter** and measure out the batter in 2-oz (¼ c) ladlefuls; cook till golden brown, turning once. Place on individual serving plates.

Garnish with **corn relish, crème fraîche,** and **fresh basil leaves.**

NOTES AND TIPS:

For Chef Lucas' favorite corn relish recipe, see p. 171.

For the Ark crème fraîche recipe, see p. 13.
The cakes are good with whipped butter as well.
Serves: 4 to 6 (2 to 3 cakes per serving)

Washington State's first important author, James G. Swan, wrote his best-known book, **The Northwest Coast or, Three Year's Residence in Washington Territory,** *about Willapa Bay. First published in 1857, the book is a day-by-day account of his time with the oystermen and Indians on the east side of the bay from 1852 to 1854.*

Seafood Frittata

A frittata is an open-faced Italian omelette. Chef Lucas reminds the reader, "Remember, frittatas are fun. So don't let a recipe limit you. Play! Play! Play!"

clarified butter
 (note)
salmon
bay or sea
 scallops
rockfish
cocktail (or
 "bay") shrimp
mushrooms
onions
garlic
lemon juice
dried oregano
white wine
eggs
half and half
Tabasco
tomatoes
cheese (note)
sour cream

In ¼ c **clarified butter**, sauté ½ c **1-inch salmon pieces, ½ c bay or quartered sea scallops, ½ c 1-inch rockfish pieces, ⅓ c cocktail shrimp, ⅓ c sliced mushrooms, ¼ c thinly sliced onions, ½ t minced garlic, 1 T lemon juice, a pinch dried oregano,** and **2 to 3 T white wine**. Set aside.

In a bowl, beat **3 eggs**. Add ¼ c **half and half** and **2 shakes Tabasco**. Beat well.

Slice one **tomato** in thin slices; set slices aside.

Heat **2 to 3 T clarified butter** in a small omelette pan. Add egg mixture.

When the eggs have begun to set around the edge of the pan, use a slotted spoon to add seafood mixture.

With a rubber spatula, work the mixture together. The technique: Tilt pan toward you and pull egg mixture from top toward center of pan. Tilt away and draw mixture from the bottom toward center.

When the egg mixture has begun to set, remove from heat.

Place the thin tomato slices on top in a circular pattern. Sprinkle with shredded and/or chunked **cheese**—about 2 T or more if you like cheese. Place pan in a 425° F oven for 4 to 5 minutes.

Remove frittata to plate; add a **dollop of sour cream.**

NOTES AND TIPS:

For how to clarify butter, see p. 13.

Chef Lucas uses goat cheeses or herb cow cheese.

If you double the recipe use a 10-inch omelette pan, and double the seafood or substitute vegetables. Use in all 2 to 3 c sauté mixture, 6 to 9 eggs, and ½ c half and half.

Oven Temperature: 425° F

Serves: 1 to 2

The smooth sand that stretches from the Fishing Rocks to Leadbetter Point, its twenty-eight miles making it the longest driving beach in the country, has been a highway since the arrival of the first settlers. Before roads were constructed on the peninsula, stage coaches carried passengers from Seaview to Oysterville at low tide. After all, why build roads when there was a cheap, accessible beach?

More Ark Entrées

Please Pass the Skunk Cabbage

In April the swampy ditches of the Peninsula are
filled with pointed yellow hoods, open on one
side to show a rough green stalk within—
beautiful to look at, but never picked for floral
arrangements. Once inside a room, their strong
odor justifies their name. But the Indians knew
that the root of the plant, boiled long enough that
most of the acrid taste disappeared, could nourish
them when other food was scarce.

According to an Indian legend, in the ancient
days they had nothing to eat but roots and leaves;
there were no salmon in the river. When the
spring salmon did arrive for the first time, a
person stood on the riverbank and shouted,
"Here come our relatives whose bodies are full of
eggs. If it had not been for me, the people would
have starved."

"Who speaks to us?" asked Salmon.

"Your uncle, Skunk Cabbage," the person said.

Then Salmon went ashore, and because Skunk
Cabbage had fed the people, he was given an
elkskin blanket and a war club, and a home in the
rich damp soil near the river. There he continued
to stand, serving the Indians not only as a fresh
vegetable in the spring but as a medicine as well.
An infusion of the boiled root was used to soothe
a stomachache and to ease the pains of childbirth.
The large green leaves served as a poultice to ease
cuts and swellings, and the heated blossoms were
good for rheumatism.

Antibiotics and analgesics have replaced Skunk
Cabbage's medicinal uses, and year-round frozen
vegetables, his function as a blood purifier after
the long winter. But he still appears, bright and
erect in the low, moist spots, one of the main
signs that spring has really come.

Chicken Stuffed with Mushrooms & Spinach

Chef Lucas observes that "so often in our profession people fear to take the risk of claiming their own style and so continually borrow exactly from someone else's work. Of course, the end result most of the time is an unfinished experience. That's generally the effect of imitating blindly rather than innovating.

"Borrowing inspiration, though, is another matter. It's a high compliment to be acknowledged as inspiration to someone else. It's not like anyone really does anything new; we've always borrowed from other styles, regions, or products. But it's exciting when you can give credit where it's due, yet sense your own creativity coming through."

*clarified butter
(note)
white onion
garlic
mushrooms
dried oregano
Madeira
spinach
Parmesan
cheese
goat cheese
breadcrumbs
chicken breasts
flour
garlic
shallot
salt
pepper*

Sauté till tender, in ¼ c **clarified butter,** ⅓ **c finely chopped white onions** and ½ **t minced garlic.** Add **1 c finely chopped mushrooms** and ½ **T dried oregano.** Without removing mixture from pan, deglaze with **3 T Madeira.** Remove from heat.

Add **2 bunches blanched and chopped spinach, 4 to 5 T Parmesan,** and **4 oz goat cheese** while mixture is still hot. Add ½ **c breadcrumbs (enough to bind the mixture).**

Set stuffing aside for several hours to cool and allow flavors to marry (*note*).

Bone 4 to 6 half **chicken breasts.** Slit pockets into the breasts and divide the stuffing among them.

Lightly dust stuffed breasts with **flour.** Sauté breasts in **2 to 4 T clarified butter.** Add to the pan ½ **t minced garlic,** ½ **t minced shallot, salt and pepper to taste, 1 t grainy Pommery mustard, 2 T lemon juice, 3 T brandy,** ¼ **c chicken stock** (*note*), and ⅓ **c heavy cream.**

Reduce till sauce is slightly thickened.

*grainy
  Pommery
  mustard
lemon juice
brandy
chicken stock
  (note)
heavy cream*

Finish with **2 T Madeira**, cooking only till alcohol evaporates.

NOTES AND TIPS:

For how to clarify butter, see p. 13.

For the Ark chicken stock recipe, see p. 186.

Chef Lucas suggests that the dressing mixture will keep (refrigerated) for 4 to 5 days.

Serves: 4 to 6

Lamb Chops with Green Peppercorn–Madeira Sauce

For Chef Lucas, "Seafood is a love that always excited me. There are two meat items that wake this excitement as well: lamb and veal.

"I probably do more with those two items than I do with all the rest of the traditional cuts—though sometimes filets or New York–cut beefsteak steals the limelight.

"The buttery sweetness and the delicate richness of lamb and veal lend themselves to both subtlety and bold combinations. When I develop a new recipe for either, I don't want to camouflage the flavor but to explore some complements—a little bitey here, smoothed over there, finished off elegantly with a touch of cream or a lacing of liquor like cognac or Madeira.

"Cooking is a sensual act: looks, feels, smells, and tastes combined by common sense, with portions of excitement."

lamb chops *salt*	Season **8 lamb chops** lightly with **salt** and **fresh-cracked pepper**.
cracked pepper *red wine* *olive oil* *lemon*	Mix well ½ c **red wine**, ⅓ c **olive oil, the juice of one lemon,** and ¼ t **minced garlic**. Pour over lamb chops. Set aside at room temperature for 1 to 2 hours.
garlic *clarified butter* *(note)* *green bell pepper* *red bell pepper* *green peppercorns*	Pat the chops dry, and sauté them in ¼ c **clarified butter**. Turn them and add **1 T minced garlic**, ⅓ c **diced green bell pepper,** and ⅓ c **diced red bell pepper**. Continue cooking chops till rare (and remove); cook vegetables till tender. Add **1 T green peppercorns**.
Madeira *lamb stock* *(note)*	Deglaze the sauté pan with ⅓ c **Madeira**; cook a couple of minutes to thicken. In a food processor, purée the ingredients well. Return them to the pan over heat and add ½ c **lamb stock**, ½ c **red wine**, and ¼ c **cognac**. Reduce by one-third.

cognac
heavy cream
fresh herbs

Add **3 to 4 T heavy cream**. Cook briefly and swirl in a pat of butter—no more than 1 T.

Pour sauce onto a serving plate and arrange the chops. Garnish with **fresh herbs**, such as rosemary, sage, and thyme.

NOTES AND TIPS:

For how to clarify butter, see p. 13.

For the Ark lamb stock recipe, see p. 188.

Serves: 4

Lamb Loin with Apple-Date Stuffing

At The Ark, guests are treated like friends because The Ark is about people and place and good times. The Peninsula is populated by two groups: Those who have lived here since birth—their parents and grandparents probably did too—and those who have moved here, fleeing careers, to live in the wild beauty on this little sand spit. In the nontourist season, you'll find both groups at The Ark, trying out Chef Lucas' latest new dish. One Sunday it may be an all-Greek dinner and the next week, when lamb is available, it may be a dish like this one that was created for the 1987 Garlic Dinner.

If you're planning a large dinner party, Lamb Loin with Apple-Date Stuffing might be just the elegant entrée or meat course you're looking for.

garlic

apples

fresh mint

yellow onions

butter

Madeira

dates

lamb loins

shallots

flour

lamb stock
 (note)

cracked pepper

salt

Sauté, in **½ pound butter, ½ c finely chopped garlic, 7 finely chopped apples, 2 c chopped fresh mint,** and **2 finely chopped yellow onions.**

With the mixture still in the pan, deglaze it with **½ c Madeira.**

Add **2 c pitted, ground dates,** and set stuffing aside.

Work a steel through the center of **4 ½- to ¾-lb lamb loins** to make one lengthwise hole in each.

Fill a pastry bag without a tip with stuffing; pipe into loins (*note*).

Sear loins in **butter** to brown them. Reserve juices.

Finish lamb in the oven at 425° F for 15 to 20 minutes.

For the sauce, add **6 to 7 minced cloves garlic, 3 minced shallots,** and **1 T chopped fresh mint** to pan juices. Sauté till flavors are full—1 to 2 minutes—agitating pan so ingredients do not burn.

Add **3 T flour,** stirring constantly to keep from burning.

Deglaze with ¾ **c Madeira.**

Add **3 c lamb stock, fresh-cracked pepper,** and **salt to taste.** Simmer till reduced by half.

NOTES AND TIPS:

For the Ark lamb stock recipe, see p. 188.

Extra stuffing might be rolled in blanched spinach leaves and steamed.

This recipe can be cut proportionally for fewer servings.

Oven Temperature: 425° F

Serves: 10 as entrée; 20 as meat course

North End Prime Rib of Beef

This recipe requires a party, according to Chef Lucas. "I am including North End Prime Rib of Beef in this cookbook in honor of my bartender, Jan, whose creative contributions to our business keep me in awe, and to my local winter clientele, whom I appreciate deeply. Jan buzzes in and out of the kitchen letting us know who's arrived with "Sontags are here," "Jon and Debbie are here." Of course I already know Debbie is in because the echo of her laughter has rung through the kitchen. Jeannie's at her resident space at the end of the bar, David wants an end cut, Gordon and Roy have traveled all the way from Long Beach. And on and on till the bar becomes festive. Tables get pushed together, and the prime rib of beef from my kitchen becomes a rack of rib bones." The Ark bar, at these times, is its own community center.

prime rib of beef *salt* *pepper* *granulated garlic (note)* *Worcestershire sauce*	Place a **10- to 13-lb Hollywood cut of prime rib** in a roasting pan. While the oven heats to 500° F, season meat with **salt, pepper to taste**, a **sprinkling of granulated garlic**, and ¾ c **Worcestershire sauce**.
	Roast for 15 to 20 minutes at 500° F, or till top is browned—no longer than 30 minutes.
water	Reduce heat to 350° F. Roast for 2 more hours.
dry vermouth *horseradish sauce (note)*	Remove meat from roasting pan and let stand.
	Pour **3 qts water** into juices. Scrape up the crusty bits, and simmer atop the stove for 10 to 15 minutes.
	Strain juices through a fine sieve. Skim off fat, and pour juices into a saucepan. Add **3 c dry vermouth**; simmer gently for 10 minutes.
	Serve the prime rib *au jus* but with the *jus* and also horseradish sauce each in a container on the side.

NOTES AND TIPS:

For an Ark horseradish sauce recipe, see p. 183.

Reheat cuts of meat *au jus*.

Oven Temperature: 500° F, 350° F

Serves: 12 to 15 people, with enough left over for cold prime rib sandwiches the next day

Leadbetter Point lies at the northern tip of the Peninsula at the end of Stackpole Road. A haven for hikers, the park is a wildlife refuge where amateur naturalists can find more than a hundred kinds of birds, among them brandts, herons, and the rare snowy plover.

Sweetbreads with Garlic Madeira Sauce

"Sweetbreads, like oysters," says Chef Lucas, "can turn a lot of people off just because of what they are. Sweetbreads are the thymus gland, located in the throat of veal or lamb. They are delicate and rich, intensely rich. They have become a once or twice a year tradition for me. There are very few people who request sweetbreads, but one woman who lives nearby in Nahcotta, Pat Schlafle, says, 'When you have sweetbreads, dear, call me.' And I do.

"In selecting sweetbreads, look for ones that are white and free from bloodstains. Wash them well under running cold water; then they're ready to blanch. The blanching firms up the flesh and keeps the meat from falling apart when it cooks. Once it's thus prepared, why not make the sauce as rich as the sweetbreads? One of my favorite ways to cook and eat this delectable meat follows."

Step 1: Blanch the Sweetbreads

sweetbreads
water
salt
beer

Put **2 to 3 lb sweetbreads** in a saucepan; cover with cold water. Add **1 t salt** and **8 to 12 oz beer**. Bring to a boil; cook 3 to 5 minutes. Immediately drain and run cold water into the pan to cool the meat.

Once the meat is cool, remove the membrane around the sweetbreads; cut away any cartilage, tubes, or connective tissue.

Step 2: Finish the Sweetbreads in Garlic Madeira Sauce

blanched sweetbreads
flour
clarified butter (note)

Slice **2 to 3 lb blanched sweetbreads** in ¼-inch pieces. Dust in **flour**.

Heat **¼ to ⅓ c clarified butter** in a sauté pan. Add sweetbread pieces, and **salt** and **white pepper to taste**. Brown lightly; turn.

salt
white pepper
garlic
shallot
lemon
cognac
heavy cream
Madeira

Add ¼ t minced garlic, ¼ t minced shallot, and a squeeze from one lemon wedge. Sauté till the garlic and shallot come to full flavor. With the sweetbreads still in the pan, deglaze it with 3 T cognac.

Add ⅓ c heavy cream; reduce slightly. Add 3 T Madeira, cooking only till alcohol evaporates.

Remove sweetbreads to a serving plate. Pour the sauce over them and sprinkle with chopped parsley.

NOTES AND TIPS:

For how to clarify butter, see p. 13.

Chef Lucas: "As long as we're being decadent, accompany this with one of my favorite winemaker's rich and robust Semillons: Blackwood Canyon. Enjoy yourself."

Serves: 4 to 6

Notes

Pickling, Ark Style

The Pleasures of Beachcombing

Walking the beaches in search of treasure has
always been a favorite pastime. When shipwrecks
were common, the local inhabitants were out in
search of salvage, legal or illegal, and went home
with everything from silk dresses to kitchen sinks.
When that source of largesse disappeared, there
were still things worth seeking.

Glass floats, broken loose from Japanese fishnets
two thousand miles across the ocean, were prized
finds for many years. Slightly irregular blue or
green balls, in any size from three inches to three
feet in diameter, rewarded beachcombers who
were early on the shore after a winter storm.
Modern technology has replaced the old floats,
and those that still come in, very rarely these
days, have been tossing around in the sea for
many years. In the houses of old residents,
however, the beautiful handblown glass balls can
still be seen, some of them made into lamp bases,
some merely out on display.

After Mt. St. Helens erupted, in 1980, pieces of
pumice became the objects of search. Washed
down from the Cowlitz River into the Columbia
and carried north from the mouth of the river by
the tide, pumice, like the heaps of driftwood,
washed up on Peninsula beaches. Today,
discovering a piece of pumice half buried in the
sand is unusual; it, too, has mostly been picked
up and come to rest in souvenir collections.

Nowadays, sand dollars are likely to be the
favorite treasure. Found in the greatest numbers
north of Ocean Park, these flat, rounded, white
skeletons of what were once living sea creatures
are prized for their beauty. In life, the shells are
covered by thick, hairlike fuzz, and sometimes
those (still lifelike) wash ashore. Collectors,

however—children and their grandparents—
prefer their sand dollars bleached. They search
among the pieces crushed by tires and feet and
tide till suddenly the cry arises, "Here it is! I've
found a whole one!"

Chef Lucas' Advice on Pickling

Pickling is one of the oldest forms of preserving fish. But with so much emphasis on freshness and cooking to order, pickling has been put on the back shelf. There's something satisfying about the wait for the pickling process to reach completion, something exciting about the explosion of flavors, that gives a particular sense of accomplishment—especially when I stand back to view an attractive arrangement of fish and julienne vegetables, and when I take my first taste.

Though there are traditional steps one must follow to ensure that the product is handled safely and correctly, pickling is relatively a simple process. The main ingredients are vinegar, water, salt, and spices. Salt and vinegar are the major working ingredients. Salt firms the flesh and draws out moisture, whereas vinegar softens it.

Pickling is a means of preserving, not camouflaging. So it is essential to use high-quality ingredients. The fish should be fresh, firm, and clean. Oily fish works best, and you should take care to know the breeding season of the product. A spawned-out fish or one that is about to spawn will not have enough oil, and its meat is inferior in quality. Herring, the most common pickled fish, does not have enough oil to be high in quality till late summer or early fall.

About Vinegar

White distilled vinegar with 4% to 6% acidity is recommended for pickling. For most uses, malt and fruit vinegars vary too much in acid concentration. The fruit esters sometimes give unpleasant flavors and dye the fish—not attractive. If a recipe calls for boiling, bring the liquid to a boil and then reduce the heat below the boiling point, or it will lose its preservative qualities.

Remember that most of the vinegar needs to be white distilled—as a general rule, three-quarters (some exceptions are reflected in recipes). That gives you flexibility with one-quarter, for which you can use dry wines or burgundy. I use champagne as well. Still, I do not use dark fruit vinegars. Rice vinegar works well.

About Spices

Use whole spices: Ground spices cloud the pickling solution. If you're using garlic, let the cloves simmer with other spices for best flavor. Garlic is highly susceptible to bacterial action, so it is a good practice to remove the cloves before what's pickled goes into the jars.

About Herbs

Oftentimes, instead of adding herbs to the boiling brine, I will add sprigs of fresh herbs as I pack the jars. It looks more attractive and sacrifices none of the flavors.

About Salt

If your pickling calls for salt, use the recommended salt, called canners' salt or kosher salt, either in ground form or in flakes. You want noniodized salt for pickling. Other salts have additives that can leave a bitter flavor and cloud the brine.

About Containers

To me this is part of the tradition of pickling. I have a special crock that's used for pickling *only*. Naturally, because the salt and vinegar combination can corrode metal, I make it a policy *not* to use any metal with the exception of stainless steel. My preference, however, is no metal at all; other choices are glass or plastic-lined kegs. *Always* remember to clean the container thoroughly.

About Storage

I like to let the pickle set at least five days to age before serving. Of course, I taste it every other day. That has a lot to do with my own impatience and is possible because the pickle isn't "canned," for long-term storage. I recommend tucking it away in a corner of your refrigerator where it won't be moved all the time. If properly stored and covered in a cold area, the shelf life can be months. If you notice any peculiarities—fizzing, discoloring, mold—better to exercise caution and let it go. Adding a label and date to your pickling is also a good idea. I indicate the fish and process used as well.

Final Notes About It All

Once you're comfortable with basic recipes, don't be afraid to play. That doesn't mean "kitchen sink cooking"—standing back and throwing so many ingredients together that your taste buds get confused. Look for balance and complements in all cooking, including pickling.

My favorite products for pickling are salmon, sturgeon, black cod (often referred to as sablefish), oysters, prawns, littleneck clams, mussels, medleys of garden vegetables, King Bolete mushrooms, and Bing cherries.

Pickled Black Cod

Whenever I use a heavy vinegar like a malt vinegar, as can be used in this dish, it's because I know it won't be around long. An attractive way to present this dish is on a bed of lettuce with a dollop of sour cream or crème fraîche and diced avocado.

black cod

peach vinegar

  (note)

star anise

peppercorns

pickling spices

whole allspice

garlic

beer

fennel seed

Lightly salt **5 lb skinned black cod**; let stand refrigerated for 24 hours. Gently rinse away the salt, and pat dry. Slice cod in ½-inch chunks (the size of pickled herring).

Bring to a near boil (*note*) and cook for 10 minutes **2 qt peach vinegar, ½ t star anise, 1 T peppercorns, 3 T mixed pickling spices, 1 T whole allspice, the peeled cloves of 1 small bulb of garlic, 8 oz beer, and 2 T whole fennel seed** (*note*).

Remove the spices from the pickling mixture and pour it over the cod in a nonmetal container (*note*).

Cover tightly. Refrigerate.

NOTES AND TIPS:

To substitute for peach vinegar: mix 1 ½ qt white vinegar, 1 c peach brandy, and 1 c malt vinegar.

Be sure to use the pickling spices in cheesecloth, since the mixture contains some pieces that are quite small. They can sometimes work their way into the fish. In addition, they look unappealing in the final pickled fish.

Do not bring solution to a high boil at any time during the cooking.

For more about appropriate ingredients, containers, and storage, see "On Pickling," p. 117.

Yield: 5 lb pickled fish

*ᵛᵉᶜ Fort Colum-
bia, on the site of an
army post, was built on
the 1843 homestead of
Captain Scarborough,
the first permanent
settler north of the
Columbia. For years the
promontory, just west of
the present Columbia
River Bridge at the south
end of the Long Beach
Peninsula, was a land-
mark for the safe cross-
ing of Columbia Bar. As
a coastal fort, its guns
guarded the mouth of the
river from 1896 till the
end of World War II.
Now carefully restored,
its officers' quarters and
barracks give a glimpse
of what life was like in
an army post at the turn
of the century. More
appealing to kids, how-
ever, are the old cement
bunkers where they can
crawl around with the
cobwebs and spiders.*

Pickled Salmon

"When a flower goes on a plate, you can eat it." That's the rule at The Ark. Taste that little starlike blue borage flower on your salad, and don't eat around those golden yellow daisylike petals from the calendula sprinkled over your salmon. The orange, red, or yellow nasturtium flowers are as spicy as that plant's leaves. Even the violas on your dessert parfaits are meant for your complete enjoyment. Experiment then, when you prepare the Ark Pickled Salmon, and serve it garnished with three or four borage flowers or a bright red nasturtium.

salmon fillets
canners' salt
white vinegar
pickling spices
whole allspice
dried red chili
  peppers
garlic
beer (note)
bay leaf
carrots
red onions

Remove any remaining scales on the skin side of **6 to 8 boned fillets of king/Chinook salmon, 4 to 5 oz each.** Layer the fillets, skin side down, in a crock or hard plastic container. Sprinkle each layer generously with **canners' salt.** Place plastic wrap loosely on each layer of salted fish. Continue to layer, salting and covering each layer with plastic wrap. Set about 1 lb of even weight on top cover, and press.

Refrigerate three days. Test every day to see if flesh remains firm. Rinse gently under cold water, dry, and cut into ¼-in pieces.

Bring to a slow boil **2 qt white vinegar, 3 T mixed pickling spices** tied into a cheesecloth bag (*note*), **1 T whole allspice, 3 whole dried red chili peppers, 6 to 8 large peeled garlic cloves,** and **8 oz beer.** Boil slowly 5 minutes. Cut the heat, and cool brine to room temperature. Remove the bag of pickling spices and the garlic cloves.

In jars with **1 bay leaf each,** layer fish and **2 c julienne-cut carrots** plus **2 small red onions, thinly sliced.** Distribute the allspice and chili peppers. Pour brine over, and refrigerate.

NOTES AND TIPS:

Do not use dark beer.

Be sure to use the pickling spices in cheesecloth, since the mixture contains some pieces that are quite small. They can sometimes work their way into the fish. In addition, they look unappealing in the final pickled fish.

For more about type of fish, storage, and other points, see "On Pickling," p. 117.

Yield: Brine is sufficient for 1 ½ to 2 ½ lb salmon.

⁚ℭ The mouth of the Columbia is the most dangerous stretch of ocean on the Pacific Coast. The Columbia Bar, more than seven miles long, stretches out into the ocean and up into the river. Over the years, its unpredictable sands have proved dis-astrous for nearly a hundred ocean-going ships. Most of those early wrecks lie deep on the ocean floor or covered by the drifting sand on the nearby beaches.

Pickled Cherries

For several years The Ark's own herb garden, just to the south of the restaurant on the edge of the tide flats, has been the source for many of the herbs and edible flowers the chefs use in salads and as garnish for entrées and desserts. From sage and oregano to borage and rosemary, the home-raised delicacies sometimes come to the kitchen or the table within minutes of their picking.

fresh Bing cherries
fruit vinegar
Madeira
port (note)
sticks of cinnamon
star anise
whole allspice
whole cloves
orange
garlic
red onion

Wash and stem **5 lb Bing cherries**.

In a saucepan, mix **1 quart fruit vinegar, 2 c Madeira**, and **2 c port**. Tie in cheesecloth and add **3 sticks cinnamon, 6 star anise, 1 T whole allspice,** and **1 t whole cloves**. Bring this to a rumbling boil, and reduce heat to simmer. Cook for 20 minutes.

Slice **1 orange** very thin (skin included). Peel and thinly slice **1 small red onion.** Cut a slit in the center of **6 large garlic cloves** so they stay whole while bleeding flavor. Mix with cherries.

While brine is still very hot, add it to cherry mixture. Let stand at room temperature for an hour. When cold, cover and let marinate for 2 to 3 weeks or longer in the refrigerator.

NOTES AND TIPS:

Use a heavy, fruity port such as Ficklin.

Pickled cherries are great as a complement to various patés, as a garnish on salads, or in such relishes as Pickled Cherry and Orange Relish for White Fish, p. 170.

For more about storage, containers, and other points, see "On Pickling," p. 117.

Yield: approximately 3 qt pickles

Pickled Peppers

This recipe has, according to Chef Lucas, no shelf life at all. It's a recipe to be used soon after the preparation.

malt vinegar

white vinegar

whole allspice

coriander seed

star anise

sticks of
 cinnamon

dried red chili
 peppers

beer (note)

brown sugar

garlic

red bell peppers

green bell
 peppers

yellow bell
 peppers

red Christy
 peppers (note)

carrots

red onion

jalapeño
 peppers

Cook together for 10 to 15 minutes **2 c malt vinegar, 4 c white vinegar, 1 T whole allspice, 2 T coriander, 6 star anise, 2 sticks cinnamon, 8 whole dried red chili peppers, 12 oz beer,** and **½ c brown sugar.** Remove from heat and set aside to cool for at least 5 minutes.

Prepare a variety of garden peppers. Remember: Colors and flavors are an exciting and important part of the presentation. Mix well in a bowl **12 whole garlic cloves, 9 seeded julienne-cut bell peppers (3 red, 3 green, 3 yellow), 6 seeded sweet red Christy peppers cut lengthwise in strips, 2 c julienne-cut carrots,** and **1 red onion sliced into ⅛-inch rings.**

Divide the vegetables among pint jars, and add **1 whole jalapeño** per jar. Pour hot brine over vegetables. Cool for 5 minutes, and refrigerate.

NOTES AND TIPS:

Do not use dark beer.

If red Christy peppers are unavailable, Anaheims may be substituted.

For more about storage, spices, and other points, see "On Pickling," p. 117.

These pickled peppers make a fine gift.

Yield: 3 to 4 pints pickles

Pickled Vegetables

"'Yes' is the experience I like best about The Ark." Polly Friedlander of Seattle and Oysterville requests vegetarian meals at the restaurant regularly. "Jimella, can you fix a vegetarian dinner for me? 'Yes, Yes, Yes,' at least a thousand times 'Yes'—except once just before closing on Friday night before a holiday when I asked for a veggie burger, not on the regular menu. There was a hush in the restaurant when Marianne returned to the table and stammered, 'She can't do it.'

"Yes—the 'yes' I always feel there is the experience I like best about The Ark."

Whether the chefs are serving a banquet like the Garlic Festival Dinner or preparing a special vegetarian meal garnished with the Ark pickled vegetables, that "yes" remains their hallmark.

malt vinegar
white vinegar
whole allspice
coriander seed
star anise
sticks of
  cinnamon
dried red chili
  peppers
beer (note)
brown sugar
new red
  potatoes
brussels sprouts
cauliflower
green beans
green bell
  pepper

Cook together for 10 to 15 minutes **2 c malt vinegar, 4 c white vinegar, 1 T whole allspice, 2 T coriander seed, 6 star anise, 2 sticks of cinnamon, 8 whole dried red chili peppers, 12 oz beer, and ½ c brown sugar.**

Blanch separately **8 to 10 small new red potatoes, 8 to 10 brussels sprouts, flowerets from 1 medium head cauliflower, and ½ lb green beans.** Shock them in an ice water bath immediately after cooking.

Mix the above vegetables with **1 seeded green pepper cut in chunks, 1 large seeded red bell pepper julienne-cut lengthwise, 2 c carrots julienne-cut, 1 medium red onion sliced thin, and 12 whole garlic cloves.**

Divide vegetables among jars. While brine is still hot, pour over vegetables. Let cool, and refrigerate.

red bell pepper

carrots

red onion

garlic

NOTES AND TIPS:

Do not use dark beer.

For more about storage, vinegars, and other points, see "On Pickling," p. 117.

Yield: 2 qt pickles

Notes

Desserts from the Ark

Four Old Churches

Peninsula pioneers were convinced that, once they had the beginnings of a town, their next need was a church to provide stability and moral tone. By the last quarter of the nineteenth century, most settlements had erected simple frame buildings. Although most of the early structures have fallen victim to fire, hurricane, or merely time, three of them still exist on the Peninsula, witness to the fact that those early settlers built something besides shelter and saloons.

Standing lonely on Highway 101, just west of the Astoria Bridge and far from any other buildings, is St. Mary's Catholic Church, built in 1904 by Patrick McGowan on the site of an early Catholic Indian mission. The mission had been only partly successful; one priest said as he left the Chinook area that "the whole known fruits of my labors [consist] of the various names with which I had baptized them." McGowan's church, built for the settlers, did better. Mass is still said there during the summer.

Probably the earliest church building was in Oysterville, where a circuit-riding Methodist minister completed the construction of a church in 1876. According to one story, when he asked a mill owner to donate lumber he was promised as much as he could carry away in a sailboat on one tide. He loaded the boat so heavily that he got home with all the timber he needed. That little church blew down in 1921, but a nearby Baptist church, built in 1892, has been carefully restored and is open to the public.

Chinook had two early churches, one Evangelical Lutheran (1901) and one Methodist (1906), until the 1980s, when the Lutheran church succumbed to fire. The Methodist church is still there, but religious services are not held in it.

No trace is left of the original Methodist
Campground established at Ocean Park in 1883,
but a brown shingle Methodist church, completed
there in 1914 for a little over three thousand
dollars, still stands. In its belfry is the bell from
that old Oysterville church, inscribed "1876."

Apple Dumplings with Caramel Sauce

"I love caramel apples," says Chef Main. "So as usual I started meddling with a recipe, and this old favorite turned into a dumpling mirrored in a rich caramel sauce—an excellent treat to bring to the dinner table."

Step 1: Make the Crust

all-purpose flour
baking powder
sugar
salt
butter
milk
vanilla
grated lemon zest

Sift together **2 c flour, 2 t baking powder, 2 T sugar**, and **1 t salt**. Cut **½ c butter** into flour mixture till crumbly. Combine **½ c milk, 1 t vanilla**, and **1 t grated lemon zest**. Add milk mixture to flour mixture till just incorporated. (Dough should be like biscuit dough.) Wrap and chill 30 minutes to an hour.

Step 2: Prepare Apples and Filling

green apples
sugar
cinnamon
nutmeg
vanilla

Peel and core **6 small green apples**.

Combine and set aside **¼ c sugar, 2 t cinnamon, ½ t nutmeg**, and **1 t vanilla**.

Step 3: Assemble the Dumplings

butter

Divide dumpling dough into 6 equal portions. Roll one portion into an 8-inch square. Trim edges, and reinforce center of square with the extra dough in a circle about 1 inch in diameter. (Sometimes stretching the dough around the apple weakens the seal underneath. Reinforcement helps prevent breaking.)

Place 1 apple in the center of a dough square. Fill center of apple with filling, using a narrow spoon or knife blade to funnel it in. Top with **½ t butter**.

Pull dough up around apple, starting with opposite corners and moistening edges with water to seal. Trim away any excess on top to prevent a thick bulb of dough from forming.

Repeat this process for each apple.

Place dumplings at even intervals in a lightly greased baking pan.

Bake 30 minutes at 350° F or till tender. Check for doneness by piercing with a sharp paring knife.

Step 4: Make the Caramel Sauce

butter
all-purpose flour
brown sugar
cream
vanilla

Melt ½ **c butter**. Whisk in **2 T flour** and **1 c brown sugar**. Add **1 c heavy cream** slowly, whisking constantly. Cook till thickened. Remove from heat. Add **1 t vanilla**.

Whip ½ **c heavy cream** with ½ **t vanilla** till soft peaks form.

Step 5: To Serve

cream
walnuts

Ladle ¼ c caramel sauce into each of 6 large shallow bowls. Put a warm dumpling in each on top of sauce, make 1-inch cross cuts on top of dumplings, and gently pull them apart.

Dollop **whipped cream** onto tops of dumplings and garnish with **chopped walnuts**.

NOTES AND TIPS:

If you prefer to use less caramel sauce, reserve what's left for ice cream topping. (People have been known to eat this sauce directly from the bowl with their fingers, too.)

Oven Temperature: 350° F

Yield: 6 dumplings and 1 ½ c caramel sauce

Megler, across the Columbia River from Astoria, although it was listed as a Washington town, was never much more than a ferry and railroad terminus. Its usefulness ended when the bridge was built, and like so many other one-time towns it is now only a name, a highway rest stop and a visitor's center open during the summer.

Black Walnut-Custard Tart with Seasonal Fruit

When she completes a new dessert such as this Black Walnut–Custard Tart, Chef Main carries samples around the kitchen for all the staff to taste. Her smile of anticipation as she watches the tester try her latest effort and her laugh of delight when that tester asks for more are legend among those who have worked at the restaurant.

Step 1: Make the Crust

butter
sugar
salt
eggs
vanilla
grated orange zest
bourbon
cream of tartar
black walnuts (note)
all-purpose flour

Cream **½ c softened butter**. Add slowly **½ c plus 2 T sugar** and a **pinch of salt**. Continue creaming till light yellow. Beat in **2 egg yolks**, scraping bowl. Add **1 t vanilla, 1 t grated orange zest**, and **1 T bourbon**.

Beat **2 egg whites** till foamy. Add **⅛ t cream of tartar**. Gradually add **½ c sugar**, continuing to beat till whites are stiff.

Combine **½ c finely ground walnuts** and **1 c sifted flour**.

Fold egg white mixture alternately with flour into egg yolk mixture, one-third at a time.

Spread dough over bottom and 1 ½ inches up sides of a 10-inch tart pan.

Step 2: Bake Custard in Crust

eggs
sour cream
sugar
brown sugar
grated orange zest
orange juice
flour

Beat together **2 eggs, ¾ c sour cream, 3 T sugar, 3 T brown sugar, 2 t grated orange zest, ¼ c orange juice, 3 T flour, 1 t bourbon, 1 t vanilla**, and **1 t finely minced fresh ginger root**.

Arrange in the unbaked crust **1 c sliced peaches** and **1 c pitted cherries**.

Pour the custard gently over fruit in crust. Bake

bourbon
vanilla
fresh ginger
 root
peaches
cherries

on middle rack in oven at 350° F for 30 minutes or till set.

NOTES AND TIPS:

Any combination of complementary seasonal fruit can be substituted for the suggested peaches and cherries.

If black walnuts are not available, English walnuts will do.

Oven Temperature: 350° F

Serves: 8 to 10

Buttermilk Raspberry Pie

Buttermilk pie is a traditional dessert. Its tartness joined with the richness of a shortbread crust and the lushness of raspberries melts the hardest heart.

Step 1: Make the Crust

all-purpose flour

pecans

powdered sugar

butter

egg yolks

Using an electric mixer, combine **2 c flour, ¼ c chopped pecans**, and **6 T powdered sugar**. Beat in **1 c softened butter**. Add **2 egg yolks**, and beat till just mixed.

Chill dough 1 hour. Pat into a lightly greased 9-inch pie pan. Freeze till firm. Lightly grease a sheet of foil and fit it over the crust, greased side down. Prebake 10 minutes at 350° F. The foil should lift right off (*note*). Set crust aside.

Step 2: Fill the Crust

butter

eggs

sugar

all-purpose flour

mace

salt

buttermilk

vanilla

Melt and cool ½ **c butter**. Separate **3 eggs**.

In the bowl of an electric mixer, combine **1 c sugar**, ¼ c **flour**, ¼ t **mace**, and ¼ t **salt**.

In a separate bowl, beat the 3 egg yolks till light yellow. Add **2 c room-temperature buttermilk, 1 t vanilla**, and the melted butter. Make sure the buttermilk is not chilled or it will not blend well with the butter and yolks.

Using the electric mixer, add buttermilk mixture to sugar mixture one-third at a time.

Beat the 3 egg whites till they form soft peaks. Using a spatula, gently fold them into the batter.

Pour the batter into the prebaked pie shell. Bake for 30 to 40 minutes at 325° F, or till set like a custard. It will jiggle slightly in the center, but it will set up when the pie has been chilled. If you overcook it, the pie will be slightly dry in texture, but don't worry, the raspberry topping will help cover this.

Cool pie to room temperature and chill for at least 2 hours.

Step 3: Add the Topping

cornstarch
water
fresh raspberries
(note)
sugar
grated lemon
zest
butter

Dissolve **3 T cornstarch** in ¼ c **water**.

In a heavy-bottomed saucepan, stir together with a wooden spoon **2 c raspberries**, the dissolved **cornstarch, 1 c sugar**, and **1 t grated lemon zest**. Cook, stirring over medium heat till the sauce begins to simmer and thicken.

Remove from heat; add **1 T butter**.

Cool till lukewarm, then fold in **2 c raspberries**.

Spread topping gently over chilled pie. Chill an additional 30 minutes or till set.

NOTES AND TIPS:

If after prebaking the crust you have a problem with it sticking to the foil, use a paring knife to clear it. Any pieces of crust can be gently pressed back into place while still warm.

Other topping variations: You can use frozen raspberries, but remember to drain them to remove the extra juice that frozen berries give off. Blackberries with a touch of cinnamon or blueberries with lemon and orange zest are good substitutes for raspberries.

For a variation, try "Fudge Buttermilk Pie": Melt 2 oz unsweetened chocolate with the butter. This will make a firmer custard with a fudgelike texture. You can top this with raspberries or simply pipe whipped cream onto it and top with chocolate curls.

Oven Temperature: crust, 350° F; filling, 325° F

Serves: 8 to 10

There has always been an ethnic mixture on the Peninsula—New Englanders, Midwesterners, Swedes, Norwegians, and Finns. Many of them hung onto the backgrounds and customs they brought with them; some of the older residents in Naselle still speak Finnish. The descendants of those early settlers still live in the area, and many of their names survive in the names of Peninsula places.

Centennial Torte

Chef Main developed this recipe in celebration of the Centennial of the State of Washington in 1989. Two big fans of The Ark were intimately involved with that memorial event. Mrs. Jean Gardner served as cochair of the Centennial Committee, and her husband Gov. Booth Gardner was elected to his second term in office during the centennial year.

The Gardners write: "Each visit to The Ark is a special moment—from our first visit to the Garlic Festival, having dinner and singing 'Garlic, Garlic' to the tune of 'Louis, Louis,' to the special visit celebrating our twenty-seventh wedding anniversary. As they say, 'It's worth the trip!'"

Step 1: Make the Apple Filling

apples (note)
butter
honey
brown sugar
vanilla
rum
cinnamon
nutmeg
walnuts
raisins

Lightly sauté **6 cups peeled, cored, and sliced apples** in **4 T melted butter, 1 T honey,** and **2 T brown sugar**. Remove from heat just as apples begin to soften, and transfer to a bowl.

Combine **1 t vanilla, 1 T rum, 1 t cinnamon, ½ t nutmeg, 1 c chopped walnuts,** and **½ c raisins**. Gently toss the apples with their liquid in this combination and set aside to cool.

Step 2: Make the Cherry Filling

fresh sour
  cherries (note)
almond extract
vanilla
brown sugar
lemon juice
cornstarch

Wash, stem, and pit **3 c sour cherries**. Combine them in a bowl with **1 t almond extract, ½ t vanilla, 2 T brown sugar,** and **1 t lemon juice**. (Increase sugar if cherries are very sour.)

The sugar will cause the cherries to release about ½ c of juice; drain it off and, in a small saucepan, whisk with **2 t cornstarch** to dissolve. Whisk constantly while you bring this to a boil and let it thicken. Remove from heat and gently coat cherries in the glaze. Set aside.

Step 3: Construct and Bake the Torte

butter

vanilla

phyllo dough
  (note)

cake crumbs

Lightly grease a 10-inch springform pan.

Melt ¼ **lb butter**. Add **1 t vanilla**.

Lay **phyllo** out flat, covered completely with a damp cloth (*note*).

Brush one sheet of phyllo with melted butter and lay it in the springform pan, gently fitting it up the sides and allowing extra to hang over. From a total of **2 ¼ c fine cake crumbs**, sprinkle phyllo with about 2 T crumbs. Repeat this process four times, crisscrossing phyllo sheets to cover pan completely.

Spread half of apple mixture over phyllo in bottom of pan.

Trim 12 sheets of phyllo into 9 x 9 inch squares.

Alternate atop the apples 4 squares that you brush with melted butter and sprinkle with 2 T cake crumbs, fitting the squares into the center of the pan over the apples.

Spread the cherry mixture gently over the phyllo layer. Alternate over the fruit, as before, 4 phyllo squares brushed with butter and more crumbs.

Spread remaining apples gently on phyllo.

Bring the overlapping edges of the first-placed phyllo sheets in toward the center, brushing butter between the edges to seal. Alternate atop this the last 4 buttered squares of phyllo and crumbs as before. Sprinkle remaining cake crumbs over top.

Bake in an oven preheated to 350° F for 50 minutes. Let rest 10 minutes. Gently release sides of springform pan.

Step 4: To Serve

heavy cream

sugar

rum

Cut the torte with a serrated knife. Start at an angle at the outside edge, gently working toward center.

Set each slice on a plate in a pool of softly whipped **cream** that has a touch of **sugar** and **vanilla** in it. (A little **rum** is very tasty also.)

NOTES AND TIPS:

Use green cooking apples for texture and flavor. Red delicious look good but don't give the same flavors.

Frozen (thawed) or canned cherries may be substituted for fresh cherries. Simply drain them and reserve ½ c of their juice.

Usually phyllo dough is available, frozen, in stores. Thaw it slowly, still wrapped, and use all exposed sheets immediately.

Tissue-thin phyllo is like parchment when it dries. Work quickly and keep it covered with a damp (not wet) cloth.

This torte is best served warm, but good the next day for breakfast.

Oven Temperature: 350° F

Serves: 10 to 12

California Torte

Chef Main dedicates this lemon génoise with its citrus buttercream and lemon Grand Marnier syrup to her home state. "I was raised in the San Francisco Bay Area. Although I now have the webbed feet of a Northwesterner, I still miss the lovely experience of having orange and lemon trees right outside in my sunny yard. The torte is in honor of that special privilege Californians have."

Step 1: Make the Lemon Génoise

eggs
egg yolks
sugar
cake flour
cornstarch
butter
grated lemon
  zest
vanilla

In the mixing bowl of an electric mixer, combine **4 eggs**, **3 egg yolks**, and **½ c sugar**. Use a hand whisk to mix them till combined, then set the bowl over hot water and stir till the mixture is lukewarm and bright yellow. Keep scraping from the bottom of the bowl to prevent the eggs from cooking. (The chef says, "I whisk with my hands in the egg mix at this point to stay sensitive to the heat.")

Remove egg mix from over hot water; use the electric mixer to whip it at high speed till it has cooled and become light, and soft peaks form. It will be almost tripled in bulk.

Sift **½ c cake flour** and **½ c cornstarch** together twice.

Sprinkle one-third of the flour over the whipped eggs, using a rubber spatula to fold it in gently. Repeat twice, till all flour has been absorbed.

Combine **¼ c melted butter**, **1 T grated lemon zest**, and **1 t vanilla**. Fold this into flour-egg mixture.

Grease and lightly flour 2 9-inch layer pans.

Gently pour the batter into layer pans. Smooth the tops, forming a higher ridge around the edges of the pans to make for more even baking.

Bake at 350° F for 25 to 30 minutes, till the génoise is golden brown and springs back from the impression of your fingers when you lightly press the top.

Remove the génoise from pans to a rack after 5 minutes, and let cool. Wrap delicately in plastic and freeze (*note*).

Step 2: Make the Citrus Buttercream

sugar
glucose or corn syrup
water
eggs
unsalted butter
vanilla
grated lemon zest
grated orange zest
Grand Marnier

In a heavy-bottomed saucepan, combine **2 c sugar, 2 T glucose or corn syrup**, and **½ c water**. Using a candy thermometer, heat the syrup to 235° F (the soft ball stage). Be sure to keep the sides of the pan washed down with a pastry brush dipped in water, or crystals will form in your syrup.

Meanwhile, whisk **2 eggs** and warm them in the large bowl of an electric mixer (just as they were warmed for the génoise).

Again using the electric mixer, whip at high speed till eggs are cool. (The sugar syrup should be reaching 235° F about now. Timing this step takes familiarity with your equipment. For instance, electric and gas burners perform quite differently.) Quickly transfer the hot sugar syrup to a large, heat-proof measuring cup.

Reduce mixer speed to medium and add the syrup to the eggs in a thin stream toward the middle of the bowl. (Remember to go slowly or you will have scrambled egg buttercream.) Continue to beat till cool (about 5 minutes).

Continue mixing and slowly add **1 ¼ lb cold unsalted butter** cut in small chunks. Small chunks will incorporate slowly and make the process easier on your equipment. At first the mixture will appear to separate, but don't worry, it will recombine and smooth out. Add **1 t vanilla, 2 T grated lemon zest, 2 T grated orange zest,** and **1 T Grand Marnier** (*note*).

Step 3: Make the Lemon Grand Marnier Syrup

sugar
water
Grand Marnier
lemon juice

Whisk **½ c sugar** into **½ c water** in a small saucepan over medium heat, till sugar completely dissolves. Remove from heat, and cool.

Stir in **2 T Grand Marnier** and **2 T lemon juice**.

Step 4: Assemble the Torte

If you have chilled the buttercream, beat it back to a silky smooth consistency. Don't overbeat it, or you will have air bubbles interrupting the smooth surface when you frost.

Unwrap the génoise and slice it while still frozen. Use a serrated knife to trim the rounded tops of the layers so they are flat. Rotating each layer, make a slight cut around the outside edge at two levels, to portion it into even horizontal thirds. Then cut each layer through (*note*). Stack the six layers, and cover them lightly with a towel as you work.

Place the first layer on a platter. Gently brush it with syrup. Be cautious; too much syrup will make the torte soggy. Spread with buttercream. Lay the next layer on, and press very lightly to level it and seal it with the layer below. Continue this procedure with each layer, but do not put buttercream on the top layer yet.

Using a serrated knife, very gently trim around the outside of the torte. Gently brush the sides with syrup and then frost top and sides.

Chill torte till firm, and then frost one more time to finish and refine.

Using a pastry bag with a star tip, pipe a swirled rosette border of buttercream, and decorate with fresh mint leaves and candied lemon or orange slices. Keep chilled.

To serve: Let the torte soften 15 minutes or so before cutting and serving. The texture of the frosting will be creamier and the citrus flavors will bloom. Then cut with a hot, dry, serrated knife. Dip the knife in very hot water (or run under hot tap water), dry with a cloth, and then gently divide torte into portions, letting the hot knife do the work. Pressing too hard will tear the cake and mar your presentation.

NOTES AND TIPS:

The génoise can be frozen for up to a week.

The buttercream can be refrigerated for up to a week, or frozen for up to two months. Be sure to wrap it tightly in either case to preserve its pure delicate flavor.

If you have a turntable or lazy susan, cutting the cake into six layers is much less challenging.

Oven Temperature: 350° F

Serves: 10 to 12

Chocolate Caramel Black Walnut Tart

"Fritz Schlatter," says Chef Main, "taught me pastry making at South Seattle Community College. His German Nut Bars, which have long been one of my favorite sweets, serve as the inspiration for this tart. I feel honored to have been his student and pleased that he continues to teach and share in his own particular artistic style."

Step 1: Make the Tart Shell

all-purpose flour
salt
baking powder
butter
sugar
egg
vanilla
black walnuts

Sift **1 ¼ c flour** with a **pinch of salt** and **1 t baking powder**.

Using an electric mixer, cream **¼ c softened butter** till light yellow. Slowly add **½ c sugar, 1 egg,** and **½ t vanilla.**

Add to the creamed mixture the dry ingredients and **¼ c ground black walnuts**. Chill for 1 hour. Pat this into the bottom and sides of a 10-inch greased tart pan till shell is ¼ inch thick.

Step 2: Fill and Bake the Tart

butter
honey
sugar
black walnuts

In a heavy-bottomed saucepan, bring to a boil **½ c plus 2 T (or 5 oz) each of butter, honey,** and **sugar**. Add **2 ¼ c coarsely chopped black walnuts,** and let come back just to a boil. Remove from heat. Let cool 15 minutes and pour into the tart shell.

Bake tart at 350° F on the middle rack of the oven till the filling begins to bubble (approximately 15 minutes) and turns a rich honey color. Allow the tart to cool.

cream
butter
sugar
bittersweet
 chocolate
black walnut
 halves

Step 3: Add the Ganache

In a heavy-bottomed saucepan, bring to a boil ½ **c cream**, **2 T butter**, and **2 T sugar**. Remove from heat. Stir in **4 oz bittersweet chocolate slivers** till dissolved.

Cool ganache to room temperature and spread over cooled tart.

Garnish with a circle of **black walnut halves,** and chill.

To Serve: Cut the tart with a serrated knife, dipping it in very hot water and drying the blade after each slice. This will give a good clean cut. The most refined desserts are often the most easily desecrated by sloppy serving.

NOTES AND TIPS:

If black walnuts aren't available, substitute English walnuts.

Oven Temperature: 350° F

Serves: 8 to 10

Chocolate Bread Pudding with Kahlua Ganache Sauce

Says Chef Main, "This is a cross between a chocolate soufflé and a custard pudding. The reassuring thing about this recipe is that it is forgiving of most mistakes and it will not fall as you present it!"

Step 1: Prepare Chocolate Bread Pudding

French bread cubes (note)
half and half
vanilla
Kahlua
salt
unsweetened chocolate
strong coffee
butter
egg yolks
sugar
grated lemon zest
cinnamon

Soak 4 c French bread cubes in **3 ½ c half and half, 2 t vanilla, 1 T Kahlua,** and a **pinch salt** for 2 hours at room temperature.

Melt together in a small saucepan **2 oz unsweetened chocolate, ½ c strong coffee,** and **1 T butter.** Stir into bread cube mixture.

Using an electric mixer, whip **3 egg yolks** till light. Gradually add **1 c sugar,** scraping the sides of the bowl as needed.

Continue beating the egg mixture. Strain 2 c of the cream mixture from the bread cubes and add it to the egg mixture, scraping the bowl several times. Stir remaining bread and cream mixture into egg and cream mixture with ¼ t **grated lemon zest** and a **pinch of cinnamon.**

Grease a 9 x 13 inch baking pan; fill with pudding mixture. Cover it with foil, and set it in a larger pan with enough water to reach ⅔ up the sides of the inner one. Bake at 350° F for 35 to 45 minutes (*note*) or till pudding is set like custard. It will shake slightly in the center. Let it rest at least 15 minutes to set more firmly before serving.

Step 2: Prepare Kahlua Ganache Sauce

heavy cream
unsalted butter
sugar

Stir and bring to a simmer in a heavy-bottomed saucepan ¾ c **heavy cream, 1 T unsalted butter,** and **1 T sugar.**

semisweet
chocolate
Kahlua
black walnuts
(note)

Remove from heat.

Stir in ¼ **lb shredded semisweet chocolate, 2 T Kahlua, and ½ c coarsely chopped black walnuts.**

Step 3: To serve

whipping cream
vanilla
chocolate
*   shavings*

Fill dessert dishes with about 1 c chocolate Bread Pudding; pour Kahlua Ganache Sauce over each. Whip **1 c chilled heavy cream** with **1 t vanilla,** and use a pastry bag with a star tip to pipe this over the sauce. Top with **chocolate shavings.**

NOTES AND TIPS:

Either sourdough or sweet French bread may be used, so long as the bread is firm.

If you adjust the baking pan size in arranging the water bath, also adjust the time for baking; more time for a smaller pan.

English walnuts substitute well. Chef Main prefers black walnuts because of their distinctive flavor. She says, "purely a matter of taste."

The pudding can be warmed in the microwave just before serving without losing its light texture.

Chef Main: "If you are not serving this sauce the day you make it, garnish with the walnuts instead of stirring them in, or stir them in just before serving. Otherwise they will lose their crunch to the sauce."

Oven Temperature: 350° F

Yield: 8 1-c servings of pudding; 1 ½ c sauce

Gingerbread Torte with Spiced Apples

This cake is soft and spicy. With a pot of fresh strong coffee, it's a comfortable beginning to good conversation.

Step 1: Make the Cake

all-purpose flour
baking powder
baking soda
salt
cinnamon
cloves
nutmeg
pepper
dry ground ginger
butter
brown sugar
egg
fresh ginger root
dark molasses
buttermilk
powdered sugar

Sift together **1 c flour, ½ t baking powder, ½ t baking soda, ¼ t salt, 1 t cinnamon, ½ t cloves, ½ t nutmeg, ¼ t pepper,** and **½ t dry ground ginger**.

Using an electric mixer, cream **¼ c butter**. Gradually add **¼ c brown sugar**. Scrape the bowl and add **1 egg**, mixing till incorporated. Stir in **1 T minced fresh ginger root**.

Add the dry ingredients to the creamed mixture alternately with **½ c dark molasses** and with **½ c buttermilk**. Do this in three stages, scraping bowl and beaters or paddle often.

Grease and flour a 9-inch round cake pan. Pour batter in and gently tap the cake pan on a counter to release bubbles.

Bake at 350° F for 25 minutes on center rack of oven.

Let cool 10 minutes and remove cake from pan. Dust top with powdered sugar.

Step 2: Make the Topping

apples
butter
brown sugar
sugar
salt

Peel, core, and cut **apples** in ⅛-inch slices to make **2 ½ c**. Melt **⅓ c butter** in a sauté pan. Sauté apples till they begin to give up their juices, shaking pan often or lifting apples with a wooden spoon.

cinnamon
nutmeg
brandy
vanilla
heavy cream

Add ½ c **brown sugar,** ½ c **sugar,** ½ t **salt, 1 t cinnamon,** and ½ t **freshly grated nutmeg.** Continue sautéing till apples are tender.

With the apples still in the pan, deglaze it with **2 T brandy** poured around the edges (*note*).

Remove pan from heat and add ½ t **vanilla.**

To serve: While both are still warm, slice ginger-bread into wedges and arrange apples alongside them. Add to each **a bit of soft whipped cream** and **a grate of fresh nutmeg.**

NOTES AND TIPS:

If cooking on a gas stove, keep the brandy away from the open flame as you add it and, while cooking, till the alcohol evaporates.

Oven Temperature: 350° F

Serves: 8

Lemon Cake Olga

In September of 1988, Chef Main "was privileged to travel to the Soviet Union with 'Peace Table,' a group of culinary diplomats led with unending enthusiasm by Jerilyn Brusseau. Our belief was that the seeds of peace can be planted by sharing meals and secrets of cuisine with our Soviet neighbors.

"Olga was our guide the entire three weeks. She became my first Soviet friend and gave me a precious gift, a family recipe that she makes at her home in Moscow."

eggs
butter
baking soda
apple cider vinegar
flour
lemons
sugar

Separate **4 eggs**. Put 4 yolks in one bowl and 3 whites in another.

Melt ¾ **c butter**, and cool.

Dissolve ½ **t baking soda** in **2 t apple cider vinegar**. (Allow it room to foam.)

Using an electric mixer, mix butter and the 4 egg yolks. Slowly add **1 ½ c flour** and dissolved soda to form a moist dough.

Divide dough in thirds. Put one-third in freezer till hard "like a stone." Lightly grease an 8 x 8 inch cake pan. Pat the remaining two-thirds of dough evenly on the bottom. Chill this dough while waiting for the stone to harden.

Grate the zest from **2 lemons** and squeeze the juice. There should be about ¼ **c juice** and a **heaping tablespoon zest**.

Beat the 3 whites till foamy. Gradually add **1 c sugar**. Beat till thick and quickly stir in the lemon juice and zest.

Spread the lemon mixture on the dough.

Using the coarse side of a grater, grate the stone of dough evenly over the batter.

Bake at 350° F for 30 to 35 minutes on middle oven rack.

To serve: Cool the cake and cut into even squares.

Oven Temperature: 350° F

Serves: 6

One ethnic group that arrived, worked, and departed the Peninsula leaving almost no trace of its presence was the Chinese laborers who performed the hard work in the canneries once lining the river, from Ilwaco past McGowan. The old men and young boys who came from China without their families first labored on the railroads, later washed for gold in the mountains, and ended up as the mainstay of the flourishing canneries.

Fresh Fruit with Lime Devonshire

Try this elegant combination for a light dessert or a brunch compote.

sour cream (or yogurt)
brown sugar
lime zest
lime juice
heavy cream
fresh fruit

Combine **1 c sour cream or yogurt** with **2 T brown sugar** in a small bowl, and whisk till the lumps are dissolved. If they don't dissolve immediately, let it sit 5 minutes for the sugar to soften, then whisk again.

Whisk in **1 t grated lime zest** and **2 T lime juice** (*note*). Fold in ¼ c **heavy cream** that has been whipped to soft peaks.

Arrange **sliced fresh fruit** in parfait glasses. It is visually pleasing to start with darker tones and work up into lighter shades—for instance, strawberries, then kiwi, then pineapple. (If you have frozen berries, put them on the bottom, and by the time the sauce and juices from the fruit on top have coated them they will make a pleasing finish to the compote.) Top with a generous dollop of sauce.

NOTES AND TIPS:

Grate the limes and then roll them on the table under pressure from your palm before juicing, to get the maximum amount of juice.

For a dramatic variation, use large flat plates and fan apples, pineapple, papaya, and melon in a circle. Put a few tablespoons of sauce in the center, and garnish with strawberries and/or raspberries. Grate a light dust of fresh nutmeg over the fruit, and place edible flowers along the side of the plate; try nasturtiums, geraniums, or rosebuds.

Yield: 1 ½ cups sauce (sufficient for 8 to 10 servings)

As one writer has described the settlement of the Chinese cannery workers in McGowan, on the Columbia River, "Their settlement was complete with a theater, firecrackers on occasion, and opium that was sold openly in flat round cans....The Chinese were not allowed to fish, ever. They filled all the inside cannery jobs, such as making the cans and cutting up the fish....A picture of the time shows two-score Orientals, pigtails wrapped neatly up on the backs of their necks, going about their work in a huge room steaming from the cooking apparatus."

Snicker Mousse

"Ah! Those memory sweets of childhood! I remember risking recognition by going back twice to a house on Halloween when they gave out this candy bar. Sometimes I made it a part of my school cafeteria 'lunch money booty' on the way to school. It was one of my favorites," recalls Chef Main as she serves up another childhood treat, grown up.

Though this recipe seems quite complicated, it's laid out in simple individual steps and requires only that you follow them as described, in order.

Step 1: Make the Peanut Mousse Base

cream cheese

sugar

creamy peanut
    butter

butter

whipping cream

vanilla

Whip **2 oz softened cream cheese** till fluffy. Slowly add ¼ c **sugar**, ¼ c **creamy peanut butter**, and **2 t softened butter**. Whip till well incorporated and light. Transfer to a bowl.

Whip ¾ c **cream** with ¾ t **vanilla** till firm but not dry.

Stir one-third of the whipped cream into the peanut butter mixture. Use a whisk at this point in order to blend the different textures. Once they are initially combined, it is easier to fold in the remaining whipped cream with a spatula, so that the mousselike quality remains.

Chill the mousse base.

Step 2: Make the Caramel

sweetened
    condensed milk

Pour **2 c sweetened condensed milk** into a small heavy-bottomed saucepan. Bring it just to a boil over medium high heat, whisking constantly. Reduce heat to a simmer and continue whisking (*note*) till milk turns a honey blond color and begins to thicken (5 to 8 minutes). Be sure to contact the entire surface of the pan bottom, as the sugar will caramelize quickly there and form small lumps. (If this happens, put the milk through a fine mesh strainer and proceed.)

When milk is slightly thickened, set it aside to cool to lukewarm, stirring with a whisk occasionally to prevent a crust from forming on the caramel.

Step 3: Finish the Mousse Layers

unsweetened chocolate heavy cream peanuts

Melt **4 oz shredded unsweetened chocolate** in a heat-proof bowl over barely simmering water. (Do not let the water touch the bottom of the bowl.) When the chocolate is half-melted, turn off the heat and allow it to continue melting over the hot water.

In another bowl, whip ¾ **c heavy cream** till thick and mousselike. Using a whisk, incorporate one-third of the whipped cream into 1 c of the caramel. Follow the same procedure as for the peanut mousse, folding in the remaining two-thirds. Stir in the melted chocolate.

Stir 1 c of the caramel and **1 ½ c chopped peanuts** into the peanut mousse.

Whip ¾ **c heavy cream** till thick and mousselike. Put into a pastry bag with a star tip.

Step 4: Assemble the Snicker Mousse

In parfait glasses, arrange six layers altogether. Start with the chocolate caramel, then the peanut mousse, then a piped layer of whipped cream (*note*). Repeat the three layers.

NOTES AND TIPS:

Chef Main uses the name "meditation step" for the caramel preparation because you must stand in one spot and focus on circles of motion.

It is easier to layer in clean lines if you use pastry bags for the chocolate caramel and peanut mousse as well as the whipped cream. Don't use a tip.

Chef Main often top-glazes this dessert with melted semisweet chocolate and a sprinkle of chopped peanuts. When you put your spoon through this top glaze it's like breaking into the first bite of a candy bar—the complete experience!

Serves: 6 to 8

Vanilla Cream Cheesecake

Nadene Peterson of San Antonio, Texas, might legitimately be called a "dessert freak." She recalls one of those glorious sweet moments at The Ark, "At the second Garlic Festival they served, at the very end of the meal, apricot halves dipped in chocolate with a dollop of raspberries. One was not enough! Soon word got back to the kitchen that someone was nearly intimidating other guests out of their apricot halves. When Nanci learned that I was the culprit, she decided to name the specialty Apricots Nadene, in honor of either my good taste in food or my crazed greed for the fabulous combination."

Here's one more sweet treat for this friend from Texas.

pound cake
cream cheese
sugar
flour
eggs
vanilla
*finely grated
 lemon zest*
*finely grated
 orange zest*

Cut **½-inch lengthwise slices of pound cake**; fit them into the bottom of a greased 10-inch springform pan, cutting pieces so bottom is completely covered.

Using an electric mixer, beat **2 ½ lb softened cream cheese** till smooth. Gradually add **1 ¾ c sugar,** scraping often.

Add **2 T flour,** a tablespoon at a time, **3 eggs,** one at a time, **1 T vanilla, 1 T finely grated lemon zest,** and **1 T finely grated orange zest.**

Smooth cream cheese mixture into the pan.

Bring heavy foil up around the bottom and sides of the pan. Place it in a larger pan with enough water to reach 1 inch up the sides.

Bake 10 minutes at 350° F, then 1 hour, 15 minutes at 275° F. Cheesecake is done when it jiggles like a firm custard.

Cool cheesecake to room temperature; chill at least 4 hours.

NOTES AND TIPS:

Chef Main serves this cake with Spiced Apricot-Ginger Sauce (see recipe p. 184). It also goes well with the raspberry topping from the Buttermilk Raspberry Pie recipe (see p. 138) or a chocolate ganache sauce such as for Chocolate Caramel Black Walnut Tart (p. 148).

Oven Temperature: 350° F, 275° F

Serves: 10 to 12

Wild Blackberry Cobbler

If there's a perennial hit from among the Ark desserts, it's this cobbler. We use local wild blackberries, picked for us from the woods around Willapa Bay, and serve it warm, topped with French vanilla ice cream. The biscuits for this cobbler are exceptionally light and delicate, a nice balance to the tart berries.

Step 1: Make the Blackberry Filling

blackberries
all-purpose flour
sugar
lemon zest

In a saucepan, bring **8 c blackberries** to a simmer. Mix **2 T flour** and ¾ c **sugar**, and stir into fruit. Add the **zest of 1 lemon** and add sugar if necessary. Cook till slightly thickened.

Step 2: Make the Biscuits

all-purpose flour
salt
baking powder
sugar
cinnamon
butter
milk
vanilla

Sift **1 scant c flour**, ¼ t **salt**, 1 ½ t **baking powder**, **2 t sugar**, and ½ t **cinnamon** into a mixing bowl.

Cut **3 T chilled butter** into the flour mixture till it has the consistency of cornmeal.

Make a well in the center of the mixture and add ⅓ c **cold milk** and **1 t vanilla** all at once. Mix till just blended; do not overwork. Divide into 8 biscuits.

Step 3: Assemble the Cobbler

Pour the blackberry mixture into a greased 9 x 13 inch baking pan. Dot with **2 T butter**. Using two tablespoons, scoop up the 8 biscuits and space them on top of the blackberries.

Bake at 400° F till the cobbler is bubbling and biscuits are done (20 to 30 minutes).

To serve: The cobbler is best warm, with a scoop of French vanilla ice cream.

NOTES AND TIPS:

You can warm this cobbler successfully in the microwave oven, but remove the biscuits first so they don't toughen.

If Northwest wild blackberries are not available, substitute your own local berries. Raspberries and marionberries also work well in this recipe.

Oven Temperature: 400° F

Serves: 8

Ark Basics

Getting There: The Early Days

In the early days it was not easy to get to the beach. A century ago, a stern-wheeler down the Columbia from Portland to Astoria was the only choice. Starting in 1871, the *Emma Hayward* was the first ship to make the run. As summers at the beach, and even quick weekends, became more popular, the *Emma Hayward* was replaced by the better known *T.J. Potter* in 1888, and then by the *Georgiana*, a propeller ship that was in use from 1914 to 1939, when the steamboating days came to an end.

All the ships on the river run were well fitted and comfortable, but the *T.J. Potter* was particularly elegant, with elaborately furnished cabins, tables set with white linen and silver, and a grand piano in the saloon. She had been designed for the river. When her owners tried to transfer her to Puget Sound, she rolled and lifted so badly that the dizzy, seasick passengers protested. But when she was returned to her home on the river, she worked the summer run smoothly for thirty years.

By 1888, visitors to the Peninsula could ride the *Potter* down the Columbia, take a smaller boat to Ilwaco, transfer to the narrow gauge train, and ride, if they wished, as far as Nahcotta. So many working fathers brought their families down on Saturday, went back to Portland by the night boat on Sunday, and returned to the beach the next weekend that the Saturday run of the railroad-that-ran-by-the-tide became known as "the papa's train."

Early in this century an alternate way of getting there appeared when the S.P. & S. Railroad began operating a passenger train between Portland and Astoria. Then it was possible to ride the train down the Oregon side, take a ferry to Megler, and go on by the narrow gauge train.

The forty-five minute ferry ride disappeared when the Astoria Bridge opened in 1966. Now they are all gone—the steamboats, the passenger trains, the ferries. To get to the beach, you have to have a car.

Apple, Currant, & Wild Mint Chutney with Merlot

tomatoes
wild mint
  (note)
apples
red bell pepper
green bell
  pepper
jalapeño
  peppers
honey
balsamic
  vinegar
brown sugar
Merlot
currants
raisins
tomato sauce

In a saucepan over medium heat, mix **1 ½ c chopped tomatoes, 2 T chopped wild mint, 3 c cored, chopped apples, 2 T chopped mixed red and green bell peppers, 4 seeded and diced jalapeño peppers, 2 T honey, 3 T Balsamic vinegar,** and **3 T brown sugar.** Add **1 ½ c Merlot, 1 c currants,** and **½ c raisins.**

Increase heat to high; bring mixture to a boil. Lower heat to simmer; reduce the mixture by one-quarter.

Add **⅓ c tomato sauce.**

NOTES AND TIPS:

Mint from your supermarket's produce section may be substituted if wild mint is unavailable.

Chef Lucas serves this chutney at The Ark with broiled swordfish, marlin, and even broiled fillets of albacore.

This chutney will keep for up to 6 weeks, if refrigerated in an airtight container.

Yield: 2 to 3 c chutney

Pickled Cherry & Orange Relish for White Fish

oranges
red bell pepper
yellow bell
 pepper
red onion
celery
cucumber
fresh oregano
garlic
pickled cherries
 (note)
Tabasco
pepper
salt
cornstarch

Mix together **2 peeled, sliced, and chopped oranges, 1 T red bell pepper, 1 T yellow bell pepper, 3 T diced red onion, 2 ribs diced celery, ¼ c peeled, seeded, and diced cucumber, 1 T chopped fresh oregano, 1 t minced garlic, ½ c diced pickled cherries, 4 shakes Tabasco, and freshly ground pepper** and **salt to taste.**

In a small saucepan, bring to a boil **1 c pickled cherry juice;** add **1 T cornstarch,** stirring till the cornstarch is dissolved. Remove from heat; stir into other mixture.

NOTES AND TIPS:

For the Ark pickled cherry recipe, see p. 124.

This relish will keep for 2 weeks in the refrigerator.

Yield: 3 to 4 c relish

Corn Relish

This recipe has become a favorite of Chef Lucas. "It was given to me by Kathy Casey, whose culinary craziness and creativeness it has been my pleasure to experience. This is great simply eaten out of a dish. Or it's complementary to swordfish, ahi, or seafood cakes (*note*) with a dollop of crème fraîche (*note*).

olive oil	Heat ½ c **olive oil**; add ½ **small diced onion, 2 T minced garlic, 1 seeded, diced red bell pepper, 1 seeded, diced green bell pepper,** and **1 qt corn cut from the cob.** Mix thoroughly.
onion	
garlic	
red bell pepper	
green bell pepper	When mixture, still in the pan, is thoroughly heated, deglaze it with ½ **c balsamic vinegar.**
corn	Add ¼ c **brown sugar.**
balsamic vinegar	Remove mixture from heat. Add **2 T chopped fresh basil, 6 to 8 seeded and diced jalapeño peppers,** ¼ c **lime juice,** and **salt** and **pepper to taste.**
brown sugar	
fresh basil (note)	
jalapeño peppers	
lime juice	
salt	
pepper	

NOTES AND TIPS:

For the Ark seafood cakes recipe, see p. 95.

For the Ark crème fraîche recipe, see p. 13.

1 T chopped fresh cilantro can be used instead of basil. Chef Lucas: "I prefer the basil: It balances the tartness of the vinegar and the sweetness of the corn."

In a covered airtight container in the refrigerator, this relish will keep well for a month.

Yield: 1 qt relish

Cranberry Mint Confit

Here's a wonderful accompaniment to lamb chops, or, of course, the traditional holiday turkey. Even if the turkey isn't served on a traditional holiday, this confit makes the meal a holiday meal.

onions	Cook **2 large onions**, sliced lengthwise, and **½ c sugar** in **½ c butter** till lightly browned.
sugar	
butter	Add **1 ½ t minced garlic** and **2 T chopped fresh mint**. Cook briefly to let flavors marry.
garlic	
fresh mint	With mixture still in the pan, deglaze it with **½ c red wine vinegar**.
red wine	
vinegar	Add **4 c whole cranberries, 1 bay leaf,** and **½ t dried rosemary**. Cook over medium heat, stirring occasionally, for 15 minutes or till the mixture thickens. Remove bay leaf.
cranberries	
bay leaf	
dried rosemary	

NOTES AND TIPS:

This confit will keep for up to 2 months in an airtight container in the refrigerator.

Yield: about 4 c confit

Cranberry Orange Pecan Relish

For Chef Lucas, "Tradition plays a leading role in so much that I feel and do with food. As long as I can remember, the tradition of having cranberry sauce with Thanksgiving turkey has stimulated a quest every time I smell the roasting aromas of the turkey.

"The traditions of slaughtering the turkeys, cleaning the pumpkins, pulling the fall vegetables together, helping with the baking, yes, even the cleaning of the house for company are an important part of the day. Finally the early-morning Thanksgiving aromas filling the house lead to one last day of anticipating the meal.

"When all the proper dishware is cleaned, polished, and prepared for use, I recall myself as a child filled with amazement and wonder at seeing a jiggling treat, this perfectly shaped cylinder of crimson called cranberry sauce, and pondering if it grew that way. And so, each year, I give the real stuff of the cranberry a cameo role. Here is one of the latest renditions of this traditional favorite."

cranberries
brown sugar
cranberry juice
raspberry
 vinegar
Madeira
white onions
orange
toasted pecans
 (note)
fresh ginger
 root

Mix in a saucepan **4 c whole cranberries, ½ c brown sugar, ½ c cranberry juice, ½ c raspberry vinegar, ¼ c Madeira, ½ c finely sliced white onions, 1 orange, finely ground (with peel) in a food processor, ½ c toasted and coarsely chopped pecans**, and **2 T ground fresh ginger root.**

Bring all ingredients to a high boil. Reduce heat, and cook 20 minutes.

NOTES AND TIPS:

For how to toast nuts, see p. 12.

This relish will keep for up to 4 weeks in the refrigerator.

It's Thanksgiving, enjoy!

Yield: 3 ½ c relish

Mango Pear Caper Relish

clarified butter
 (note)
onion
garlic
cumin
rice wine
 vinegar
lime juice
mangos
pears
tomato brunoise
 (note)
capers
salt
pepper
Tabasco
pineapple juice
sake
fresh mint

Sauté in **6 T clarified butter**, over very high heat, **1 chopped onion, 1 T minced garlic,** and **½ t cumin**. Remove from heat.

Combine with the sautéed mixture **¾ c rice wine vinegar, ½ c lime juice, 1 ½ c peeled, chopped mango, 1 c peeled, cored, chopped pear, ½ c tomato brunoise, 3 T capers, salt and pepper to taste, 4 shakes Tabasco, ½ c pineapple juice, ¼ c sake,** and **3 T chopped fresh mint.**

NOTES AND TIPS:

For how to clarify butter, see p. 13.

Tomato brunoise: The outside flesh layer of the tomatoes only, chopped in perfect squares.

Don't limit this richly flavored relish to grilled fish entrées. Chef Lucas sometimes serves it on a plate of mixed vegetables (such as grilled vegetables and vinaigrette green beans) and with cheeses and an assortment of crackers.

This relish will keep for 2 weeks in the refrigerator.

Yield: 2 to 3 c relish

Yakima Beefsteak Tomato-Orange Salsa with Ginger

jalapeño
 peppers
tomatoes
onion
garlic
fresh cilantro
ground cumin
coriander seed
chili powder
oranges
lime juice
fresh ginger
 root
salt
olive oil

Mix **3 to 4 seeded and diced jalapeño peppers, 3 to 4 diced tomatoes, 1 finely chopped red onion, 1 T minced garlic, 2 T minced fresh cilantro, 1 ½ t ground cumin, 1 T whole coriander seed, 1 T chili powder, the zest of one orange, the flesh of 2 oranges, peeled and sectioned and chopped, ½ c lime juice, 1 T ground fresh ginger root, salt to taste,** and **3 T olive oil.**

Allow the mixture to rest 2 to 4 hours to set the flavors.

NOTES AND TIPS:

Chef Lucas serves this salsa with grilled fish, such as salmon, shark, or marlin.

This salsa will keep for 2 to 3 weeks in the refrigerator.

Yield: 2 to 3 c salsa

Zucchini Relish

Chef Lucas finds "This recipe is quite complementary to sturgeon and swordfish. It is a great side for seafood frittatas (*note*).

clarified butter (note)
garlic
fresh ginger root
onions
zucchini
red bell peppers
green bell peppers
yellow bell peppers
brown sugar
whole allspice
pickling spice
curry powder
mustard seed
cayenne
cider vinegar
balsamic vinegar

Heat in a large saucepan, in **½ c clarified butter, 4 T minced garlic** and **3 T minced fresh ginger root**. Add **2 onions thinly sliced lengthwise**. Cook till tender.

Add **1 gal ⅓-inch-cubed zucchini, 2 c seeded, julienne-cut mixed red, green, and yellow bell peppers, 2 c brown sugar, 1 t whole allspice, 2 t pickling spice, 2 T curry powder, 1 t mustard seed, 1 t cayenne, 3 c cider vinegar**, and **1 c balsamic vinegar**.

Bring mixture to a boil and cook 5 minutes, stirring frequently.

Reduce heat; cook 20 to 25 minutes, or till sauce is syrupy.

NOTES AND TIPS:

For the Ark seafood frittata recipe, see p. 97.

For how to clarify butter, see p. 13.

This relish will keep for 2 to 3 weeks in the refrigerator.

Pint jars of this relish make great gifts.

Yield: approximately 3 qt relish

Dill Butter

Don't let the simplicity of this butter mislead you; it's an elegant topping for a number of grilled fish or vegetable preparations.

butter
Dijon mustard
lemon juice
fresh dill

Mix well **½ lb softened butter, 1 T Dijon mustard, 2 T lemon juice,** and **3 T chopped fresh dill.**

NOTES AND TIPS:

Good especially on steamed carrots or on glacé grilled salmon.

Yield: ½ c dill butter

Garlic Béchamel Sauce

butter
garlic
flour
milk
salt
white pepper

Heat ¼ c **butter** in a saucepan. When it's hot, add **2 T minced garlic,** and brown it carefully (don't let it burn). Add **4 T flour,** stirring constantly, and cook 3 to 4 minutes.

Add **2 c milk,** and **salt** and **white pepper to taste.**

Cook for about 5 minutes.

NOTES AND TIPS:

Besides Oysters Scentiva (p. 66) and other recipes that call for béchamel, here's a fine use for this elegant sauce: Toast bread, and spread it with chopped celery and green onions. Add a mound of hot shrimp, and ladle garlic béchamel sauce over it.

Yield: 2 c sauce

Roasted Garlic-Prawn Sauce

This hearty, rich sauce can be served over steamed salmon or white-fish, seafood crêpes, or vegetable timbales; use it over Steamed Petrale Sole with Seafood Mousse. Try it also with grilled veal or lamb.

prawn shells
salt
white pepper
clarified butter
  (note)
garlic
shallots
Dijon mustard
white wine
fish stock (note)
heavy cream

In 450° F oven, roast **prawn shells from about 4 lb prawns** with **salt** and **white pepper** for 10 to 15 minutes, or till browned. Set aside.

Place **6 T clarified butter, 2 T minced garlic,** and **1 T minced shallots** into an oven-proof stainless steel saucepan. Pan roast at the same hot oven temperature, till the garlic starts to brown.

Quickly add to the garlic mixture **2 T Dijon mustard.** Deglaze the roasted garlic with ½ c **white wine.** Add the prawn shells to the pan; mix well.

Add **1 c fish stock** and **1 qt heavy cream.**

Bring to a near boil; reduce heat.

Stirring frequently, reduce sauce by half or till it reaches the desired thickness, 35 to 45 minutes.

Strain the sauce.

NOTES AND TIPS:

For how to clarify butter, see p. 13.

For the Ark fish stock recipe, see p. 187.

If you need to reheat this sauce, pour it into a double boiler. As you heat it, it will break. At that point, add about ½ c heavy cream; it will bind itself again. Once it binds, remove it from the heat or it will break again.

Oven Temperature: 450° F

Yield: 2 to 3 c sauce

*McGowan, on
the banks of the river not
far from the Astoria
Bridge, grew up around
the salmon saltery and
cannery owned by the
businessman for whom it
was named. In 1868 it
caught fire and houses,
sheds, barrels of fish, and
a cooper shop went up in
flames. Rebuilt, the town
lasted until 1902, when
heavy storms wrecked
the mess houses along
the river, uprooted big
trees, and caused the
"China House" to be
moved farther up the
bank, away from high
water. Then, as the sal-
mon canneries vanished,
so did the town. Now
there is nothing to show
where it once stood.*

Ginger-Lime Mousseline

clarified butter
(note)
fresh ginger
root
garlic
lime juice
Madeira
egg yolks
white wine
heavy cream

Sauté, in **2 T clarified butter,** ½ **t grated fresh ginger root** and ½ **t minced garlic.** Add ⅓ **c lime juice.** Let cook 1 to 2 minutes.

With ingredients still in the pan, deglaze with **2 T Madeira;** allow liquid to reduce by half.

Place the mixture in a round-bottomed stainless steel bowl, and allow to cool at room temperature.

Add the **yolks of 4 eggs** and **2 T white wine.** Heat the mixture in the top of a double boiler while whisking vigorously (the technique for basic hollandaise).

When you see marks from the whisk and the mixture has turned pale yellow, remove it from the heat; slowly add ¾ **c clarified butter** that's a bit warmer than room temperature.

Whip and fold in ½ **c heavy cream.** Adjust flavor by adding the juice of up to one lime, if desired.

NOTES AND TIPS:

For how to clarify butter, see p. 13.

Have ice water handy; if the sauce starts to break, add drops of water. Keep the water level low enough in the bottom half of the double boiler that it can't touch the top half. For further protection, keep a cotton towel between the steam and the bowl.

The sauce turns a simple poached white fish into an elegant entrée.

Yield: about 2 ½ c sauce

Hollandaise Sauce

egg yolks
dry white wine
clarified butter

While heating water in the bottom of a double boiler (*note*), whisk vigorously in the top **4 egg yolks** with **1 T dry white wine**.

When the sauce turns pale and the whisk marks appear, remove from heat and drizzle in ¾ **to 1 lb clarified butter** (*note*) that's a bit warmer than room temperature.

Whisk sauce till stiff.

NOTES AND TIPS:

The top pan should not sit in the water in the lower pan.

For how to clarify butter, see p. 13.

Keep ice water handy; if the sauce starts to break, add drops of water.

Yield: 1 ½ c sauce

Horseradish-Cream Sauce

whipped cream
sour cream
prepared
 horseradish
lemon
salt
white pepper

Mix **2 c whipped cream, 1 c sour cream, ½ c prepared horseradish, the juice of ½ lemon,** and **salt** and **white pepper to taste.**

NOTES AND TIPS:

Serve Horseradish-Cream Sauce with North End Prime Rib of Beef. For recipe, see p. 108.

Yield: 2 ½ to 3 c sauce

Spiced Apricot-Ginger Sauce

dried apricots *brown sugar* *water*	In a 2-qt saucepan, combine **1 c dried apricots, ¼ c brown sugar,** and **1 ½ c water.** Simmer 30 minutes or till tender, stirring often.
white wine *vinegar*	Add **½ c white wine vinegar, 1 c water,** and **¼ c brown sugar.**
sticks of *cinnamon* *fresh ginger* *root*	Wrap in a piece of cheesecloth and immerse in the saucepan **1 ½ sticks cinnamon, 2 t coarsely chopped fresh ginger root,** and **2 t whole cloves.** Simmer 30 minutes. Remove cheesecloth bundle.
whole cloves	Purée sauce and press through a strainer.
Grand Marnier *candied ginger*	Add **¼ c Grand Marnier** and **3 T chopped candied (or "crystallized") ginger.**

NOTES AND TIPS:

Chef Main serves this over her vanilla cream cheesecake (see p. 161 for recipe), on ice cream, or drizzled over poached fruit, topped with a dollop of crème fraîche.

Yield: 1 ¾ c sauce

Candied Lime & Orange Zest

Candied citrus zests are a wonderful garnish for both entrées and desserts. They add that little extra something that makes a dish really extraordinary.

Lime Zest

clarified butter (note)
lime zest
Chambord

Heat **2 T clarified butter** in a sauté pan. Add the **zest of 2 to 3 limes**, turning it constantly to prevent burning.

Without removing the zest from the pan, deglaze it with **3 T Chambord**. Remove and drain zest.

Orange Zest

clarified butter (note)
orange zest
Drambuie

Heat **2 T clarified butter** in a sauté pan. Add the **zest of 1 large or 2 small oranges,** turning it constantly to prevent burning.

Without removing the zest from the pan, deglaze it with **3 T Drambuie**. Remove and drain zest.

NOTES AND TIPS:

For how to clarify butter, see p. 13.

Store zest in an airtight container in the refrigerator.

Yield: scant ¼ c lime zest; scant ¼ c orange zest

Chicken Stock

water
chicken parts
gizzards
onion
whole cloves
garlic
carrot
celery
parsley
dried thyme
bay leaves
peppercorns

Combine, in **4 qt water, 3 lb chicken parts and trimmings** (*note*), **2 lb chicken gizzards, 1 large quartered onion studded with 6 cloves, 3 split cloves garlic, 2 large carrots, coarsely.chopped, 2 c coarsely chopped celery, including tops, 1 c coarsely chopped parsley, 1 t dried thyme, 3 bay leaves, and 2 t peppercorns.** Bring ingredients to a boil, and reduce heat.

Simmer stock about 3 hours; strain it through cheesecloth.

Cool the stock at room temperature, refrigerate, and skim off the fat. Store in refrigerator, or freeze.

NOTES AND TIPS:

Whenever you prepare chicken, save the trimmings and freeze them for use when you make stock.

Yield: 3 qt stock

Fish Stock

water
fish scraps
onion
carrot
fresh fennel
bay leaves
star anise
peppercorns

Combine, in **2 to 3 qt water, 1 lb fish scraps** (*note*), **1 large onion, coarsely chopped, 2 large carrots, coarsely chopped, 1 c chopped fresh fennel, 2 bay leaves, 4 to 6 star anise** (*note*), **and 1 ½ t peppercorns.** Bring ingredients to a boil, and reduce heat.

Simmer stock about 3 hours; strain through cheesecloth.

Cool stock at room temperature, and refrigerate, or freeze.

NOTES AND TIPS:

Do not use gills. Also do not use sturgeon. Aside from these restrictions, any raw fish heads, tails, bones, and trimmings are fine to use for stock. (Freeze the extra bits whenever preparing fish, for later use). Salmon, snapper, and halibut are Chef Lucas' favorites.

The star anise adds a delicate sweetness to the fish flavor of the stock but may be omitted.

Yield: 1 ½ to 2 qt stock

Lamb Stock

lamb bones
pepper
water
carrots
yellow onions
whole cloves
parsley
peppercorns

Bake **3 lb lamb bones,** seasoned with **pepper,** at 450° F till browned.

Combine, **in 3 to 4 qt water, the lamb bones, 2 to 3 carrots, cut into chunks, 2 whole yellow onions, peeled and studded with 4 whole cloves, 1 bunch parsley stems and tops,** and **2 t peppercorns.** Bring ingredients to a boil, and reduce heat. Simmer stock for 3 hours. Skim the pot regularly to clear impurities that collect on the top.

Strain the stock through cheesecloth. When it has cooled to room temperature, refrigerate; skim off fat. Store in refrigerator, or freeze.

NOTES AND TIPS:

Chef Lucas never salts basic stocks while making them; she adds salt when using them.

Yield: 2 ½ to 3 qt stock

Notes

Notes

Index

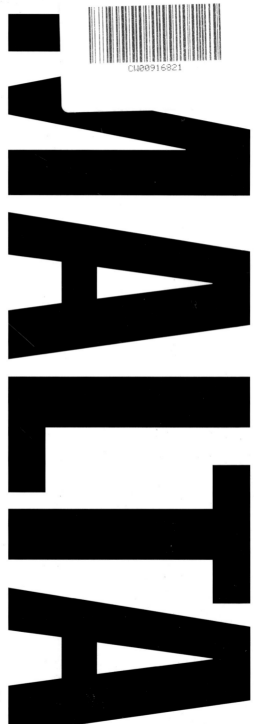

SPIRAL GUIDE

MALTA

CW00916821

AA
Publishing

Contents

the magazine **5**

Finding Your Feet 31

Valletta, Sliema and St Julian's 41

The South 81

Written by Paul Murphy

Produced by Duncan Baird Publishers, London, England

Published by AA Publishing, a trading name of Automobile
Association Developments Limited, whose registered office is
Millstream, Maidenhead Road, Windsor, Berkshire, SL4 5GD.
Registered number 1878835.

ISBN 0 7495 3557 1

All rights reserved. No part of this publication may be reproduced,
stored in a retrieval system, or transmitted in any form or by any
means – electronic, photocopying, recording or otherwise – unless
the written permission of the publishers has been obtained beforehand. This book may not be sold, resold, hired out or otherwise
disposed of by way of trade in any form of binding or cover other
than that in which it is published, without the prior consent of the
publisher.

The contents of this publication are believed correct at the time of
printing. Nevertheless, AA Publishing accept no responsibility for
errors, omissions or changes in the details given, or for the conse-
quences of reader's reliance on this information. This does not affect
your statutory rights. Assessments of the attractions, hotels and
restaurants are based upon the author's own experience, and contain
subjective opinions that may not reflect the publisher's opinion or a
reader's experience. We have tried to ensure accuracy, but things do
change, so please let us know if you have any comments or correc-
tions.

A CIP catalogue record for this book is available from the
British Library.

Cover design and binding style by permission of AA Publishing
Colour separation by Leo Reprographics
Printed and bound in China by Leo Paper Products

Find out more about AA Publishing and the wide range of travel pub-
lications and services the AA provides by visiting our website at
www.theAA.com

First published 2003
Reprinted Jun 2004

© Automobile Association Developments Limited 2003
Maps produced under licence from map data © RMF Publishing and
Surveys Ltd (Malta)
Maps © Automobile Association Developments Limited 2003

A02279

the magazine

ROMANCING

Malta's temples and ancient sites, which include the oldest freestanding structures on earth, are some of the island's most impressive but least understood visitor attractions. Here are the bare facts.

Around 7,000 years ago Man first came to Malta, then sometime between 3600 BC and 2500 BC he decided to embark on an enormous temple-building spree. Some 23 classifiable temples remain today, though how many more have been lost or destroyed will never be known. The principal survivors are the Ħal Saflieni Hypogeum (► 86–88), Tarxien (► 89–90), Ġgantija (Gozo, ► 144), Mnajdra and Ħaġar Qim (► 94).

We know, from the discovery of statues and statuettes, that the temples were built in honour of a deity, probably the Mother-Goddess of Fertility, and they were divided into private inner sanctums and public outer areas. Imagine them roofed, plastered and painted in bright ochre. The inner sanctums were curtained off and had "oracle holes" where the priesthood would confer with the deity before reporting back to the people. Animal sacrifice was practised, but all evidence points to a peaceful civilisation. Then, quite suddenly, in around 2000 BC, these temple-builders simply disappeared. From evidence excavated at Tarxien, it appears that in the 400 years between their disappearance and the Bronze Age inhabitants who followed them, the island may have been deserted.

Questions abound. Why were there so many temples given that the island population cannot have been more than around 11,000 – were the islands on some kind of Mediterranean pilgrim's route? Why did it all end so suddenly – were there religious upheavals? Had the inhabitants been so busy building temples that they had neglected to look after more secular matters?

Did You Know?

Each temple is built to a similar ground plan, with a corridor leading beneath a huge stone trilithon (an arch consisting of two uprights and a lintel) through kidney-shaped rooms to the altar enclosure. Giant stones weighing up to 20 tons form the protective outer walls.

TIMELINE

c 3600 BC	*c* 2550 BC	*c* 2500 BC
Ġgantija (oldest temple)	**The Great Pyramids of Egypt**	**Tarxien** (youngest temple)

THE STONES

And had this led to war, drought, plague, invasion or other calamities? Mass suicide or even tidal waves? No evidence of struggles has been found, but could there have been wholesale abduction of the populace by pirates (as was to happen on Gozo in 1551)? Or did climatic changes cause crop failures and force the people to leave the island?

As with many temples of the ancient world, there is more here than meets the eye. It is said that an astronomical calendar is carved into one of the blocks at Mnajdra, and it has been proven that light once shone straight into its inner sanctum on the equinox.

Above: Ancient altars at Ġgantija, Gozo

Left: The Mnajdra Temple, a survivor of several millennia

c 2300 BC	c 2000 BC	
Stonehenge, England	**Palace of Knossos, Crete**	**Acropolis, Athens, Greece**

Like Stonehenge (in England's west country), Macchu Picchu (in Peru) and a dozen other places, it seems that the ancient scholars of Malta understood, precisely calibrated and celebrated the importance of the seasons.

Below: The porthole door at Hağar Qim

Bottom: The huge stones at one of Hağar Qim's temples

Visiting the Temples

Unless you have your own personal guide to show you around Malta's temples, the lack of guidebooks, signs and general visitor information is almost guaranteed to frustrate your intentions. The best tactic is to visit the Hal Saflieni Hypogeum (► 86–88) first. With its intact roof, excellent state of preservation, video presentation and above all a superb guided tour, it provides a perfect introduction to the subject.

Quite the Craftsman

The craftsmanship of the temples, given that the only tools available were flint and obsidian (a hard glassy stone), is quite remarkable. Moreover, the design is completely home-grown. There is nothing like them anywhere else in the world. How such giant blocks of stone were transported and erected can be explained by primitive rollers and levers, but it must have taken a monumental effort to erect them, particularly given the relatively small number of people involved.

The Two Great Sieges

> **"So long as Malta remains in the hands of the Knights [of St John] so long will every relief from Constantinople to Tripoli run the danger of being taken or destroyed."**

In 1565 all Europe trembled. The Ottoman Empire under Suleiman the Magnificent was at its peak. The shores of North Africa and most of Eastern Europe lay in his thrall and the Turks were camped at the gates of Vienna. Thwarted by the Austrians, Suleiman turned his European invasion plans to Italy, via Sicily. Just one thing stood in his way. "So long as Malta remains in the hands of the Knights [of St John]", his advisers warned, "so long will every relief from Constantinople to Tripoli run the danger of being taken or destroyed." They were right. The Knights of St John were the most formidable seafarers in the Mediterranean, and more, as Suleiman knew of old. The Knights, originally the Hospitaller Order, of Crusades fame, had dedicated themselves to an eternal war against his religion, and like his own, men had no fear of death in battle against the unbeliever.

And so, in April 1565, a fleet of 181 ships carrying 40,000 of the Ottoman Empire's finest warriors sailed for Malta. Waiting for them was Grand Master Jean Parisot de la Valette, some 600 Knights and around 8,000 soldiers. The "Great Battle of the Cross and Koran" was about to begin. The Knights, who had long expected the onslaught, retired to their fortifications of St Elmo, Birgu and Senglea, and sent word to Sicily requesting reinforcements.

Malta George Cross

In April 1942 King George VI made a unique award to the whole island. "To honour her brave people, I award the George Cross [the highest award for civilian gallantry] to the Island Fortress of Malta to bear witness to a Heroism and Devotion that will long be famous in History." The George Cross was incorporated into the Maltese Flag and the actual medal can be seen in the National War Museum (▶ 58).

Above: in an
engraving after
a painting by
Larivière, the
siege is raised,
the Knights are
victorious

The First Great Siege

The Great Siege began on 18 May, 1565 with the onslaught against Fort St Elmo. The Turks expected it to fall within days and bombarded it with a fury never seen before in any theatre of war. Reliable eye-witness accounts say 6,000 to 7,000 shots were fired daily. The bombardment and attempts to scale the walls continued for five weeks and still no troops from Sicily arrived. The rulebook of warfare was torn up and no quarter was given nor expected. On 23 June, St Elmo finally fell, defended literally to the death. The Turks counted 8,000 dead, the Knights 1,500, with just five men swimming to safety. It is said that the Turkish commander surveyed the

Below:
Suleiman the
Magnificent,
the scourge of
16th-century
Christendom

SOLIMANVS III.

ruins of St Elmo, looked towards Birgu and Senglea, and cried out, "Allah, if so small a son has cost us so dear, what price shall we have to pay for so large a father."

Birgu and Senglea braced themselves for the next onslaught. After ten more weeks of bloody fighting the Knights had been reduced to just 600 men and were on the point of collapse when at last the relief from Sicily arrived. The Turks, decimated by disease and sapped of morale, fled. In all they had lost around 30,000 men.

The hitherto almost invincible Sultan had been defeated, Europe was saved and Malta became the toast of Europe.

The Second Great Siege

Four centuries passed, weapons of mass destruction now replaced sword and musket, and once again tiny Malta was at the fulcrum of

The Ottoman army gathers for the Great Siege

the struggle for Europe. Just as in 1565, the deep-water harbours of Malta served as the base from which enemy shipping was attacked during World War II, in this case breaking Field Marshal Rommel's supply line from Naples to North Africa. If the Allies were to lose Malta then this vital battleground would surely also be lost. But was the island tenable in modern warfare? Like La Valette before him, Britain's prime minister, Winston Churchill, decided that it would be defended at all costs. In June 1940 the first Axis bombs fell – on St Elmo of all places – and by December Italian planes had mounted around 200 raids. The defenders, however, were so well dug in that, as with the Turks, it made little initial impression.

Frustrated, Hitler stepped into the fray, dismissed Mussolini and introduced the

"The hitherto almost invincible Sultan had been defeated"

Europe was saved and Malta was the toast of Europe.

Essential Reading and Viewing

- *The Great Siege, Malta 1565* by Ernle Bradford. Sounds like a boring history lesson? Not a bit of it! This is gripping, edge-of-your-seat narrative. It really brings alive the epic story of how the Knights held on to the island and will help you see their historical sites in a new light. A gripping account of the battle, drawing heavily on the first-hand account of one of the few Christian survivors.
- *Siege: Malta 1940–1943* by Ernle Bradford. Bradford, a navigating officer on a British destroyer, missed this one too, but only by a few months. Not as epic as the first Great Siege, but still very entertaining.
- Audio-visual shows: Malta George Cross; The Wartime Experience and The Valletta Experience (▶ 78).

Below: The
smoking ruins
of the Opera
House, Valletta

Bottom: The
British Fleet in
Grand Harbour,
1937

might of the Luftwaffe, Germany's airforce. By a combination of *blitzkrieg* and blockade he attempted to starve the island into submission. In just the two months of March and April 1942 twice the tonnage of bombs that fell in a whole year during London's more famous Blitz rained down on Malta. Once again this tiny rock became the most assailed place on earth. Raids went on continuously for 154 days and nights (London endured just 57) and by 10 May, 1942, the beleaguered island recorded its 2,000th air raid. Supplies were dwindling and Malta, unbeknown to Hitler, was within two months of capitulation.

Just in time, the tide of aerial warfare began to change. British Spitfires were now controlling the skies and with two weeks to spare, on 15 August, 1942, a convoy of five supply ships finally broke through the German blockade. For over two years Malta had withstood everything that the most powerful adversary on earth could throw at it. Britain's Field Marshall Montgomery went on to defeat Rommel in Africa, and the rest, as they say, is history.

Below: The smoking ruins of the Opera House, Valletta

Bottom: The British Fleet in Grand Harbour, 1937

1940

Festa!

BANGS, BANNERS, BULBS AND BRASS BANDS

Boom! An explosion rends the air and rattles the window panes. Was it thunder? A bomb (there is a puff of smoke over the next village)? Or perhaps artillery practice – it sounds and feels just like mortar fire. And that's basically just what it is, though here they call them *pétards*, and you needn't worry, it's all in honour of the local saint. Welcome to the *festa*!

Right: The marching band at the Feast of St Philip, Żebbuġ

Below: Bright lights, big crowds at Rabat

Below right: The processional statues at Valletta can be really impressive

It's pretty obvious when it is *festa* week in a village. Huge, brightly coloured banners, statues of saints and thousands of coloured electric lights illuminate the main streets. The parish church is an eye-catching sight. White lights sparkle on the façade, while inside pillars are draped with red damask, and gorgeous floral arrangements decorate the aisles which gleam with silver treasures brought out of safekeeping especially for such celebrations.

Street revelries begin on the eve of the feast day, Saturday night, when the local brass band parades through the village or town. The whole community, neighbouring villagers and curious tourists fill the streets, which are lined with fast-food sellers and beautifully crafted old-fashioned brass-and-glass stands selling nougat. At around 10 or 11 pm it's time for fireworks and *pétards* (► 13).

On Sunday there's more of the same, though this time the atmosphere is more religious; the statue of the village or town's patron saint is carried shoulder-high through the streets, while the crowds throw confetti. More *pétards* and fireworks round off the night.

Festas take place throughout the year (except January), but the vast majority are between June and September. There are over 100 each year (many villages and towns have more than one patron saint!), so wherever you are you'll always be within earshot of one (► 80).

Booking a Seat

It's easy enough to visit a *festa* by yourself, but if you want to get the full inside track, professional guides offer their services. For heavily attended celebrations, particularly on Good Friday or Easter Sunday, some tours may include seats booked ahead. The price is well worth paying if you want a good view without having to scrummage with the locals! Ask your nearest tourist office for details. Normally a small village *festa* has more atmosphere than one held in a larger town. The biggest is held on 15 August, celebrating The Assumption of Our Lady (at various towns and villages), and attracts ex-pat Maltese from all over the world.

Warning!

Despite the atmosphere, not all Maltese enjoy *festa*. The crowds bring disruption and the *pétards* are disliked by the very young and older people. And it's not just the noise: *pétards* sometimes go wrong, spraying deadly shrapnel over a large area.

Rule Britannia

Maltese people may look Mediterranean, they may speak a strange Mediterranean language, they may even gesticulate and behave like Mediterraneans as they do the *passegiata* (promenade) on summer evenings – but, as British visitors know, they also speak perfect English, have red letter boxes, blue police lamps, drink pale ale and bitter shandy in British-style pubs, and (mostly) support Manchester United. Clearly Britain has had a tremendous influence on this island.

The British first arrived in 1798, ousting the hated Napoleon, and stayed in Malta for almost 200 years, including the second "Great Siege" during World War II (► 10). In 1979 Britain and Malta amicably shook hands and island independence was granted. During that time the British established an infrastructure, commerce, government, laws, employment in the great naval dockyards and many customs that have embedded themselves in the Maltese psyche. Above all, strong emotional ties were forged that will probably last for many more generations.

Driving Passions

When many British cars and buses failed their roadworthiness tests in the 1960s and '70s they were shipped to Malta. The Ford Capri, Cortina, Anglia, Prefect, Triumph Herald, Hillman Minx and Hunter, along with other outmoded models, came to Malta for an Indian summer, which in some cases has lasted nearly 40 years. A lot of the British buses that still operate here are older still. Thanks to the warm dry climate and *laissez-faire* transport regulations, they run on...and on...and on... rattling the bones of their passengers and belching out plumes of diesel. No wonder some of them sport stickers proclaiming "In God We Trust".

As in Britain, the Maltese drive on the left, though any similarity with British driving (or indeed that of most of mainland European) ends there. For some reason it seems that the British Highway Code never quite made it to Malta.

The Great Wall of Malta

If statues of Queen Victoria and Winston Churchill and shops bearing names such as Commonwealth Stores and Coronation Stores are obvious relics of the days of the British Empire, there is a much larger legacy of British rule about which visitors, and even many Maltese, are ignorant.

A natural fault runs across Malta from Fomm-ir Riħ (southwest of Mġarr) in the west to Fort Madliena in the east. The Knights of St John first built watch-towers along this route, and the British reinforced them, linked them with a parapet and named them the Victoria Lines. Because of British naval superiority they were never put to the test, however, and have since fallen into disrepair. The best stretch is the 3km between Nadur (west of Rabat) and the point known as the Falka Gap on the Żebbiegħ–Mosta road.

Left to right from top: Great British exports; Buses on the seafront at Sliema; A blue lamp and red telephone box in Għarb; Queen Victoria sitting majestically in Valletta

Left: Xagħra village square on Gozo

The Way we Were

Malta and Gozo are home to many people from around the world who have fallen in love with the islands.

Ann Monserrat

Among some long-time residents is Ann Monserrat, widow of Nicholas Monserrat (both above), author of the acclaimed novel *The Cruel Sea* (1951). When Ann and Nicholas arrived from Canada to visit the remote island of Gozo in 1969, the *"landscape was almost biblical, dotted with donkeys and great flocks of sheep and goats – there was this tremendous sense of peace."*

John Ripard

A native Maltese, John Ripard is chairman of the Port Cottonera Consortium (► 49), head of Malta's foremost shipping agents and one of Malta's greatest ever yachtsmen. He is a highly respected judge in international yachting. *"When I was growing up in the 1950s the island had a very gracious, laid-back lifestyle. My grandfather had a summer house in Sliema, which in those days was quite separate from St Julian's and Valletta. There was no urban sprawl, so Mosta was a separate village, St Paul's was positively remote and there was very little traffic. In those days yachtsmen were at the forefront of our tourism. They were mostly English, mostly very rich. Then, in the 1970s Dom Mintoff (the present president) had an anti-British stance because he had been put off the old school of holiday-makers. He said we were under the yoke of the British, but British rule had brought us telephones,*

> ## "When I was growing up in the 1950s the island had a very gracious, laid-back lifestyle."

They fell in love with the island and bought an old farmhouse in the village of San Lawrenz. The documents had to be signed by candlelight, but in the intervening 30 years the island has seen radical changes in wealth and lifestyles. *"Nowadays we have too much traffic, but at least we have some reliable electricity (the romance of candles soon wears off!), some very good restaurants, airline links with everywhere in the world and the islanders' push to get into the electronic age has been remarkable. But the most important thing is that most Gozitans are remarkably down to earth and the spirit of Gozo is still very strong."*

electricity and infrastructure which was decades ahead of our neighbours."

Tourism is now Malta's major industry but with huge numbers visiting each year, John Ripard feels great concern *"for the environment. I have been very critical of our governments for their lack of planning and foresight. And the biggest change of all is in the quality of the sea. The problem is that an island the size of Malta was never meant to cater for such numbers. Of course, we have to look after and nurture our existing tourism. No doubt we have made incredible strides, but it has been at a price."*

BESTS, IFS AND MOSTS

Best Tours
Helicopter tour of the archipelago (►98), Grand Harbour Cruise (►46–48).

"And on your right..." – cruising Grand Harbour gives a great overview

Best Food with a View
Bobbyland at Dingi Cliffs (►97); Caffe Raffael (or any one of several places on the front) at Spinola Bay (►73–75); Ciappetti (►111) or Fontanella, Bastion Square, Mdina (►112); De Mondion Roof Garden, Xara Palace, Mdina (►112); Il-Veduta, Rabat (►113); Hotel L-Imgarr, Mgarr, Gozo (►149).

Spinola Bay is very attractive when lit up at dusk

Best Bar with a View
Gleneagles Bar, Mgarr, Gozo (►137).

Best Island View
From a helicopter (►98); from Bastion Square, Mdina (►161); from Upper Barrakka Gardens, Valletta (►47); looking back from Vittoriosa on a Grand Harbour Cruise (►46–48).

The view from Upper Barrakka Gardens in Valletta

The gorgeous little sandy beach of San Blas on Gozo

Neptune's Courtyard, Grand Master's Palace, is a triumph of architecture

The bright lights of Paceville, the best place for lively nightlife

Best Beach
San Blas on Gozo (▶ 145) is a little piece of heaven out of season.

Best Places to Watch the Sunset
Dwejra Point, Gozo (▶ 148); watching the buildings turn golden from Senglea.

Best Village Squares
Gozo has many contenders including Għarb (▶ 147) and Xagħra (▶ 144).

Best Hotels for Maltese Atmosphere
Ta' Ċenc, Gozo (▶ 149); Xara Palace, Mdina (▶ 111).

Best Building
Grand Master's Palace (▶ 55–57) or St John's Co-Cathedral, (▶ 52–54).

Best Maltese food
Barbecued fish with sauce Maltaise (▶ 24).

Best Maltese drink
Kinnie (▶ 24).

Best Places for People-Watching
Café Ta'Karun at the Traditions and Crafts of Malta, Valletta (▶ 71), or any outdoor bar on the front at Sliema or Marsaskala when the *passegiata* is in full swing.

Best Place If You're 18–25
Paceville (▶ 78).

Best Place to Get Away from it All
Self-catering in a converted farmhouse in the countryside in Gozo (▶ 36).

Best Place for Swimming
Mġarr-ix-Xini, Gozo (▶ 146), and Peter's Pool, near Marsaxlokk (▶ 94).

Best Natural Sights

The Azure Window, Dwejra Point, Gozo (► 148); the salt pans and rock formations at Qbajjar, Gozo, particularly at sunset (► 167–168).

A natural treasure: the Azure Window, Dwejra Point, Gozo

Best Island Activity

Diving. Warm clear waters, expert English-speaking instructors to guide you and wartime wrecks to explore.

If You Only See One

temple make it the Hypogeum (► 86–88). The atmospheric underground tour will tell you most of what has been uncovered about the ancient island temple builders.

If You Only See One

museum on Malta make it the National Museum of Archaeology in Valletta, for boning up on the temples (► 62).

If You Only See One

museum on Gozo make it the Folklore Museum at Għarb (► 147).

Most Controversial Building

The brand new "Big Blue", the 18-storey Portomaso Business Tower, lording it over St Julian's.

Most Atmospheric Backstreets

Mdina (► 104–106) and Vittoriosa (► 49–51).

Most Unusual Bar

The Gun Tower, Valletta, a café-bar in a World War II gun emplacement.

Most Hyped, Most Expensive Bar

The Pub in Archbishop Street, Valletta, where the legendary hellraising actor Oliver Reed (in Malta filming *Gladiator*) was drinking before he died.

A charming quiet street in "The Silent City" of Mdina

Pasta, Pastries and Pale Ale

The Maltese really do have their own cuisine, though you would never guess it from walking into the majority of island restaurants. Neighbouring Sicily and Italy contribute the main culinary influences, with just a hint of North Africa.

Above: Island tastes on a plate

Below: Maltese *antipasti*

Pasta and Pastry

These ingredients figure highly in the Maltese diet, usually borrowed from Italy, but the island has its own pasta dishes, such as *timpana* (macaroni, bolognese sauce, egg and cheese, with flaky or puff pastry on top). Take away the pastry and you have *mqarrun fil-forn*; substitute rice for macaroni and you have *ross fil-forn*.

Come mid-morning it's time for a *pastizzi*, a savoury pastry pocket filled with either ricotta cheese and/or spinach, or *pizelli*, yellow mushy marrowfat peas. *Qassatat* (pronounced *ass-a-tat*) are round flaky or shortcrust pies with the same fillings as *pastizzi*. They are on sale in cafés, bars and from street vendors.

The taste of Malta for many visitors is the similarly rustic *hobz biz-zejt*, a roll of the local bread (*ftira*) rubbed with tomatoes, which is drizzled with olive oil, filled with salad and tuna, then dressed with olives and capers.

Rabbit, Rabbit, Rabbit

The Maltese national dish is *fenek* (rabbit), stewed, fried or roasted. Wild rabbits were hunted to extinction years ago, so all rabbits destined for the table are now specially bred (you may see them on sale in the markets). The meat is marinated in red wine and bay leaves, cooked with onions and garlic and cut into portions. There is a high bone-to-meat ratio, so it can get rather fiddly. On feast days some restaurants, typically those that cater mostly for locals, offer a special *fenkata* ("rabbit feast") menu. The starter is spaghetti with rabbit sauce (rabbit liver, diced pork, tomatoes, onions and garlic) then rabbit stew with chips or roast potatoes. Wash it down with copious draughts of local red wine.

Filling Dishes

Braġioli are strips of topside filled with a mixture of minced pork, ham, cheese and egg, cooked in red wine. It's rich, but tasty. *Tiġiega mimlija* is boned chicken stuffed with a similar mixture as above, then roasted. Stuffed vegetables include *bzar adhar* (peppers), *qargha baghli* (marrows/courgettes) and *bringiel* (aubergines). On a menu, the suffix *mimli*, indicates that the dish is stuffed. If you are vegetarian ask what the stuffing is.

Qubbajt, Mqaret and Other Sweet Things

These are a bit of a mouthful in every sense, but do try to get your teeth around

Simple pleasures: Bread, pies and cakes are best eaten straight from the oven

sometimes accompanied by sauce Maltaise, a robust mixture of tomatoes, onions and capers. *Qarnitta* (octopus) is another favourite, also served in a rich tomato sauce.

Saha! (Cheers!)

In the last decade, Maltese wines have come of age. The biggest brands are Marsovin and Delicata. The latter has garnered rave reviews from the foreign press – try its award-winning Grand Vin de Hautville range – but both labels produce excellent wines, especially if you are willing to pay a little more. Gozo is renowned for its high-alcohol, gutsy local red wines.

A legacy of British rule is Hop Leaf Pale Ale and Farson's Bitter Shandy. The ubiquitous local lager is Cisk (pronounced *chisk*). Cisk Export is a stronger and much tastier version.

The island's favourite soft drink is Kinnie, a sort of Coca-cola for adults incorporating a delicious hint of bitter herbs. It makes for a perfect aperitif.

qubbajt (sweet nougat, pronounced *oo-buy-at*) and *mqaret* (deep-fried date pastries, pronounced *im-arr-ay*). Except during the summer, the gorgeous sweet Arabic smell of sizzling *mqaret* is a familiar aroma to visitors at the front gate of Valletta. *Qubbajt* really comes into its own at festival time (► 15).

From top:
Nougat on sale at festival time

Seafood

Local specialities include *aljotta* (fish broth) and *lampuka* (dorada/dolphin fish), though this is only available from late August onwards, and is often put into a pie (*torta tal-Lampuki*). There is a wide variety of local fish, usually simply grilled or barbecued and

Gotcha!
Octopus destined for the pot at Marsaxlokk

A taste of Britain

Malta in the Movies

The summer of 1999 was a bittersweet time for Malta's fledgling film industry. Having pledged its resources to *U571*, the U-boat movie featuring American rock star Jon Bon Jovi, it could only watch as just up the road at Fort Ricasoli, the Colosseum was rebuilt for Ridley Scott's multi-Oscar-winning *Gladiator*. "It was unfortunate that both came along at the same time", recalls Mediterranean Film Studios production manager, Malcolm Scerri-Ferrante, "but when two major films are shooting here simultaneously, it reflects the strength of Malta as a service provider to the film industry".

The sexiest man in sandals: Russell Crowe in *Gladiator*

Malta and the movie world can be traced back to the 1950s when the Rank Organisation came here to shoot *The Malta Story* (1951), a wartime epic starring Alec Guinness. But it was not until 1964 that the studio's unique surface water tank was built on the site of Fort Rinella by the edge of the Mediterranean. Measuring 91m by 122m and up to 2m deep, it was built to blend seamlessly with sea and horizon and offered a controlled environment for shipwrecks, sea battles, hurricanes and any other sort of mayhem at sea that a film director wished to create, with models or full-size ships.

speaking, particularly useful for the Americans. The weather also is vital. The K-value (ie brightness) of the sun in Malta is exactly the same as in Los Angeles, which means that outdoor production here and in Hollywood can be almost seamlessly blended. The stability of the weather is also important in Malta. From June to September we can almost guarantee film crews uninterrupted sunshine. And finally, we have some of the best model construction craftsmen in the world living locally."

So what's next?

The prison from the 1977 film *Midnight Express* at Lower Fort St Elmo, and, left, its fictional inmates

It was supplemented in 1979 by a deep water tank with a depth of 50m, built for *Raise the Titanic* (1980).

"Nine out of ten movies which are filmed here come especially for our water tanks," concedes Scerri-Ferrante, "but Malta offers many other advantages. Its Mediterranean architecture enables it to transform into several countries (*Midnight Express*, for example, was shot entirely on location here, [Fort St Elmo], although it was supposed to be set in Turkey). It also has many economic advantages, including relatively cheap local labour, and it is English-

Following in the sandals of *Gladiator* came *Julius Caesar*, a US TV series, and stars shooting on the island in 2001 included Madonna in the comedy *Love, Sex, Drugs and Money* and Guy Pearce and Richard Harris in *The Count of Monte Cristo*. Keep an eye out for the latter, which includes shots of Vittoriosa and Comino.

Maltese Turkeys

Malta not only played the part of Turkey (in *Midnight Express*; 1977), it has produced its share of "turkeys" (movie flops). Ironically the set of one of these, *Popeye* (1979), has become a major island attraction (► 125).

DOMES, DUCKS AND THE DEVIL

At first glance Malta may seem a rather conservative sort of place, but when you take into account that this is a small island, floating between two continents, with some 7,000 years of recorded history, then it really is no surprise that it abounds in legends and curiosities.

Devil's Island

The creation of the islet of Filfla, off Malta's southwest coast, is one of the more bizarre legends. Apparently God was so displeased with the inhabitants of nearby Il-Maqluba (near Qrendi), that he tore out the ground beneath them and sent them down to Hell. They were so evil, however, that the Devil didn't want them either, and he threw the piece of earth back up and into the sea.

Whatever, one very special inhabitant of this lonely rock is a species of large green-and-red spotted lizard, found nowhere else in the world. It must be hardy as for some 25 years the British Navy and RAF used the rock as target practice. Today no-one is allowed to land here for fear of unexploded bombs and shells.

The Mosta Dome is (arguably!) the third biggest dome in Europe, after the Pantheon and St Peter's in Rome

Left and below: Xewkija, perhaps now the biggest dome in Malta

Eggs-Traordinary Domes

Malta is not only remarkable for the size of its churches, but in particular for two enormous domes. Until very recently Mosta Dome, the third largest in the world, reigned supreme in the archipelago. But then the inhabitants of Xewkija in Gozo got together and decided to build a dome that was ever so slightly bigger. The good people of Mosta, understandably miffed, countered by pointing out that their dome was still bigger in terms of cubic capacity.

Likewise there are two contenders for the strangest dome in the islands. You might think it should go to the ovoid-shaped cupola of the "Egg Church" in Mgarr (the final detail of which was a second *trompe l'oeil* clock, painted so that the hands show two minutes to midnight, thus avoiding the Devil's hour).

And what about the dome that's not a dome? Enter the cathedral of Gozo in Victoria (▶ 141), and above the altar appears the cupola of a fine handsome dome. On closer inspection, the dome is nothing more than a *trompe l'oeil* painting – much cheaper than the real thing!

Cart Ruts

The only thing that is debated more in Maltese archaeology than its temples are its bizarre "cart ruts". These have the appearance of tramlines hewn into solid rock and can be found in the southwest of the island and on Gozo (they have also been reported elsewhere in the Mediterranean). The densest concentration has been christened Clapham Junction after the British railway network's busiest station. Experts conclude that they were almost certainly communication routes, probably of agricultural vehicles, but what kind and how they were propelled remains a mystery.

The Indestructible Grotto

It is said that stone scraped from the walls of St Paul's Grotto in Rabat (➤ 107–108) has healing powers. Furthermore, and quite conveniently for religious souvenir hunters, it is also claimed that no matter how much of the magical stone is scraped off, the grotto never changes in size. Scoff as you may, it is none the less intriguing that after decades, if not centuries of being nibbled away, the grotto remains hermit sized.

Shopping the Easy Way

Itinerant grocers and fruit- and vegetable-sellers are quite common in Malta. They often announce their presence with a prolonged blast of the horn. Sometimes to save the bother of coming down all those stairs, the people on upper storeys drop down a basket on a rope with their order and money inside. The vendor fills it up and the shopping is hauled back up.

Duck Village

The Maltese may be beastly to most feathered creatures unlucky enough to fly into their air space (➤ 121) but someone on the island is a bird lover. Cross the causeway from Sliema to Manoel Island and immediately on your left is the bizarre Duck Village, with little pens and shelters turned into model village-like houses and shops for a small colony of ducks!

The enigmatic "cart ruts" at Clapham Junction still baffle everyone

What to do with the Kids

A perfect opportunity for a close encounter

Given the huge numbers of families who visit Malta, there are surprisingly few attractions geared for children. The resorts mostly only offer lidos, while Valletta is mainly concerned with history, culture and architecture, though the **Great Siege of Malta** (➤ 66) is a favourite among young visitors.

The most unforgettable experience for children (minimum age nine) is surely at **Mediterraneo Marine Park** (➤ 126) which offers the opportunity to swim with its dolphins at a very reasonable price. You must book in advance, as only eight guests are allowed in the water at a time.

After your close encounter, keep your swimming gear on and trot across the car-park to **Splash & Fun** (➤ 126). Also here, for younger children, is a play area with model dinosaurs, a bouncy castle and various mini fairground rides, including a small roller-coaster and bumper cars.

Older ones will get more of a thrill at the Badger Karting go-karting track at **Ta' Qali** (Duramblatt Street, tel: 21 421838 to book a session, minimum age eight, minimum height 4 feet 6 inches).

Ghoulish teenagers will no doubt enjoy the **Mdina Dungeons** (➤ 160) where depictions of death, disease and torture are the star attractions.

On a more wholesome historical note, don't miss **In Guardia** (➤ 59), a spectacular Knights-of-old re-enactment with lots of flashes and bangs and colourful characters. Enquire at the tourist office (➤ 33) for dates and times of shows.

Four Good Restaurants for Older Children

TGI Fridays
Il-Fortizza, Tower Road, Sliema
Piccolo Padre
195, Triq il-Kbira, St Julians (➤ 74)
Henry J Beans
Corinthia San Gorg, St George's Bay
World Sports Café
The Mayfair Complex,
Lower St Augustine Street,
St George's Bay

Finding Your Feet

SALVS IN PERICVLIS

First Two Hours

Arriving by Air

- **Malta International Airport**, at Luqa, is the archipelago's only international terminal. It lies 7km from Valletta, 13km from St Julian's, 22km from Mellieħa and 8km from Marsaskala. Outside rush hour nowhere on the island is more than a 30- to 45-minute drive from the airport.
- For **airport enquiries** tel: 21 249600 or click on www.maltaairport.com

Getting to Valletta from the Airport

- Valletta is a 20- to 30-minute ride on **bus No 8** with departures every 20–30 minutes from 5:30 am to 8 pm.
- From the Valletta terminus you can get a bus to **anywhere** on the island.
- If you want to go anywhere other than Valletta from the airport you will have to get a **taxi or hire a car**.

Taxis from the Airport

- **Fares** from the airport are regulated. Pick up a sheet of fares from the tourist office in Arrivals for your destination and note that the price covers up to four persons "with normal sized luggage" at any time of day.
- Make sure you **agree this fare** with the taxi driver before you set off.
- To **pre-book a taxi** call the Public Transport Authority, tel: 21 438475.

Getting from Malta to Gozo

Most tour operators include onward transport to Gozo from Malta, but if you are travelling independently there are three options.

- The quickest, most spectacular, and most expensive option, is by **helicopter**. The flight to Gozo (it lands near Mġarr) takes just 15 minutes with a check-in time of 30 minutes. Local travel agents will make the booking for you, or contact **Malta Air Charter Ltd**, tel: 21 559341.
- The vast majority of people cross the Gozo Channel by **ferry** from Ċirkewwa (at the northern tip of Malta) to Mġarr on Gozo. The service runs every half an hour or so through the day and less frequently through the night. From July to September it runs 24 hours, from October to June it runs from 5 am to 11 pm. The journey takes 25–30 minutes and also transports vehicles. It is very cheap for pedestrians and inexpensive for drivers, too. Confusingly there is no ticket for the journey going out to Gozo, but you must buy a return ticket at the kiosk at Mġarr harbour before boarding for the return trip; tel: 21 561622 (Mġarr), tel: 21 580435 (Ċirkewwa).
- There are also two ferry services from Sa Maison (Msida, near Valletta) to Mġarr on Gozo. A high-speed **catamaran**, the SES *Victoria Express* (foot-passengers only) takes 45 minutes and operates daily (except Sunday), departing approximately every one to two hours from 6:30 am to 5:15 pm. There is also a conventional **vehicle and passenger ferry** which takes 1 hour 15 minutes and sails once a day, Monday to Friday, departing Mġarr at 12:15 pm and Sa Maison creek at Msida at 2:15 pm. To confirm times, tel: 21 243964/5/6.
- On Gozo the Mġarr to Victoria **bus schedule** follows the ferry timetable so that connections link up.

Getting from Malta to Comino

- Crossings for **Hotel Comino residents** are arranged by the island's one and only hotel (► 149).

■ Numerous **pleasure boats** from all over Gozo and Malta also visit
  Comino on day-trips. Contact the tourist information office nearest you
  for details.

Tourist Information

■ Arrivals, Malta International Airport, tel: 21 249600.
■ There are tourist information offices in Valletta, tel: 21 237747, and
  Mġarr Harbour, tel: 21 553343.
■ Victoria, Gozo, tel: 21 561419.

Getting Around

Both the main islands are so small that getting from A to B is relatively
easy. Buses are the only form of public transport, and can either be fun and
comfortable or frenetic and crowded, depending on the route. Driving on
Malta is rarely less than an interesting experience.

Orientation

■ **Road signs** are not as comprehensive as in some parts of Europe. They
  often only signpost the most immediate location, not general directions
  or larger towns in the same direction. Although Valletta is well signposted
  from the airport, other major tourist destinations are not mentioned. It is
  therefore important that you study a good road map before you set off.
  Having said that, the Maltese people are friendly and will always help you
  out with directions.
■ **Malta & Gozo 1:40,000 Miller Guides/Intermap** is recommended and is
  usually available in the Departures area of the Malta International Airport.
■ The **maps** handed out by car hire companies are not very comprehensive.

Driving

■ Drive on the **left**.
■ **Speed limits** in built-up areas are 40 kph, and on other (main) roads
  65 kph.
■ **Seat belts** are compulsory.
■ **Children** aged between nine months and four years must by law sit in
  the back. **Babies** under nine months must occupy a baby seat (available
  from car-hire companies).
■ There are **no motorways** and only a few miles of dual carriageway.
■ **Road surfaces** are of a reasonable quality around the major conurbations,
  but elsewhere they are variable. Secondary roads tend to be bumpy and
  pot-holed.
■ Driving in Malta can be very **stressful**. It may be best to get a bus or taxi
  from the airport to your destination and get to know the road conditions.
■ In theory drivers should **give way to the right**, in practice anything can,
  and does, happen. Local drivers are famously impatient, have little
  consideration for other road users and, by mainland European standards,
  road discipline is poor.
■ **Roundabouts** are particularly chaotic. It is said that the vehicle already
  on the roundabout has priority but "might is right" usually prevails.
■ Surprisingly, in the circumstances, the use of the horn and the
  phenomenon of **road rage** are rare.
■ **Gozo** has much less traffic and travelling around is therefore less
  stressful.

Car Hire

- Car hire in Malta is the **cheapest in Europe**, and as the standard of public transport is rather basic it is a good idea to hire a car, particularly if you intend to sightsee independently.
- All **major car-hire companies** are based at the airport or will bring your car to the airport.
- Usually you must be **25 or over**.
- You will need either a **national or an international driving licence**, and a credit card.
- **Local operators** often undercut nationals. Look out too for **special offers**.
- In summer (particularly July–August) **air-conditioning** is highly recommended.
- Always **lock** your car and remove valuables from sight. In tourist areas theft from cars is common.
- **Comprehensive insurance** is vital. Minor accidents are quite common so if you have the option to pay a little more to cover your excess then it is strongly advised that you do so.
- Car hire is an even more attractive option in **Gozo** as it is less well served by buses than Malta.

Traffic

- Traffic is **frequently congested**, and very long queues form on the main coastal routes from around 5–7 pm as people leave the beaches and head for home.
- St Julian's (➤ 60–61) is very busy at night and there are traffic jams even into the early hours in Paceville (➤ 78).

Parking

- Parking is often **difficult**.
- Note that only the **top hotels** have their own spaces, so if this is a consideration check first before hiring.
- When parking your car near a beach, by a market or in any unofficial car parking area, an "**attendant**" will often appear from nowhere, beckon you into a space, offer to "look after" your car and expect a tip for his services.
- **Parking tickets** are given to offenders, so be very careful where you park, and check road markings and nearby signposts.
- **Clamping** occurs in some areas.

Pedestrian Crossings

- Cars which have stopped at pedestrian crossings are frequently **overtaken** by other cars. As a driver beware that these are potentially dangerous points.
- As a **pedestrian**, never set foot on a pedestrian crossing before traffic has completely stopped both ways and you have made sure that no one is about to overtake from either direction.

Buses

Malta's public buses are almost a museum attraction in their own right, with many dating back to the 1950s. They are uncomfortable, hot and crowded, but very cheap.

- 1-day, 3-day, 5-day and 7-day **Saver** tickets can be bought at the bus termini at Valletta, Buġibba and Sliema Ferries, or from any branch of BOV Bank.
- All **single-journey tickets** are bought on board. Drivers do give change but try to have some small coins to hand.

- Services **connect most parts of the island** and run regularly on Malta (less so on Gozo).
- On Malta most services run to and from **Valletta** and on Gozo all services run to and from Victoria.
- There are additional "**Direct Route Buses**" on Malta from Sliema and Buġibba/Qawra to other points of interest.
- **Late buses** operate out of Paceville (except in July and August).
- **Timetables and routes** can be picked up at any one of the three bus information kiosks outside Valletta City Gate, or from tourist offices, or on www.atp.com.mt

Taxis

- Taxis are **white**.
- They are relatively **expensive** (about the same as western European fares) and rarely work on the meter.
- Always **agree the fare** before you get in.

Admission Charges
The cost of admission for museums and places of interest mentioned in the text is indicated by the following categories:
Inexpensive = under LM1
Moderate = LM1–2
Expensive = over LM2

Accommodation

The majority of Malta's visitors are package tourists and the accommodation reflects this. In recent years the trend has been to move up-market. There are relatively few provisions for independent travel.

Hotels

The majority of hotels are moderate to high class, catering largely for **package tours**, and many are block-booked for the summer months. Typically they are medium to large high-rise impersonal blocks erected in the 1970s and 1980s.

Over the last few years several **new luxury hotels** have sprung up, most notably in the St George's Bay area. These are almost self-contained resorts. There are also a number of "**villages**", holiday complexes and aparthotels, from cheap and cheerful to luxury, all of which offer variations on the theme of self-catering within a hotel complex environment.

Gozo

The accommodation situation is quite different on Gozo, which has just ten hotels (compared to around 120 on Malta), though three of these are in the luxury bracket. Here **quality is rated above quantity** and properties are generally low-rise and unobtrusive.

Gozo specialises in **characterful self-catering accommodation** and in recent years a good number of its sturdy stone-built farmhouses, some several centuries old, have been converted into self-catering villas and apartments. These are relatively expensive.

Cheap Sleeps

- Malta has **never been on the backpackers' trail** and as the current trend is for accommodation to go up-market so crash pads have become more scarce.
- The tourist office has a list of hotels, hostels and guest-houses offering **cheap accommodation**. If they are not too busy they may even ring up and make a booking for you for free.
- Malta has **five youth hostels**, plus one on Gozo; contact Malta Youth Hostels Association, tel: 21 244983.
- There are **no official campsites** on Malta and Gozo.

When to Go

- In **summer** (Easter–October) prices increase significantly. You should book well ahead if you intend travelling during the school holidays.
- **August** is the busiest period, with Italian holiday-makers increasing the numbers of visitors.
- The busiest weekend of the year (next to Christmas) is **15 August** when the whole archipelago celebrates the Feast of the Assumption (➤ 15).

Gozo Farmhouses and Village Complexes

- Dotted around several rural locations on the island are **rustic farmhouses, beautifully converted** to self-catering holiday homes, most equipped to a good standard. Some have their own swimming pools, the setting is invariably quiet and peaceful and many have wide-ranging views.
- In a similar vein, though without the same character, are **"village" complexes**, comprising a small number of houses or apartments built in local farmhouse style, set around a communal swimming pool.
- **Gozo Farmhouses**, 3 Imgarr Street, Għajnsielem, tel: 21 5612801.
- **Gozo Village Holidays**, Kapuccini Street, Victoria, tel: 21 563520.

Prices
Price categories below are for a double room per night and are based on hotel "rack" rates (the published rate). Package rates, however, can be considerably less.
£ under LM15 **££** LM15–30 **£££** LM31–50 **££££** above LM50

Food and Drink

A typical Maltese restaurant menu might be described as a hybrid of Italian and Mediterranean dishes, including a small range of Maltese specialities. Don't be fooled by all those pizzas, pastas and steaks – rabbit and chips or barbecued whole fish is the real taste of the islands.

Opening Hours

- Restaurants are usually open **noon–3 pm** and **6–11 pm**, though some establishments open throughout the day.
- During the **summer** most places open daily but some have a day of rest (often Monday). Some restaurants also close for a couple of weeks in January or February.

Five Good Places for a Relaxing Coffee Break
- **Café Diva**, Manoel Theatre, Valletta (➤ 70)
- **St James Cavalier Centre for Creativity**, Valletta (➤ 66)
- **Trattoria AD 1530**, Mdina (➤ 112)
- **Ciappetti**, Mdina (➤ 111)
- **Lanċa**, Sliema Ferries (➤ 73)

Practical Tips

- It's best to **book ahead** at more popular restaurants, certainly at weekends in the summer, and especially at Sunday lunchtime.
- A handy eating out reference is **The Definitively Good Guide to Restaurants in Malta & Gozo**, available from most bookshops. Its choice of places is generally reliable, and there's lots of detailed information.
- **Service charge** is not usually included and it is customary to tip around 10 per cent of the final bill.
- **Fresh fish** is likely to be available at any Italian or Mediterranean restaurant. The fresh whole fish on display are at market price and it is these that will be "pushed" by the waiter or waitress. It's a good idea to ascertain the price before you order as it is unlikely to be cheap.
- Main courses are often very large, and it is quite possible, particularly in more formal restaurants, that you will be served a **"complimentary" snack**, such as bigilla (➤ below) or bruschetta (Italian-style toasted bread with tomatoes and olive oil). A cover charge, usually quite small, is made for this, and also for bread and butter.

Dress Code

- It's generally only in the international restaurants of top hotels and some of Malta's more business-orientated eating houses (mostly in Valletta) where you need to think about a dress code. **Most places are casual**.

Vegetarians

- The ubiquitous **minestra** is a thicker version of minestrone soup. **Soppa ta l-Armla** (literally Widow's Soup), is another vegetable soup, appearing on the menu in winter.
- **Stuffed vegetables** may often be found in Maltese restaurants, though check that there is no minced meat in the stuffing.
- **Bigilla**, a purée of broad beans, served as a dip with crackers, is a Maltese speciality, though something of an acquired taste.
- Apart from fish, many Italian restaurants serve **pasta** with vegetarian sauces and **meat-free pizzas**.
- **Gbejna** is the local fresh goat's cheese. It's a mild variety, but there is also a peppered version with more kick.
- **International restaurants** nearly always have a vegetarian option or two and if all else fails there are the pastries known as pastizzis and qassatats (➤ 22) to fill up on.

Prices
The symbols indicate what you should pay per person for a three-course meal, excluding drinks and service charge.
£ under LM8 ££ LM8–12 £££ over LM12

Shopping

On Malta, international chain stores predominate, along with sports' and "20-something" fashion shops. If you want bargains and local colour, avoid the modern malls and seek out independent shops. Until recently Valletta had the monopoly on shopping on the islands. It still has the most variety and easily the most interesting shops, and new developments such as the Bay Street Mall at St Julian's (► 76) attract younger shoppers.

Practicalities

- Most shops **open** around 9 am, observe a siesta from 1–4 pm and reopen from 4–7 pm. On Saturday they close at 1 pm. In **tourist centres**, however, shops are open all day and throughout the weekend.
- **Credit cards** are widely accepted.
- July and August are the months for **bargains**. Some fashion shops discount everything by 50 per cent or even more. Bear in mind, however, that prices were probably high to begin with.

Food

- Try a *qaghaq tal-ghasel* – a ring of sweet pastry filled with treacle and candied fruit. You can buy them loose from good-quality *pastizzerias* or gift-boxed from Caffe Cordina on Republic Square in Valletta (► 71). They are also on sale at the airport.
- Look out for pickled and conserved **Maltese specialities**; capers, vegetables, goat's cheese, honey and jams.
- Gift packs of **local wines** are good value. Pick them up at the airport.

Footwear

- With Italy as a neighbour it is not surprising that **stylish footwear** is widely available. There are many good and reasonably priced shoe shops in Valletta.

Crafts

- **Lace, wool, glass and filigree silver and gold** are the mainstays of Malta's craft industry.
- Both Malta and Gozo have their own **"craft village"** where you can see artisans at work (► 114 and 152).

Markets

- Valletta's **Sunday morning market** is really the only open-air market worth a special trip (► 76).

Unusual Local Souvenirs
- A knight's **suit of armour** from Ta' Qali (► 114)
- Pickled **goat's cheese**
- A bottle of *bajtra*, Maltese prickly pear liqueur
- Thick **woollen jumpers** from Gozo (► 152)
- A hand-made **tin windmill** (hole-in the wall workshop, Republic Street, Gozo)
- A **brass or iron door-knocker** in the shape of a dolphin, from Mdina or any large souvenir shop on Malta

---

Entertainment

What's On

See the local newpapers, *The Malta Times* and *The Malta Independent*, for details of all entertainment and sporting events. Both papers also have weekend supplements worth browsing.

Nightlife

- **Paceville** (pronounced *par-chay ville*), tucked just off the seafront of St Julian's (► 78), is the undisputed champion when it comes to nightlife on Malta. There are dozens of music bars, vast discos and nightclubs, cinemas, and a major ten-pin bowling alley all within a few blocks of each other.
- **Buġibba** is the only other place on Malta that has any concentration of bars and clubs, though most resorts have at least one disco/nightclub, often aimed at locals as much as visitors.
- Elsewhere on Malta **hotels** are the main providers of nocturnal fun, ranging from frothy folklore shows to nightclubs.

Theatre and Other Entertainment

- The **Manoel Theatre** in Valletta (► 63) stages classical concerts from September to June (www.teatrumanoel.com.mt for latest events).
- Victoria in Gozo has two **opera houses** (► 140).
- The **St James Cavalier Centre for Creativity** in Valletta (► 66) has an eclectic programme covering many aspects of the performing arts.

Casinos

- There are **three casinos** on Malta: the **Dragonara Palace**, St George's Bay (► 80); **The Oracle** at Qawra (► 132); and the **Casinò de Venezia** at Vittoriosa (► 78).
- Note the age, dress code and proof of identification **regulations** at each establishment.

Cinemas

- The main cinema is the **IMAX** at St George's Bay (► 79).
- There are also cinemas at **St George's Bay** (Eden Century, 16 screens), **Buġibba** (Empire, eight screens) and **Victoria, Gozo** (The Citadel, two screens).
- **St James Cavalier Centre for Creativity** in Valletta screens foreign and art-house films (► 66).

Sport

Watersports

- The absence of tide, sand and pollution creates very **favourable conditions for diving** just off the coast of Malta. As well as marine life such as groupers, gurnards, octopus and parrotfish, labyrinthine caves and wartime wrecks (both planes and ships) provide added interest. There are several dive schools on Malta, Gozo and Comino (► 98 and 152). For further information check out this website: www.holidays-malta.com/diving.htm
- Other watersports around the islands include **windsurfing**, **waterskiing** and **jetskiing**. Small boats can be hired from several marinas.
- **Inflatables** and **paragliders** provide alternative thrills.

Other Sports

- Click on **www.maltaweb.com** for information on Malta's many sporting opportunities.
- Malta's only golf course is the **Royal Malta Golf Club** at Marsa (➤ 114).
- The **Marsa Sports Club** at Marsa (➤ 114) also has 18 tennis courts, five squash courts and an open-air swimming pool.
- Elsewhere luxury hotels offer **tennis courts**.
- **Horse-riding** is on offer at various locations on Malta; probably the nicest venue is the **Golden Bay Horse Riding School** (➤ 132).

Spectator Sports

- **Waterpolo** is a national speciality, taking up plenty of column inches in the daily newspapers. Matches take place throughout the summer at the national pool near the University. See *The Malta Times* and *The Malta Independent* for details.
- **Horse-racing** is another island passion – with a twist. Here jockeys don't ride the horse but sit in a flimsy-looking trap behind it, and are dragged along at Ben-Hur speeds (➤ 114).

Festivals

Aside from the island's religious *festas* (➤ 13–15 and 80), there are a number of other well-established secular festivals:

- **February**: Carnival in February has the usual floats and dance troupes. The celebrations in Nadur on Gozo are infamous for their wild behaviour.
- **31 March**: Freedom Day is marked with a traditional regatta in Grand Harbour, Valletta, featuring local rowing clubs.
- **29 June**: Mnarja is Malta's most important folklore festival (➤ 98), taking place at Buskett Gardens.
- **Mid-late July**: Valletta hosts the acclaimed Malta Jazz Festival.
- **Late July–August**: The Farsons International Food and Beer Festival is held close to Ta' Xbiex.
- **8 September**: Our Lady of Victories is celebrated with a traditional regatta in Grand Harbour, Valletta. It commemorates not only the Great Siege of 1565 but also the lifting of the siege in 1943 (➤ 9–12).
- **Late September**: Malta International Airshow.
- **Late October**: The Middle Sea Yacht Race, from Marsamxett Harbour (Sliema) to Sicily and back, attracts top international yachtspeople.

Gay and Lesbian Malta

- There is a small gay scene on Malta, mostly around the **Paceville** area (➤ 78), and in the larger resorts most people are tolerant of low-key gay behaviour. Beware of displays of gay affection in small conservative-minded villages, however.
- **Homosexuality is legal** throughout Malta from the age of 18. For more information log on to www.gaymalta.com
- **Bars and clubs** frequented by gays and lesbians include City of London, Nix Bar (lesbian) and Lady Godiva, all in Paceville/St Julian's, and Tom's Bar in Floriana, just outside Valletta. Didies at Buġibba is a lesbian bar.
- Popular **gay beaches** are Ferro Bay, Tower Road, Sliema (near the TGIF restaurant) and Tigne Point, Sliema. Also try the gay nudist "beach" – in reality an isolated large slab of rock – between Ġnejna Bay and Għajn Tuffieħa.
- **Gozo** is predictably more conservative, but try the gay-friendly Taverna del Ponte at Xlendi. By day check out Blata il-Bajda, a 15-minute walk south of Ramla Bay (➤ 145).

Valletta, Sliema and St Julian's

Getting Your Bearings

Valletta, the "City built by Gentlemen for Gentlemen", is one of the great sights of the Mediterranean. Prepare to be surprised by its scale and beauty. A visit here is imperative in order to understand the remarkable history of this little island.

The quiet streets of Vittoriosa (Birgu) and Senglea lie just across Grand Harbour from Valletta. These are the "old cities", where the Knights of St John made their famous stand against the Ottomans (▶ 9–10).

Tourism came to Sliema and St Julian's long ago and has transformed these two areas into Malta's premier resorts. Sliema Ferries faces Valletta, its front lined with a bewildering array of pleasure boats. St Julian's clusters around the pretty harbour of Spinola Bay. Behind the harbour Paceville is the throbbing night-time epicentre. On the fringes the luxury hotels of St George's Bay stand aloof.

**Previous page:
The rich
interior of the
Grand Master's
Palace in
Valletta**

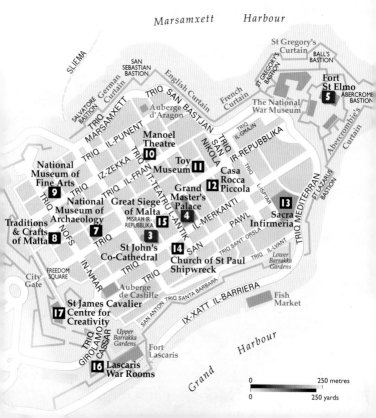

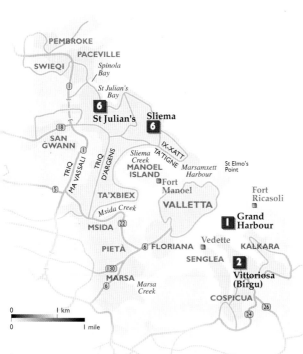

43

★ Don't Miss

1. Grand Harbour ➤ 46
2. Vittoriosa ➤ 49
3. St John's Co-Cathedral ➤ 52
4. Grand Master's Palace ➤ 55
5. Fort St Elmo ➤ 58
6. Sliema and St Julian's ➤ 60

The city skyline with the familiar dome of the Carmelite Church

At Your Leisure

7. National Museum of Archaeology ➤ 62
8. Traditions and Crafts of Malta ➤ 62
9. National Museum of Fine Arts ➤ 62
10. Manoel Theatre ➤ 63
11. Toy Museum ➤ 63
12. Casa Rocca Piccola ➤ 64
13. Sacra Infirmeria ➤ 64
14. Church of St Paul Shipwreck ➤ 65
15. Great Siege of Malta ➤ 66
16. Lascaris War Rooms ➤ 66
17. St James Cavalier Centre for Creativity ➤ 66

Although Valletta has more museums and historical sights than anywhere else on the island, Sliema and St Julian's are the holiday capitals, with shops, restaurants and nightspots.

Valletta, Sliema and St Julian's in Four Days

Day One

Morning/Lunch

1 **Grand Harbour tours** (➤ 48) are offered by several boat operators which depart from the quayside area known as **Sliema Ferries** (the stretch of Sliema on Marsamxett Harbour facing Manoel Island). Take coffee or lunch on the front at Lanċa (➤ 73) or one of the cafés along the harbour by the junction with Bisazza Street.

Afternoon/Evening

Walk up to Tower Road and spread out on the rocks or choose a **lido** (➤ 60). For more history take the Marsamxett ferry from Sliema to Valletta (below: Valletta as seen from Sliema) and visit the **15** **Great Siege of Malta** (➤ 66) or **The Malta Experience** (➤ 78). Round off the afternoon at Caffe Cordina (➤ 71). In the evening sample the restaurants and nightlife in Sliema or St Julian's (➤ 72–75 and 78–80).

Day Two

Morning/Lunch

Catch bus No 1 or 4 to **2** **Vittoriosa** (➤ 49–51) from Valletta and follow the walk (➤ 157–159). Have lunch in Café Boccaccio (➤ 70) in Vittoriosa.

Afternoon/Evening

Make your way to **Senglea** (➤ 47) and walk along the shore looking back to where you have just been. The late afternoon sun on Vittoriosa's honey-coloured buildings is a glorious sight. At the end of the Senglea peninsula is the famous "Ear-and-Eye" Vedette. Return to Valletta and have dinner at one of its restaurants (➤ 70–72)

Day Three

Morning/Lunch

Take the bus and/or ferry from Sliema or St Julian's to Valletta. Visit the **4 Grand Master's Palace** (➤ 55–57) or the **10 Manoel Theatre** (➤ 63) and have lunch there.

Afternoon/Evening

Visit **3 St John's Co-Cathedral** (above, ➤ 52–54). If the heat is taking its toll, hail a *karrozin* (carriage, left) for a quick look around the city in style. The main places to hire one are City Gate, St George's Square and Fort St Elmo. Have a night out on the town – pick up a copy of the monthly *Calendar of Events* to see what's on (➤ 77–78).

Day Four

Morning

If it's a Sunday, make an early start and visit **Valletta's Sunday market** (➤ 76) in the morning and see In Guardia at **5 Fort St Elmo** (➤ 59). Then hop on a bus to **6 St Julian's** (below, ➤ 60–61), and get off at Spinola Bay.

Lunch

Caffe Raffael (➤ 73) or one of its pretty neighbours overlooking the water are perfect for lunch.

Afternoon

Continue around the bay to chill out at one of the lidos or foreshore, either sunbathing or taking part in the watersports.

Grand Harbour

Grand Harbour is the biggest and probably most dramatic harbour in the Mediterranean. It has been the focus of two titanic battles as Malta has struggled against overwhelming odds. Taking a tour around the harbour provides a good introduction to those events and brings home the enormity of Valletta's remarkable fortifications.

Above:
Grand Harbour,
the biggest
harbour in the
Mediterranean

Right: The Ear
and Eye of
Senglea's
famous lookout
tower give it an
unusual style

Grand Harbour Tour

The tour begins in **Marsamxett Harbour**, opposite Manoel Island and the Carmelite Church. With the exception of the Royal Malta Yacht Club, a bomb disposal depot and a handful of workshops, Manoel Island is now deserted, decaying and scheduled for redevelopment. **Fort Manoel**, built in 1726 as a garrison for 500 men, is semi-derelict, as is its neighbour, the **Lazzaretto**, built in 1643 as an isolation hospital for treating plague, leprosy and other infectious diseases. It claims to be the first of its kind in Europe and was used as a hospital in World War I.

At the head of Marsamxett Harbour is **Msida Creek**, Malta's premier yachting marina, housing around 1,000 boats. The most notable is the black schooner *Black Pearl*, built in Sweden

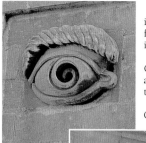

in 1909 and abandoned here after catching fire in the Suez Canal. In 1980 she was used in the filming of *Popeye* (➤ 125).

The cruise continues past the Carmelite Church, around **Fort St Elmo** (➤ 58–59), and out briefly into the open sea before turning back into Grand Harbour.

The rusting pillar at the entrance to Grand Harbour is part of a bridge that was damaged by an E-boat attack in 1941. It was said that while Grand Harbour remained under Maltese control the island could still be saved.

Turning towards Valletta, the following sights are clearly visible: the **Sacra Infirmeria** or Holy Infirmary, used by the Knights Hospitallers in their care of the sick (➤ 64); the 10-tonne, bronze **Siege Bell**, dedicated to the 8,000 victims of the 1940–43 Siege of Malta (➤ 10–12); the **Fish Market**; the elegant houses of **Santa Barbara's Bastion**; and **Upper Barrakka Gardens**, from where there is a panorama across the Grand Harbour to the "Three Cities". There is also a fine view of the land bridge that divides Valletta from its neighbouring suburb, Floriana.

Marsa Creek is the industrial heart of the docks, with huge silos, a massive power station and large cargo ships arriving from all over the world. At **Senglea** you sail right past the **Chinese Dock**, a dry dock some four storeys deep constructed by Chinese workers. Some of the world's largest ships come here for repairs. At the very tip of Senglea look up for the famous **"Eye-and-Ear" Vedette** (or look-out tower), with large ear and eye carvings, symbols of vigilance.

At **Vittoriosa** (➤ 49–51), Dockyard Creek features the Maritime Museum and Fort St Angelo. On the water you will see traditional *dghajsa* (pronounced "dicer") ferryboats. Like the *luzzus* (➤ 92), they are brightly painted and have upright prows that are of Phoenician design.

As your tour boat turns around to head back there are spendid views of Valletta to the left.

The cruise continues via Kalkara Creek, past **Fort Ricasoli**, and back out of Grand Harbour to Marsamxett Harbour. Fort Ricasoli is Malta's largest fort, and last saw action in 1999 when filming of the movie *Gladiator* took place here (➤ 25).

Vital Statistics

• Grand Harbour is 4km long and has an average depth of 36m.
• In Marsa Creek there are silos holding up to 97,000 tons of grain.
• The Chinese Dock can accommodate ships of up to 320,000 tons. At its height in 1938, some 12,000 people worked in the Maltese dockyards.
• In April 1942 over 3,000 tons of bombs hit the dockyards.

Who to Sail With

There are numerous operators. **Captain Morgan** is a reputable and long-established company with double-decker boats, knowledgeable guides and refreshments on board. Whoever you choose, make sure their tour has live commentary and visits the nine main creeks. Tours start from around 10 am to 4 pm and last approximately 90 minutes. If you are staying in Valletta you will have to catch the ferry to Sliema Ferries from the quay known as Manderiggio at St Salvatore Bastion.

Above:
Dghajsas
"dicers" are
traditional ferry
boats, seen
here at Senglea

For Landlubbers

If you don't especially like boats, you could take a walk around Valletta and see all the sights of Grand Harbour or take a tour of the "Three Cities" (► 49–51).

TAKING A BREAK

Cans of drink and crisps are usually available **on board the boat**. Back at Sliema Ferries try **Lanċa** (► 73) or one of the Italian-style cafés lining the harbour.

Above: Captain
Morgan Cruises
is one of Malta's
oldest cruise
operators

➕ 185 E1
Captain Morgan Cruises
✉ Sliema Ferries ☎ 21 343373; www.captainmorgan.com.mt 🕐 Daily tours hourly 10–4 💲 Expensive

Right: Façade
of the Maritime
Museum

GRAND HARBOUR: INSIDE INFO

Top tips Large boats not only offer more choice of seating, but are useful if you want to walk around and take pictures.

• Don't forget to take a **sunhat** and **suncream** in case you want to (or have to) sit in a part of the boat without shade.

• Most boats **depart** at regular intervals throughout the day all year round.

• **Parking** spaces can be found on the main road on Sliema Ferries quayside.

2 Vittoriosa

Vittoriosa takes its name "the Victorious" from the Great Siege of 1565, as it was here that Grand Master La Valette and his troops were based, and where they made their final stand against the Turks (► 9–10). Before then it was known as Birgu, a name that is still widely used by locals.

Vittoriosa is almost completely uncommercialised, despite a number of interesting historical sights. However, the Port Cottonera Consortium plans to develop offices, restaurants and shops in its many empty waterfront buildings and a start has already been made with the chic new **Casinò de Venezia**, opened in 2001 (► 78).

Alongside Senglea and Cospicua, Vittoriosa makes up the so-called **"Three Cities"**. The term is misleading, though, as none of the three is much bigger than the area of a village.

The Waterfront

The beautiful golden buildings of Vittoriosa's waterfront are some of Malta's most photographed sights, usually featuring the colonnaded former Naval Bakery, built in 1842. This is now the **Maritime Museum**, an entertaining collection of model ships, parts of real ships and naval memorabilia relating particularly to the Knights and the British. Almost next door is the **Church of St Lawrence**, built in the 16th century as the main church of the Knights until St John's Co-Cathedral (► 52–54) was constructed. Here La Valette prayed for victory. Behind the church in the **Oratory of St Joseph**, you can see both his hat and sword.

Death of a Hero

Fort St Angelo, nerve centre of the Great Siege, was also the place where Grand Master Jean Parisot de la Valette, its great commander, died while at prayer in 1568 at the age of 75. It is thought that he expired of heatstroke after a day's hunting.

Above: Grandest of all the inns, the Auberge de Castile et Léon in Valletta

At the end of the Vittoriosa promontory is **Fort St Angelo**, used by the Knights as their headquarters during the Great Siege, and again by the British in the siege of 1940–43 when it received 69 direct hits (► 10–12). Take the guided tour to make its vibrant history come to life.

The Backstreets

Vittoriosa's quiet, narrow backstreets are where the Knights had their *auberges* (► below) from 1530 until 1570 when they moved to Valletta. The principal sight open to the public is the **Inquisitor's Palace** (► panel below).

The Knights' *Auberges*

The Knights of St John were organised by *langues*, or nationalities (► 54). Each *langue* had its own *auberge*, or inn, in the old sense of the word, meaning accommodation. This was similar to a college campus arrangement, with lodgings, a chapel and dining hall built around a courtyard. Each of the *auberges* was designed by the Knights' master architect, Gerolamo Cassar, in the 1570s.

Below: The Inquisitor's Palace with its dreaded rack

The Inquisition

Between 1574 and 1798, Vittoriosa was the headquarters of the Grand Inquisition. Inside the **Inquisitor's Palace** (Main Gate Street, tel: 21 663731, opening times as Maritime Museum opposite; inexpensive) are some fine murals and a ceiling decorated with the coats of arms of the 62 Inquisitors who ruled from here. The doorway of the dreaded Judgement Room was built deliberately low so the prisoners entering would be forced to bow.

Valletta's *Auberges*

The Knight's *auberges* were originally built in Vittoriosa, but moved to Valletta in 1570. Today five of them survive in Valletta, though all have been considerably altered over the centuries and only the Auberge de Provence is open to the public.

The most famous is the Auberge de Castile, on Castile Place, now the office of the prime minister. Its façade, described as "the grandest and most harmonious example of Maltese baroque", was added in 1741 by Andrea Belli.

The Auberge de Provence is now occupied by the National Museum of Archaeology (► 62) and has a fine mural on the ceiling of its entrance, added in the 18th century. The beautiful upper floor, currently under restoration, was the Knight's Great Hall, and its fine coffered ceiling and painted walls indicate the privileged lifestyle of the knights.

The remaining three auberges have all been converted into government offices; the Auberge d'Aragon on Independence Square, West Street; the Auberge d'Angleterre et Baviere at the corner of West Street and St Sebastian Street; and the Auberge d'Italie on Merchants Street, until recently the main post office.

Of the others, the Auberge d'Allemagne (Germany) was demolished in 1838, while the Auberge d'Auvergne and the Auberge de France failed to survive World War II. The Valletta Walk (► 154–156) passes several of these sites.

TAKING A BREAK

There are very few refreshment outlets in Vittoriosa. **Café Boccaccio** (► 70) is the best option.

➕ 181 E2
Maritime Museum
➕ 181 E2 ✉ Vittoriosa Wharf ☎ 21 660052 ⏰ Mon–Fri 7:45–2, mid-Jun–Sep; Mon–Sat 8:15–5, Sun 8:15–4:15, rest of year 💷 Inexpensive

Church of St Lawrence
➕ 181 E2 ✉ St Lawrence Street ☎ 21 827057 ⏰ Daily 6–10, 4–7 (note it is often closed during these times) 💷 Free

Oratory of St Joseph
➕ 181 E2 ✉ Vittoriosa Square ⏰ Mon–Sat 8:30–noon, 2–4, Sun 9:30–noon (note it is often closed during these times) 💷 Free

Fort St Angelo
➕ 183 E1 ⏰ Sat 9–1, first Sun of month 10–noon; guided tours 9:15–12:15 💷 Inexpensive (also covers Fort St Elmo in Valletta; ► 58–59)

VITTORIOSA: INSIDE INFO

Top tips Early evening, when the setting sun illuminates the golden sandstones, is the best time to see Vittoriosa.
• **The best view** is from Grand Harbour on a tour (► 46–48) or from Senglea (► 47).

3 St John's Co-Cathedral

It may not look much from the outside, but inside St John's Co-Cathedral is a baroque riot of colour, shapes, textures, monuments and a marble "tombstone floor". In 1831 Scottish novelist and poet Sir Walter Scott was so impressed that he called it "the most magnificent place I ever saw in my life".

The construction of the cathedral began in 1573 under the auspices of Gerolamo Cassar, the chief architect of the Order of the Knights of St John. Valletta itself was being built at this time, preparing for the next great Ottoman attack (which never came), so it is not surprising that the exterior of the building has a military, fortress-like appearance. It was finished in 1577, though its decoration took another century or so to complete.

Above: Large door knockers were a symbol of wealth and power

Right: The Cathedral is decorated with tapestries at festival time

As you enter the church, notice the giant **door knockers**, a feature of many grand old Maltese buildings. Once inside you have to turn left and follow a "one-way system". Before doing so take a minute or two to look along the length of the 58m-long nave pavement (during services it is roped off). It is almost entirely laid with marble memorial **tombstones**, around 400 in all, dedicated to the Knights of St John. Each bears an elaborate inlaid picture (many featuring Death or a skull and crossbones), symbols of war and peace, and a glowing Latin inscription including the family name and battle honours.

The **ceiling** is no less flamboyant. Tunnel-vaulted, it is painted in 18 panels with scenes of the life of John the Baptist (patron saint of the Order). It was painted between 1662 and 1667 by the Calabrian artist Mattia Preti (1613–1699) who is buried in the first side altar that you reach.

The route round the cathedral takes in 12 richly decorated side chapels, seven of which are dedicated to each *langue of the Knights* (▶ 54). All but two of the 28 Grand Masters are buried in the cathedral, and most of their tombs are perfect examples of High Baroque art. However, you'll look in vain for that of Great Siege hero Grand Master Jean Parisot de la Valette (▶ 9). His remains lie in the crypt (rarely open to the public), along with ten other early Grand Masters.

Just before you complete the church circuit is the entrance to the **museum**. Its most acclaimed work is Caravaggio's masterpiece *The Beheading*

Spot the Skulls
Children and churches don't usually mix but here's a way to keep the kids occupied. Point out the macabre skull and crossbones or skeletons on the tombstones and ask them how many they can find.

of St John the Baptist. A brilliant study in light and shade and a landmark in European art, it is also an extremely brutal image. In fact it depicts not the actual beheading, but the moment after it has been administered (note the sword on the floor), just as the executioner is about to sever the saint's head with his knife. The apparent indifference of the onlookers behind the barred window makes the scene all the more unpalatable. Another acclaimed work by Caravaggio in the museum is *St Jerome*.

Caravaggio's bloodcurdling masterpiece *The Beheading of St John the Baptist*

A Multinational Force

The Knights of St John were organised according to their nationality or **langue**. The seven *langues* at the time of the Great Siege in 1565 were France, Provence, Auvergne, Germany, Italy, Aragon (including Catalonia and Navarre) and Castile (including Léon and Portugal). The English *langue* had been suppressed by King Henry VIII in 1534, and by 1565 England was only represented by a single, albeit very important Knight, Sir Oliver Starkey. He was Secretary, close friend and adviser to La Valette, and is buried beside him in the cathedral crypt.

TAKING A BREAK

The pleasant **Café Marquee** is opposite the Cathedral entrance. Near by are several other alternatives (▶ 70–72).

Right: The courtyards of the Grand Master's Palace – peaceful oases for men of war

✚ 182 C2 ✉ St John's Square, Valletta ☎ 21 220536 🕐 Mon–Fri 9:30–12:30, 1:30–4:30, Sat 9:30–12:30. Sun for services only 💷 Co-Cathedral free; museum inexpensive

---

ST JOHN'S CO-CATHEDRAL: INSIDE INFO

Top tip Not only is **flash photography forbidden** in the cathedral, signs warn that offenders' films will be confiscated.

One to miss For most visitors the **museum** is only worthwhile for the works of Caravaggio. They are in the first room, so if you are too tired to complete the museum tour (involving several flights of stairs), come straight back out. Alternatively take a break and return here later.

4 Grand Master's Palace

As a result of the astonishing victory over the Ottoman Empire in the Great Siege of 1565, the Grand Master of the Knights of St John became as powerful as any European monarch. As riches poured in from Europe – in gratitude for the victory and for providing further defence against invasion – so the trappings of the Order became more palatial.

Work began on the Grand Master's Palace in 1571 under the direction of Gerolamo Cassar, chief architect of the Order. It was completed in 1575 and continuously occupied by 21 Grand Masters until Grand Master von Hompesch was forced to hand it over to Napoleon in 1798.

After the French were ousted two years later it became the seat of the British governors and since 1976 it has housed the offices of the President of Malta.

Enter through the main gate off Republic Street and straight ahead is the Neptune Courtyard, an attractive area of plants and palms surrounding a bronze muscular statue of King Neptune and a fountain.

The Apartments

The Apartments are reached via a narrow spiral staircase, easily defended against an attacker, and almost impossible to negotiate when a group of determined sightseers are pushing their way down! Notice how shallow the steps are, designed with knights in heavy armour and aged Grand Masters in mind. The staircase was also built wide enough to accommodate a sedan chair, and leads to the frequently photographed **Armoury Corridor**, lined with knights' suits standing to attention.

At one end of the Corridor, roped off, is the **Chamber of Parliament** where the Maltese Assembly has sat since 1976. Off the corridor are two quite remarkable rooms. The **Supreme Council Hall** (also known as the Hall of St Michael and St George), where the Supreme Council of the Knights once met, is famous for its frieze of the Great Siege of 1565. It was painted between 1576 and 1581 by Matteo Perez d'Aleccio, a pupil of Michelangelo, and is the most reliable pictorial account of events of the Great Siege in existence. Note, too, the richly decorated timber ceiling.

There is another exquisite ceiling in the **Council Chamber** (where the Maltese Parliament sat from 1921 until 1976), but the star attractions here are the **Gobelin tapestries**, known as *Les Tentures des Indes* (*Paintings of the Indies*). They were inspired by the tales which came back from the early 17th-century hunting expeditions of a German prince in various exotic places – Brazil, the Caribbean, India and Africa to name a few – and are a romantic and fanciful vision of noble savages, wild animals and lush flora. Age has somewhat dimmed the tapestries' original vibrant colours, but they still create an impressive spectacle.

There are three other rooms usually open to the public: the **State Dining Hall**, the **Ambassador's Room** and the **Page's Waiting Room** (Yellow Room). All feature fine portraits and frieze paintings.

GRAND MASTER'S PALACE: INSIDE INFO

Top tip The Palace is on the agenda of every sightseeing group in Malta and the **narrow corridors can get very congested**. To avoid them, come first thing in the morning or an hour or so before closing time.

Hidden gem Next to the case containing the Grand Masters' suits in the Palace Armoury is a **Gonne Shield**, a round shield with a small chimney-like protrusion just big enough to fire a gun through. It is part of a donation from England's King Henry VIII. Another curious weapon is the **flintlock rocket launcher**, made around 1800 (it's in a central cabinet in the second room).

**Below left:
Suits of armour
in the Armoury
Exhibition**

**Below right:
Exotic tapes-
tries enliven
the Council
Chamber**

The Palace Armoury

Downstairs in two large vaulted rooms, formerly the stables, the Palace Armoury is one of the finest collections of 16th- and 17th-century arms and armour in the world. The main features are the lavishly engraved suits of armour. They were created, almost inevitably, for the Grand Masters and include the suits of Alof de Wignacourt (1601–22) and the Great Siege hero, Jean Parisot de la Valette (1557–68). Made in Milan, they are inlaid with gold and were worn only on ceremonial occasions.

TAKING A BREAK

There are several restaurants and cafés very close by. On the square next to the cathedral are **Caffe Cordina** and **Café Premier** (➤ 71 for both).

🔲 183 D3 ✉ Republic Street ☎ 21 221221 🕐 Mon–Fri 8–12:45, mid-Jun–Sep; Mon–Wed 8:30–3:45, Thu–Fri 8:30–4, rest of year 💰 Moderate (closed to visitors when Parliament is sitting)

5 Fort St Elmo

At the very tip of the peninsula on which Valletta sits, the small, star-shaped fort of St Elmo is today a rather modest sight. But back in 1565 Valletta did not yet exist and this was the only fort on the peninsula, commanding both Grand Harbour and Marsamxett Harbour.

When the Turkish fleet arrived in 1565 to take the island they knew they had to neutralise St Elmo if they wanted safe deep anchorage. In 1565, for 31 days of continuous siege, this small patch of ground was the focus of all-out war between East and West (► 10). By the time the Turkish flag was finally raised at St Elmo, some 1,500 Christian defenders and 8,000 Moslem attackers had died. The Knights had lost the battle, but had also inflicted such grievous losses and delayed the Ottomans for so long that they went on to win the war.

A **self-guided walking tour** leaflet shows the main points of interest, but to get a sense of what really happened here it is best to take one of the **guided tours** that depart hourly.

Despite the heroic status of the Fort, its lower barracks area (not open to visitors but clearly visible) is a squalid mess, occupied by squatters for many years now. The chilling Turkish prison movie *Midnight Express* was filmed here in 1977 and its sinister atmosphere seems to have changed little in 25 years.

Top: On Guard, nowadays only for tourists

Above: Fort St Elmo is named after the patron saint of mariners

National War Museum

Tucked around the back of the Fort (with a separate entrance), the National War Museum deals with Malta's siege of 1940–43 (► 10–12). The museum houses a small collection, with pride

of place going to the **George Cross** medal that was awarded in 1942 to the whole island in recognition of their bravery during World War II (➤ 9). The other star attraction is the **Gloucester Gladiator biplane *Faith***, one of three that helped defend the island in 1940.

TAKING A BREAK

The nearest café is at the **Malta Experience** in the Mediterranean Conference Centre (➤ 78). However, it's only a short walk back into the centre of Valletta where there is a wide choice of cafés and restaurants (➤ 70–72).

The George Cross, awarded "for a heroism and devotion that will long be famous in history"

Fort St Elmo
🕂 183 E4 ✉ Merchant Street/Republic Street 🕐 Sat 1–5, Sun 9–4
🎟 Fort only inexpensive, Fort and shows moderate (no In Guardia or Alarme shows Jul or Aug and at other times shows are subject to weather conditions – pick up a leaflet from the tourist office for exact dates and times; ➤ 33)

National War Museum
🕂 183 E5 ✉ Lower St Elmo, French Curtain ☎ 21 222430 🕐 Mon–Fri 7:45–2, mid-Jun–Sep; Mon–Sat 8:15–5, Sun 8:15–4:15, rest of year
🎟 Inexpensive

FORT ST ELMO: INSIDE INFO

Top tip On most Sundays you can see **In Guardia**, a colourful evocation of the past featuring around 90 men-at-arms and officers in period costume, performing a series of drills and discharging guns. On the last Sunday of the month In Guardia is replaced by **Alarme**, portraying a military encounter between French and Maltese troops around 1800.

6 Sliema and St Julian's

From Sliema Ferries, opposite Valletta, to St George's Bay 3km north, where the solid urban and resort sprawl finally relaxes, lies Malta's biggest, most concentrated and most popular holiday playground. St Julian's begins at Spinola Bay and includes Paceville and St George's Bay. Sliema has at least three divisions: Tower Road ("The Front"), home to the main hotels; Sliema Ferries (The Strand) where the pleasure boats line up; and a quieter, exclusive residential district inland.

Spinola Bay

Spinola Bay, with its fleet of brightly coloured **luzzus** (➤ 92) and flower-filled restaurant balconies, is a near-perfect Mediterranean fishing harbour (only slightly spoiled by the high-rise buildings). Go at lunchtime for a quiet relaxing waterside meal, or experience the buzz of a weekend evening.

The bay takes its name from Paul Raphael Spinola, Grand Prior of Lombardy, who built his **palazzo** here in 1688. It still stands, while immediately below, on the bay front, the boathouses and market-place built for the local fishermen by Spinola now house attractive restaurants.

Beaches

To a Malti "beach" really means any access to the sea. Sliema's beaches start at **Qui-Si-Sana**, the promontory, and then head around the bay, past the tall Preluna Hotel and Towers, with several **lidos** offering swimming pools, cafés and terraces with welcome parasols. Many sunbathers simply stretch out on the large, flat sandstone rocks by the water's edge; handrails set in the rocks offer a helping hand in and out of the sea.

SLIEMA AND ST JULIAN'S: INSIDE INFO

Top tips The hotels on Tower Road, Sliema and around the centre of St Julian's can suffer from road and party noise, particularly from July to August. If you want a bit of **peace and quiet**, but still want to be close to the action, choose St George's Bay.
• Sliema has more than 600 **shopping outlets**, with designer clothes, and every kind of obect for the home top of the list. Most shops are concentrated on Bisazza Street and The Strand (➤ 76).

The promenade at Sliema, the place to be at *passegiata* time

Above: On the rocks along Tower Road, Sliema

Further round the coast, between Sliema and St Julian's, is **Balluta Bay**, a pretty spot with a small square of sand. There's a little park and large, smooth rocks for sunbathing.

Valletta Viewpoint

The view from The Strand at Sliema (by the Fortina Hotel) across the water to the Carmelite Church and Valletta skyline is breathtaking. Late afternoon when it glows golden is just perfect. By night the church and bastions are softly illuminated.

Stepping Out

Step out of your Sliema hotel on any summer night and you might be forgiven for thinking that a football match has suddenly disgorged its spectators on to the street. Who are all these people and where are they going? The answer is that they are locals and they are basically going nowhere – apart from up and down the front. The *passegiata*, or Mediterranean promenade, is a nightly ritual for meeting, chatting, snacking, seeing and being seen.

TAKING A BREAK

The whole of this area is chock-a-block with places to eat and drink (➤ 72–75).

Left: Spinola Bay – quiet by day

➕ 185 E2 Sliema
➕ 184 A3 St Julian's
Tourist Information Office (➤ 33)

At Your Leisure

7 National Museum of Archaeology

Housed in the former Auberge de Provence (▶ 50), the National Museum of Archaeology is the logical starting point for anyone who is interested in Malta's ancient temples. In fact, until the long-awaited re-opening of the first floor (scheduled for 2002) documenting the Bronze Age, Punic, Roman and medieval periods, the neolithic period is as far as the exhibits go.

The displays on Tarxien, the Hypogeum and the other principal temples are well captioned and a good introduction to the subject.

One of the "ladies" statues in the National Museum of Archaeology

Almost hidden away in a corner is the museum's star attraction, the *Sleeping Lady*, a beautiful tiny statuette (12.2cm long), thought to represent eternal sleep or death. It was found in the Hypogeum and is around 5,000 years old. In a similar vein, if not so attractive, are several more "ladies" including the figure known as the *Venus of Malta*.

✚ 182 B3 ✉ Republic Street
☎ 21 221623 ⏰ Mon–Fri 7:45–2,
mid-Jun–Sep; Mon–Sat 8:15–5, Sun
8:15–4:15, rest of year 💷 Inexpensive

8 Traditions and Crafts of Malta

A reconstruction of 19th-century village life in the tunnels underneath Valletta may sound a little offbeat, but this collection of tableaux with animated figures and various sound-and-light effects is worth a visit. An audio tour tells you all about life in the village square, a typical Maltese house and, of course, local traditions and crafts, featuring the work of blacksmiths, woodworkers and carpenters. See if you can spot the 100-year-old child's scooter that bears an uncanny resemblance to today's fashionable scooters.

✚ 182 B3 ✉ St John Cavalier
Street ☎ 21 240292 ⏰ Daily
9:30–4 💷 Moderate

9 National Museum of Fine Arts

The grand building housing this museum dates from the late 16th century, and was one of the first buildings in Valletta. The collection goes back as far as early medieval times, but the bulk of its works are 17th- and 18th-century religious subjects. The most valuable paintings are by the great Calabrian baroque master Mattia Preti (1613–1699), who lived in Malta for ten

The Baptism of Christ by Malta's most famous (adopted) artist, Mattia Preti

years and painted the ceiling of St John's Co-Cathedral (➤ 52). To see how Valletta and Malta looked in the 18th century, seek out the works of French artists Antoine de Farvray and Louis du Cros. By contrast there are some interesting works by contemporary Maltese artists. Don't leave without seeing the various memorabilia in the basement area, much of it relating to the Knights.

🔲 182 B3 ✉ South Street ☎ 21 233034 🕐 Mon–Fri 7:45–2, mid-Jun–Sep; Mon–Sat 8:15–5, Sun 8:15–4:15, rest of year 💶 Inexpensive

🔟 Manoel Theatre

The Manoel, one of the oldest theatres in Europe, was built in 1732. It has enjoyed good times, when it was patronised by British royalty, and bad times, twice teetering on the brink of extinction. In 1864, Valletta's grand

new Royal Opera House was finally completed, the Manoel closed and for a time became a doss house for beggars. It reopened when the Opera House burned down in 1873, but when the Opera House was rebuilt, it was again snubbed.

In 1942 the Royal Opera House was again destroyed and this time remained in ruins (these still stand, left as a memorial, at the top end of Republic Street). The Manoel did not re-open until 1960, but in the meantime its beautifully detailed tiered boxes and 22-carat-gold ceiling had been lavishly restored. This time it was back for good. A short tour, which includes a theatre museum, brings out the finer points of this little baroque gem.

🔲 182 C4 ✉ Old Theatre Street ☎ 21 222618 or 242977 🕐 Museum: Mon–Fri 10–1, 5–7. Guided tours: Mon–Fri 10:30, 11:30, 4:30; Sat 11:30, 12:30 💶 Moderate

Five Good Places for the Kids
- Grand Masters' Palace Armoury (➤ 57)
- Toy Museum (➤ right)
- Great Siege of Malta and the Knights of St John (➤ 66)
- Malta Experience (➤ 78)
- Traditions and Crafts of Malta (➤ left)

🔟 Toy Museum

Train sets, cars, robots, dolls, miniature sewing machines and cookers…as you peruse the rows of toys from the 1950s

Kids' stuff in the Toy Museum, set in a traditional Valletta house

🚩 183 D4 ✉ 222 Republic Street ☎ 21 251652
🕐 Mon–Fri 10:30–3:30, Sat–Sun 10:30–1:30
💶 Inexpensive (child free if accompanied by an adult)

and 1960s in this small three-storey collection you can almost anticipate the hoots of derision from the kids: "Mum, Dad, you didn't have one of *those* did you?" Look out for the kitsch 1950s Japanese sci-fi items.

🔢 Casa Rocca Piccola

Built in the 1580s for a Knight of St John and subsequently occupied by many noble families, the Casa Rocca Piccola is unique for the insight that it gives into an aristocratic Valletta household over the centuries.

The current owners, the de Piro family, trace their noble Valletta lineage back almost 300 years and have been resident here for 50 of them. Family members sometimes lead the tour of the house.

Highlights include a set of ten 17th-century canvases, reputed to have been part of the barge of Grand Master Lascaris, and a wall-cabinet which functioned as a portable chapel. There is also a separate Costume Collection featuring 18th- and 19th-century costumes.

🚩 183 D4 ✉ 74 Republic Street
☎ 21 231796; www.casarocca.net
🕐 House: by guided tour only, Mon–Sat 10, 11, noon, 1, 2, 3 and 4. Costume Collection: Mon–Sat 10–4
💶 House moderate; Costume Collection inexpensive; combined ticket expensive

🔢 Sacra Infirmeria

Although the Knights of St John became famous for their military exploits, they began life in 1085 as Knights Hospitallers, a peaceful order who tended to the sick on their way to the Crusades. The Sacra Infirmeria (literally Holy Infirmary) is the embodiment of this calling. Built in 1574, its huge hospital ward, the Long Hall, was extended in the mid-17th century to measure 155m, making it the longest hall in Europe at that time. It could accommodate 563 beds in peacetime, with an emergency capacity of over 900 beds. Patients ate from solid silver plates to cut down the risk of infection, and even the Grand Master took a turn serving the food. Napoleon had the silver melted down and sold to pay for his military campaigns, but there are a few surviving pieces on display in the National Museum of Fine Arts (► 62).

The Sacra Infirmeria was heavily bombed during World War II and re-opened in 1979 as the prestigious **Mediterranean Conference Centre**. The Long Hall is open to the public (subject to conference functions) and The Knights Hospitallers Exhibition is a series of tableaux relating to the history of the Order.

➕ 183 E3 ✉ Mediterranean Street
☎ 21 224135 🕐 Mon–Fri 9:30–4:30, Sat 9:30–4 💰 Moderate

🔟 Church of St Paul Shipwreck

St Paul has strong associations with Malta (► 126) and this is the finest of many churches to take his name. The vault is decorated with frescoes depicting scenes from his life. The church also includes two remarkable

Three Unusual Places to Eat and Drink with the Locals
• The **Malta Labour Party Club**, 41 Republic Street, promises the best prices in the city, from its incredibly cheap all-day breakfast to sea bream for LM3.25.
• **Labyrinth**, 44 Strait Street, is a dusty, arty complex which includes an antiques shop and an old-fashioned tea-room.
• **Café Diva** (► 70), in a peaceful courtyard in the Manoel Theatre, is the perfect place to chill out from sightseeing and the summer heat.

relics, his wristbone and part of the column on which he was beheaded in Rome (both to the right of the main altar). The statue of St Paul is carried high through the streets of Valletta on 10 February, the Feast of St Paul. The church, built in the 16th century, is often called Malta's hidden gem, the reason for which becomes obvious when stepping inside. The façade, almost concealed, gives away nothing of the riot of colour within. Just about every square inch has been

The dazzling interior of the Church of St Paul Shipwreck

elaborately decorated with coloured marble and gilded woodwork.

🏛 182 C3 ✉ St Paul's Street
☎ 21 236013 🕐 Daily
9:30–11:45, 1:30–5 (no visits during Mass) 💰 Free

🔢 Great Siege of Malta and the Knights of St John

This is Malta's newest and most spectacular special-effects historical show. Through 45 minutes of tableaux, talking heads, videos, touch screens and other state-of-the-art special effects, it traces the history of the Knights from the Crusades, via their home in Rhodes, to Malta and the Great Siege of 1565 (▶ 10). Visitors wear special headphones which automatically begin the commentary as they walk from one area, or time zone, to another. Children will particularly enjoy it and it's a good introduction to Valletta and the Great Siege sites.

🏛 182 C3 ✉ Republic Square
☎ 21 247300 or 237574;
www.cities.com.mt/great-siege
🕐 Daily 9–4 (last admission at 4)
💰 Expensive

🔢 Lascaris War Rooms

Tucked away below the fortifications of the city, this warren of tunnels was the nerve centre from where Allied

Take a look at life in Malta as it once was at the Traditions and Crafts of Malta

air and sea operations were directed during the Siege of Malta during World War II (▶ 10–12). Not only was the defence of the island master-minded here, but also the counter-offensive invasion of Sicily in 1943. Dummy figures now staff the tunnels, map and communications rooms and an audio-tour guides you round.

🏛 182 B2 ✉ Lascaris Ditch ☎ 21 238396 🕐 Mon–Fri 9:30–4:30, Sat–Sun 9:30–1 (last admission 30 minutes before closing) 💰 Moderate

🔢 St James Cavalier Centre for Creativity

This huge, powerful fortification by the City Gate once held the Knight's armoury, and more prosaically in latter years, the government printing press. It has been beautifully restored and was re-opened in 2000 as an arts centre promoting a range of performing and visual arts. Art exhibitions are held throughout the day. For more details on its other many events and activities ▶ 77.

🏛 182 B2 ✉ St James Cavalier
☎ 21 223216, info@stjamescav.org
🕐 Daily 10–8:30, later in summer depending on events. Guided tours daily during summer by request 💰 Most art exhibitions free (charge for events)

Where to... Stay

Prices
Expect to pay per double room per night
£ under LM15 **££** LM15–30 **£££** LM31–50 **££££** over LM50

British £

This is Valletta's longest-established hotel, and something of a city institution. It may be old-fashioned, but as its devotees point out, it's also cheap, friendly, has something of the character of Valletta in its British days, and enjoys a great location, particularly if you can get a sea-view room. If not you can still eat breakfast on the balcony, taking in one of the island's finest and most famous views, overlooking the fabulous Grand Harbour.

➕ 182 C2 ◾ 267 St Ursula Street, Valletta ☎ 21 224730; www.britishhotel.com

Castille ££

This attractive traditional building dates from the 16th century, when it was the home of a noble Maltese family. In 1967 it was converted into a small hotel. The reception area is welcoming and the concierge friendly, though most rooms are a bit old-fashioned. However, the location (next to Upper Barrakka Gardens; ➤ 47) is good and there's a rooftop restaurant with views over Grand Harbour. La Cave (➤ 71) is an attractive wine cellar serving pizzas and pasta and on the ground floor there's a cosy café.

➕ 182 C2 ◾ Castille Square, Valletta ☎ 21 243677; fax: 21 243679

Le Meridien Phoenicia ££££

If you want to stay in Valletta in style then you really will have no choice but to come here as the Phoenicia is the city's only really up-market hotel. You won't be disappointed. Built in the 1920s, just outside the Main Gate, and carefully restored in the 1990s to retain its classical character, the Phoenicia has luxury rooms, beautiful public areas, manicured grounds and excellent restaurants. It's a favourite with businesspeople, luminaries and short-break holiday-makers.

➕ 182 A3 ◾ The Mall, Floriana ☎ 21 225241; www.lemeridien.com

Crowne Plaza ££££

Tucked comfortably away on the Tigne peninsula, around the corner from the main streets and noisy traffic of Sliema, the 187-room Crowne Plaza is a friendly, modern, well-equipped hotel in spacious grounds. It has more than a touch of history, too, with a 19th-century wing that once accommodated a military hospital. In the grounds next to the pool are the remains of emplacements that used to house a huge gun, similar to that at Fort Rinella. The hotel does a brisk conference trade, so business suits may be seen alongside swimsuits. Beware the adjacent building work; ask before booking.

➕ 185 F1 ◾ Tigne Street, Sliema ☎ 21 343400; www.crowneplazamalta.com

Fortina ££££

The most obvious feature of this modern, 215-room hotel is the unbeatable views from its attractive lido area, across Marsamxett Harbour to the landmark dome of the Carmelite Church. Inside it is very comfortable and stylish. The Fortina is Malta's only all-inclusive hotel, although there are many restaurants and cafés in Sliema and Valletta close to hand. The Sliema Ferries' action is just a short walk away. Try and specify a room with a view. Deluxe Jacuzzi suites and thalassotherapy packages are also available.

➕ 185 off F1 ✉ Tigne Sea Front ☎ 21 342976; www. hotelfortina.com

Howard Johnson Diplomat £££

Set about 200m from the main tourist part of Sliema, the Howard Johnson Diplomat caters for both businesspeople and holiday-makers and has a more relaxed and refined air about it than some of Sliema's more obvious tourist establishments. Full-length windows in the bedrooms offer great sea views and triple-glazing tames the noise of traffic from the main street. The hotel has no grounds but there's a small rooftop swimming pool.

➕ 185 E3 ✉ 173 Tower Road ☎ 21 345361; fax: 21 345351

Imperial ££

The smart Imperial, built in 1865, is almost equidistant (around 500m) from Tower Road, Sliema Ferries and Balluta Bay, so this is a good place to stay if you want to escape the noise and yet be within walking distance of all local facilities. A double staircase sweeps up through its period-style interior to modern rooms. A pretty courtyard leads to a swimming pool and a spacious sundeck. Holiday-makers in the know return here regularly so it's wise to book in advance.

➕ 185 D2 ✉ 1 Rudolph Street, Sliema ☎ 21 344093; www.imperialhotelmalta.com

Plevna ££

This superior, 100-room hotel is tucked away on the Tigne peninsula and has a loyal following among British visitors. Rooms have been refurbished to a good standard and although general facilities are limited, a big plus is its own lido just 200m away. There's also a small coffee shop and a piano bar.

➕ 185 F1 ✉ 2 Thornton Street, Sliema ☎ 21 331031; www.destinationmalta.com/plevna

Preluna Hotel and Towers £££

If you want to be at the heart of the action in Sliema, this well-known landmark hotel is very comfortable and has all the facilities you could wish for, including private lido, roof terraces for sunbathing, a small indoor swimming pool, fitness room and its own disco. It's very popular with package groups.

➕ 185 E2 ✉ 124 Tower Road, Sliema ☎ 21 330401; fax: 21 337281

Victoria Hotel £££–££££

In the quieter residential part of Sliema, a 10-minute walk from the seafront, this luxurious hotel is a winning combination of old and new, with sandstone walls, a traditional fire and Chesterfield sofas in the Penny Black lounge and cocktail bar. The rooms are attractively furnished, while the rooftop sun terrace and pool and Copperfield's restaurant (with live piano music) entices guests not to stray too far.

➕ 185 E2 ✉ George Borg Oliver Street ☎ 21 334711; www.victoriahotel.com

ST JULIAN'S

Cavalieri £££

Tucked away in a fairly quiet location at the end of the main Spinola Bay road, the Cavalieri is well placed for St Julian's many evening pleasures. It enjoys excellent views of the bay and there's easy immediate access to the sea. There are also two swimming pools with a large sundeck if you wish to stay in the hotel grounds. Rooms are bright and comfortable, and public areas are nicely furnished.

➕ 184 C4 ✉ 21 Spinola Road ☎ 21 336255; www.hotelcavalieri.com

Corinthia Marina ££££

This sprawling, modern complex occupying the St George's seafront is highly impressive, with excellent staff and a popular restaurant, Vinotheque (▶ 75). Rooms nudge luxury quality – all with uninterrupted sea views – and cater to holiday-makers willing to spend that bit more for a touch of class and comfort. The sweeping views from the breakfast terrace make a great start to every day. Guests may also make use of the facilities of the Corinthia San Gorg next door (▶ below). Together the two hotels are sometimes referred to as the Corinthia Beach Resort.

✛ 184 off B5 ☒ St George's Bay, St Julian's ☎ 21 381719; www.corinthiahotels.com

Corinthia San Gorg ££££

Sister to the adjacent Corinthia Marina (▶ above), the luxurious San Gorg has a large conference clientele and a more business-like air than the Corinthia, with slightly more formal décor. Executive suites offer world-class luxury and all the technical business support required. The large grounds feature a cascading pool, a state-of-the-art health and beauty spa, and a choice of first-class

restaurants, the Fra Martino (▶ 73) and the Frejgatina (▶ 73). Guests may also make use of the adjacent Corinthia Marina facilities.

✛ 184 off B5 ☒ St George's Bay, St Julian's ☎ 21 374114; www.corinthiahotels.com

Golden Tulip Vivaldi £££

This elegant establishment is St Julian's newest major hotel. The public areas and rooms are luxurious and there's an attractive modern brasserie. A rooftop hotel, indoor swimming pool and fitness centre make up for the hotel's lack of grounds, but visitors should be aware of its proximity to the noise and night-time antics of Paceville (▶ 78).

✛ 184 B5 ☒ Dragonara Road, St Julian's ☎ 21 378100; www.goldentuliphotels.nl/gtvivaldi

Hilton Malta ££££

Overlooking the burgeoning new Portomaso marina development, the chic Hilton opened in 1999 and is

arguably Malta's finest retreat. A stunning atrium opens out on to spacious, palm-landscaped grounds. The luxurious rooms are arranged in tiers and are offset from each other, giving an organic feel to the whole complex and setting it apart from some of its more boxy highrise neighbours. A choice of superb restaurants, the Blue Elephant (▶ 73) and Gazebo (▶ 74), draws many non-residents. For business travellers (or lottery winners) the executive suites are the best in Malta, and if you want to pamper yourself, the health and fitness club here is the largest in Malta.

✛ 184 B4 ☒ Portomaso, St Julian's ☎ 21 336210; www.hiltonmalta.com

Villa Rosa ££

This attractive, bright pink, old-world mansion with landscaped gardens tumbling down the hillside makes a refreshing change from the major international hotel chains around the St Julian's area. Rooms are fairly basic but also feature four

to six bunk beds and so are ideal for groups. There are indoor and outdoor pools, sports and gym facilities. Note that if you are seeking peace, it is also close to the noisy nightlife of Paceville (▶ 78).

✛ 184 off B5 ☒ St George's Bay ☎ 21 342707; fax: 21 316531

Westin Dragonara Resort ££££

Isolated from the rest of St Julian's on its own promontory with 3.5 hectares of sunbathing grounds, including a casino (▶ 80), the Westin is definitely luxurious. The interior is cool and calm, with Arabic influences and the rooms are huge luxury suites with every facility. High-rollers and business types mix with families willing to spend that bit more. There are all kinds of leisure options and the Westin Kids Club is highly regarded. Note that there's plenty of action at the popular Reef Club lido at weekends.

✛ 184 C5 ☒ Dragonara Road, St Julian's ☎ 21 381000; www.westinmalta.com

Where to…
Eat and Drink

Prices
Prices indicate what you should pay per person for a three-course meal, excluding drinks and service charge.
£ under LM8 ££ LM8–12 £££ over LM12

VALLETTA

Bologna ££
Like its neighbour, the Grand Master's Palace (▶ 55–57), the Bologna is one of Valletta's more enduring institutions. As you ascend the stairs, a serious dining-room of dark wood panelling and long traditions welcomes you. The food is what counts here, good solid Italian fare: *antipasti*, pasta, risotto, veal, lamb, giant prawns and lobster. There's a sprinkling of classic Maltese dishes too. At lunchtime fellow diners will be business types, in the evening an older clientele.

🏛 183 D4 ☒ 59 Republic Street
☎ 21 246149 ⏰ Mon–Sat lunch and dinner

British Hotel £
The view is really the thing here. If you can't get a table on the balcony overlooking the lovely Grand Harbour (and preferably a front row one), then it's probably not worth coming. Having secured your spot, the choice is easy: *fenek* (rabbit), followed by ricotta and almond cake, or whatever home-made goodies are on offer. The food is good, the price is good and the view is superb.

🏛 182 C2 ☒ 267 St Ursula Street
☎ 21 224730 ⏰ Daily lunch and dinner

Café Boccaccio ££
If you want a proper meal in Vittoriosa (or indeed anywhere in the "Three Cities") then this is your only choice. The Café Boccaccio is in a superb setting in the 18th-century courtyard of the Couvre Porte. Rustic Italian is the theme, with pasta dishes predominating. The staff are friendly.

🏛 181 E2 ☒ Couvre Porte, Vittoriosa ☎ 21 675757 ⏰ Sun–Fri 11:30–3, Sat–Sun 7–10:30 pm

Café Diva £
The Café Diva is the perfect place to take the weight off your feet and relax in very peaceful surroundings. It is set around a covered three-storey arcade, part of the Manoel Theatre complex (▶ 63). Modern art, fountains, plants and local music-lovers are all to be found here. The young, friendly staff produce typical Maltese snacks such as *timpana* (baked macaroni with puff pastry topping) and *ross fil-forn* (baked rice) and also serve traditional pastries and an excellent cappuccino.

🏛 182 C4 ☒ 72 Old Bakery Street
☎ 21 223005 ⏰ Daily 10–5

Café Jubilee £
This old-fashioned-looking pub/café attracts a friendly, chic local crowd and is a good place to get away from the heritage and tourist mainstream. They do good snacks and the mellow atmosphere is helped by eclectic world music. It's the perfect place to come if you're looking for a late-night drink.

🏛 182 C3 ☒ 125 Santa Lucia Street
☎ Daily 8 am–1 am

Café Olé £
Café Olé is a trendy new place for drinking and eating – quite unusual

Where to... **71**

in traditional Valletta. The terrace catches the sun's rays, while the barrel-vaulted interior is a good place to retreat if you've had enough sun, or later for an evening meal. Go healthy with a salad and cooling fresh lemon juice, then spoil it all with a gooey pastry and a creamy *café freddo* (iced coffee). Or try a *cappuccino bacio* (cappuccino and chocolate syrup).

✦ 182 B2 ☒ St James Cavalier ☎ 21 223200 ◷ Daily 10–5

Café Premier £–££

Owned by the company responsible for the adjacent Great Siege of Malta (▶ 66), Café Premier is putting back some quality Maltese dining into leafy Republic Square, a venue which has become more famed for its overpriced posing opportunities. The menu features plenty of local items: don't miss the *lampuki* (dolphin fish) in season (autumn).

✦ 182 C3 ☒ Republic Square ☎ 21 237362 ◷ Daily 9–6

Café Ta' Karun £

This pretty little terrace is probably the ultimate place for people-watching in Valletta. From this almost secret vantage point, you can see virtually every single person passing into and out of the main City Gate. An awning and fans alleviate the summer heat while Maltese folk music – a real rarity – creates a mellow atmosphere. Although admission to the café is by a separate entrance from the Traditions and Crafts of Malta (▶ 62), it is worth taking advantage of their good-value combined food, drink and admission ticket – tea, coffee and basic snacks.

✦ 182 B3 ☒ Traditions and Crafts of Malta, St John Cavalier ☎ 21 240292 ◷ Daily 9.30–4

Caffe Cordina £–££

Occupying pole position on leafy Republic Square, Caffe Cordina is a Valletta legend. Like the renowned cafes in St Mark's Square in Venice, sooner or later everyone sits down

here, if only to see what all the fuss is about. Cordina serves drinks, snacks, light lunches and excellent pastries and cakes. Take a look inside at the floral baroque decorations on the ceiling. You can order at the bar inside, but note you must pre-pay. Gift-wrapped goodies make tasty souvenirs or gifts.

✦ 182 C3 ☒ Republic Square ☎ 21 234385 ◷ Daily 9.30/10–8

The Carriage £££

One of Valletta's most renowned and stylish restaurants, The Carriage was set up in the 1980s by Michael Lowell, a veteran of some of the finest eateries in New York and London. Book a table at the window or on the terrace for great views over Valletta and the sea. The cuisine is modern Mediterranean: try ricotta and pumpkin ravioli with black truffle and pinenuts, followed by fillet of sea bream with artichoke and hazelnut gratin, or rabbit and fennel filo pie with a cognac sauce, and finish with warm

apricot and mascarpone cheesecake with honey ice-cream.

✦ 182 B3 ☒ 22/5 Valletta Buildings, South Street ☎ 21 247828 ◷ Mon–Fri lunch and dinner, Sat dinner only

La Cave £

Enjoy a large crusty pizza or a bowl of pasta and crunchy salad in the cosy, honey-coloured underground vaults of a 16th-century cellar (formerly stables, kitchen and mill-room) below the Castille Hotel (▶ 67). There's a good wine list both from Malta and abroad.

✦ 182 C2 ☒ Beneath Castille Hotel, Castille Square ☎ 21 243677 ◷ Mon–Fri lunch only, Sat–Sun dinner only

Christopher's £££

This famous restaurant, said to serve the island's finest food, is slightly off the beaten tourist track. It's on the marina waterfront in the embassy quarter of 'Ta' Xbiex (pronounced *tash bee-yesh*), a

5-minute taxi ride from Sliema. The owner produces classical French cuisine, with each dish a masterpiece for both the eye and the palate. The menu changes frequently depending on the season and availability of fresh ingredients. The setting is quite formal and smart casual dress is the code. Book a window seat for views across the marina to Valletta's bastions.

➕ 181 D3 ⊠ Ta' Xbiex Marina
☎ 21 337101 ⊕ Tue–Fri lunch and dinner, Fri–Sat dinner

Cocopazzo ££

Unassuming from the street, inside Cocopazzo turns out to be a colourful warm-hearted trattoria, complete with cheery staff. Fresh fish is usually on display, but the menu offers a wide Italian selection, from pastas and savoury pancakes to meat and fish. A place to come for good value.

➕ 182 B3 ⊠ Ground floor, Valletta Buildings, South Street ☎ 21 235706 ⊕ Daily lunch and dinner

Le Meridien Phoenicia Bastion Pool ££

Tucked away in the grounds of Le Meridien Phoenicia Hotel (▶ 67) is the Bastion Pool open-air restaurant. Hand-painted Venetian and blue mosaic tiles decorate the bar, while canvas awnings and teak tables and chairs give an air of relaxed Mediterranean elegance. Choose from grills, salads and pasta dishes, all presented to the very highest standards. Look out for special offers – for a set price you get lunch and the use of the pool.

➕ 182 A3 ⊠ Le Meridien Phoenicia, The Mall, Floriana ☎ 21 225241 ⊕ Mon–Fri noon–6:30 pm, Tue dinner also (closed in winter)

Da Pippo ££

This small, friendly, family trattoria displays many of the familiar Italian hallmarks, including checked tablecloths and local paintings for sale on the walls. The menu is mostly Italian, but local dishes such as fenek (rabbit) and laham fuq il-fwar (steamed meat) are the house specialities.

➕ 182 B3 ⊠ 136 Melita Street ☎ 21 248029 ⊕ Mon–Sat 11:30–4

Rubino £££

Rubino is housed in a 100-year-old shop redecorated in traditional Maltese style. The modern Maltese/Mediterranean cuisine is very popular. Start with the famous antipasto, then move on to veal with apple mustard or Maltese sausage stew, and for dessert try their renowned version of the classic Cassata Siciliana. Rub shoulders with the business elite at lunchtime, and Valletta's trendies in the evenings.

➕ 182 C4 ⊠ 53 Old Bakery Street ☎ 21 224656 ⊕ Mon–Fri lunch, Tue and Fri also dinner

SLIEMA

Café Georgio £

Among the many pavement cafés along Sliema's Strand, Georgio's is probably the best. You'll soon spot its polished chrome-and-glass fixtures groaning under the weight of a mouth-watering selection of cakes and artfully crafted snacks and sandwiches. Well-heeled chic locals sip their café latte behind designer shades and spill out on to the pavement at a busy junction overlooking Sliema Ferries. If you want peace, sit at the back.

➕ 185 E1 ⊠ Triq ix-Xatt (junction Strand and Bisazza Street) ☎ 21 342456 ⊕ Daily 9 am–midnight

La Cuccagna £

This small, family-run restaurant is tucked in a side street off Tower Road. You may be surprised to see just how busy it gets, particularly with locals. They come mostly for the crispy thin pizzas, a choice of 15 in all. Pasta and grilled meats also figure on the menu. The décor is traditional, with plenty of dark wood and glass.

➕ 185 E2 ⊠ 47 Amery Street ☎ 21 346703 ⊕ Tue–Sun dinner; Sun lunch (Sep–Jun)

Lanċa £-££

Lanċa (pronounced *lancher*) occupies an old beamed house painted
a modern dark red and decorated
with pots and plants. The tables
spill out on to a pretty terrace overlooking the busy junction of The
Strand and Bisazza Street, which
makes for some interesting people-
watching. By day the terrace is a
great place to relax with a drink:
mellow music wafts through and
the international-Maltese food is
very palatable. On summer nights
it gets very crowded, the volume is
cranked up and service slows down.

➕ 185 E1 ☒ Strand/Bisazza Street
☎ 21 338743 🕐 Daily early
morning to late at night

ST JULIAN'S AND AROUND

Barracuda £££

Set right on the corner of Balluta
Bay, and with great sea views, Barracuda has been the big fish in this
neck of the woods for many years.
It is set in a converted 18th-century

seaside villa, and if you want to
impress in the entertaining or
romantic stakes be sure to book a
table on the balcony. The mouth-
watering menu is mainstream and
modern Mediterranean, with plenty
of interest for gourmets but not at
all intimidating for the casual diner.
Try the carpaccio of swordfish,
fresh clam soup or baked rabbit.

➕ 184 C3 ☒ 194 Main Street,
St Julian's ☎ 21 331817 🕐 Daily
dinner (closed Sun in winter)

Blue Elephant £££

One of the restaurants in the Hilton
Malta (▲ 69), the Blue Elephant is
very picturesque and highly romantic. Bridges lead the way over lily
ponds into a bamboo Thai house
and low-level tables (though you
can eat at a Western table level if
you prefer). The food is superb:
try chicken satay, Thai fishcakes,
or specialities such as Bangkok fish
(deep fried fish with ginger and
garlic in a chilli sauce) or *yam nua*
(tenderloin steak with mint and

coriander dressed with lime and
chilli). Or why not experiment with
a special platter, which gives a taste
of most dishes?

➕ 184 B4 ☒ Hilton Malta,
Portomaso, St Julian's ☎ 21 383383
🕐 Daily dinner

Caffe Raffael ££

Housed in one of the colonnaded
boat-houses built for the 17th-
century Spinola Palace, Caffe Raffael
is the prettiest of the restaurants
that make up this corner of Spinola
Bay. On a quiet sunny lunchtime,
relaxing on the flower-decked
terrace by the water's edge with a
glass of wine and plate of fresh fish
is heavenly. The food is quality
Italian cuisine – pizza, pasta, grilled
meat and fish (try the octopus stew).
In the evening the atmosphere
changes to suit the trendy young
crowd and the pace quickens –
booking is essential.

➕ 184 B4 ☒ Spinola Bay, St Julian's
☎ 21 319988 🕐 Daily lunch
and dinner

Fra Martino £££

The flagship dining room of the
Corinthia San Gorg Hotel (▲ 69),
Fra Martino manages to combine
great food, luxurious surroundings
and relaxed informality. In Maltese
restaurant popularity surveys it
usually comes very near the top.
The à la carte theme is Mediterranean, featuring a signature dish
from 12 countries in the Med at any
one time. There's also a buffet of
local and Mediterranean specialities.

➕ 184 off B5 ☒ Corinthia San Gorg
Hotel, St George's Bay, St Julian's
☎ 21 374114 🕐 Daily lunch and
dinner

Frejgatina £££

A *frejgatina* is a skiff or light rowing
boat, so it's no surprise that fresh
fish is the house dish of this open-
air restaurant in the grounds of the
Corinthia San Gorg Hotel (▲ 69).
Grouper, tuna, swordfish, mussels,
langoustines, giant prawns and a
whole host of lesser-known Mediterranean fish are on offer. Let the chef

put together a fish and shellfish platter – beware, though, it's absolutely huge.

🚹 184 off B5 ⊠ **Corinthia San Gorg Hotel, St George's Bay, St Julian's** ☎ 21 374114 🕑 **Daily dinner; Sun lunch, May–Oct**

Gazebo £££

Eating under olive trees is a bit of a novelty in Malta, so you will have to forgive the fact that these are potted, and on the terrace of the Hilton Malta hotel (▶ 69). However, the atmosphere, which sits somewhere between Greece and Tuscany, along with the mouth-watering Maltese-Mediterranean *prix-fixe* menu, will soon put you in the right of frame of mind. Start with lightly grilled local seafood in lemon zest oil, three sauces and truffle salad, continue with braised Maltese rabbit on spiced cous-cous with aromatic rosemary pan juices, and finish off with the delicious summer berry and Grand Marnier Romanov. The service is first class.

sauce) or dip into *sopa t l'Armla* ("Widow's soup", made with eggs, ricotta cheese, goat's cheese and vegetables). Follow up with *tigieg tal brodu* (chicken stuffed with mincemeat) or *falda mimlija* (stuffed flank). The wine and service are both to be recommended.

🚹 184 B5 ⊠ **1 Church Street, Paceville** ☎ 21 339602 🕑 **Mon–Sat dinner**

Misfits ££

If you're up for a spot of clubbing (▶ 78–79) but don't really want a full-on rave, or perhaps you just want to catch the Paceville vibe with some good food, then this is the place for you. The music and décor are funky, with abstract images and sounds from the four corners of the world, though the food is more restrained and mostly French influenced.

🚹 184 B5 ⊠ **White House Hotel, Paceville Avenue, Paceville** ☎ 21 378016 🕑 **Daily lunch and dinner**

Henry J Bean's £–££

A branch of the famous American chain, Henry J Bean's is one of Malta's most popular meeting places. You'll either love it or hate it. The menu is barbecue-led, as well as offering good burgers (of course), ribs, nachos, *fajitas*, steaks and more. At weekends there are live bands, theme nights and DJs.

🚹 184 off B5 ⊠ **Corinthia San Gorg Hotel, St George's Bay** ☎ 21 379165 🕑 **Mon–Thu 6 pm–late, Fri–Sun 12:30 pm–late**

La Maltija ££–£££

This charming, restored old Maltese stone house seems quite out of place in brash fast-food Paceville (▶ 78), and, as if to emphasise the difference, the entire menu is traditional Malti fare. Try *bebbux bl-arjoli* (snails with special Maltese

🚹 184 B4 ⊠ **Hilton Malta Hotel, Portomaso, St Julian's** ☎ 21 383383 🕑 **Daily lunch and dinner**

Peppino's ££–£££

A St Julian's institution, Peppino's sits on three floors overlooking pretty Spinola Bay, with two floors dedicated to a restaurant and the other to a wine bar. If you are feeling flush, eat in the restaurant, where fresh lobster soup and *filletto d'agnello Peppino* (lamb fillets in port and cream sauce) are the stars on the menu. The wine bar has a cheaper bistro blackboard menu and is a lively hang-out for a smart 30-something crowd.

🚹 184 B4 ⊠ **31 St George's Road, St Julian's** ☎ 21 373200 🕑 **Restaurant: Mon–Sat 7–11 pm; wine bar: noon–3:30, 7–11 pm**

Piccolo Padre £

Tucked beneath its famous parent, the Barracuda (▶ 73), the popular Piccolo Padre is one of this area's rare inexpensive treats. It is little more than a buzzing pizzeria, but the rustic cellar setting, splashed with geraniums and corner tables enjoying windows overlooking the sea, is very atmospheric. In summer it spills out on to a much sought-after terrace, making advance booking essential. Do note that early evenings are often busy with families and lots of children running around.

➕ 184 C3 ⊠ 195 Triq il-Kbira, St Julian's ☎ 21 344875 ⏱ Daily dinner, Sun lunch in winter

Plough & Anchor ££

This ship-shape restaurant has just ten tables in a room the size of a large lifeboat, so if nothing else, you're assured of a cosy meal! There's nautical memorabilia everywhere, right down to the plates. The food is French-Mediterranean: embark with *penne Faruk* (pasta with prawns in a light curry sauce) then cruise along with fish of the day, fillet steak or pork in a variety of rich creamy sauces.

➕ 184 C3 ⊠ 1 Triq il-Kbira, St Julian's ☎ 21 334725 ⏱ Tue–Sun lunch and dinner (closed week after Easter Mon and last week Jul)

San Giuliano £££

Big brother to Caffe Raffael (➤73), San Giuliano also occupies a boat-house, immediately above its junior partner. You can't sit outside here, but floor-to-ceiling windows allow fine views over Spinola Bay. The food too, high-quality Italian, is a step up from the Raffael. Start with marinated swordfish, then perhaps indulge in a plate of spaghetti with sea urchin sauce, and follow that with fillet of beef in Marsala wine and cream.

➕ 184 B4 ⊠ Spinola Bay, St Julian's ☎ 21 332000 ⏱ Daily dinner

Terrazza ££

North Africa and the southern Mediterranean are the theme of this attractive restaurant overlooking Spinola Bay. Terrazza's dips are renowned, so order a selection, including the delicious Egyptian *foul* (don't worry, its pronounced *fool*). Then move on to Greek lamb, Spanish *paella* or try something adventurous from Lebanon or Morocco. Their salads are very good and vegetarians are well catered for. Make sure you book a table on the terrace to appreciate the full romance of Spinola Bay.

➕ 184 B4 ⊠ Spinola Bay ☎ 21 384939 ⏱ Daily lunch and dinner (closed Mon in winter)

Vinotheque £–££

If your idea of a good lunch is a simple healthy salad, a good selection of international and local cheeses and cold meats, all washed down with a glass or two of good quality wine, then this is the place for you. Vinotheque, based in the Corinthia Marina hotel (➤68), also offers other dishes and snacks, such as baguettes, and a variety of steaks and fish dishes. The dining area is cool and contemporary. This is a good opportunity to try some Maltese wines. The friendly staff will advise you if you need any help.

➕ 184 off B5 ⊠ Corinthia Marina Hotel, St George's Bay, St Julian's ☎ 21 374114 ⏱ Daily noon–midnight

XII £££

XII ("Twelve") is the latest in a line of highly regarded restaurants owned by the Barracuda (➤73) team. Its name speaks volumes – young, innovative, relaxed, stylish, confident, up-to-the minute and designer trendy. Rustic, century-old limestone walls, discrete soft lighting and music from all over the world set the tone for a feast of eclectic cuisine. Try duck Karl's style (marinated in lemongrass and ginger oil) or the adventurous fish of the day, perhaps stuffed with capers, sun-dried tomatoes, garlic, basil and marjoram. There are local dishes, too, such as *fusilli alla Maltese* (pasta with spicy Maltese sausage, spinach, chilli and tomatoes). For dessert, creme brulee is the chef's signature dish.

➕ 184 B4 ⊠ 16 St George's Road, St Julian's ☎ 21 324361 ⏱ Tue–Sun dinner (summer)

Where to...
Shop

VALLETTA

Valletta may provide the best shopping in the archipelago, but by mainland European standards it is a modest offering. Despite the recent encroachment of indoor shopping malls, independent specialist shops are the capital's forte; particularly good for shoes, books and silver and gold jewellery. Many of their shop fronts go back several decades; some are over 150 years old, and with names such as Jubilee and Coronation Stores clearly show their link with the Victorian age. There are over 60 of these shop fronts, now protected as part of the island's heritage – look out for them, particularly along Merchant's Street and St Paul Street. Specialist shop owners are usually patient,

knowledgeable and dedicated, and it's well worth visiting them.

Most shops are located on or just off **Republic Street** and around the main squares. For gold and silver filigree workshops continue towards the far end of Republic Street.

If malls are your thing, look in at the new **Embassy Shopping Complex** in St Lucia Street, with its four floors of brand-name youth-orientated shops.

Valletta Market

Valletta's famous **Sunday morning market** is held in St James Ditch, just outside the main City Gate. There's something for everyone here – towels featuring Australia's Bondi Beach, pirated CDs booming out from sound systems, pirate replica football strips, polythene bags of hatless Palitoy playfigures (the company has a factory on Malta), leather accessories, underwear, shirts, skirts, busts of Napoleon, "Old Masters", bits of motorbike, car parts, household

"antiques" and books by the barrow-load. Don't look too closely at the quality of what's on offer, just look at the "bargain" prices and enjoy the atmosphere!

Visitors, and many locals, pour in from all over the island and by 11 am it can be very crowded – arrive as early as possible for a bit of elbow room.

Alternatively wait a a day or so and you'll see much the same material on sale Monday to Friday mornings at the regular **Valletta market** just a few yards way in Merchant's Street. It doesn't have the same atmosphere, but it's much more comfortable. They start packing away around 12.30 pm.

VITTORIOSA

Until now free of shops and restaurants, major new developments by the Port Cottonera Consortium are set to transform sleepy Vittoriosa.

The first step was taken with the opening of the **Casino de**

Venezia on the waterfront in 2001. Shops and other leisure outlets are scheduled to open along the waterfront during the next couple of years. Contact the tourist information office (▶ 33) for further details.

SLIEMA AND ST JULIAN'S

Sliema's shops are concentrated on Bisazza Street and The Strand.

There are lots of British High Street regulars, such as **Marks & Spencer, The Body Shop** and **Virgin Megastore**, but prices are quite high so you may be better off shopping back in your own country.

The most notable shopping space in St Julian's is **Bay Street Mall**. It has four floors of around 40 shops, plus restaurants that stay open late and plenty of food and drink stalls. It's a lively venue (▶ 79) with frequent events such as book-signings, poetry and literary recitals, wine-tasting, make-up demonstrations, clothes shows and live bands promoting their latest CD.

Where to...
Be Entertained

For details on all performing arts, pick up a copy of the monthly *Calendar of Events* from any tourist office, or click on www.visitmalta.com/events for further information. *The Malta Times* and *The Malta Independent* also have details of many events.

Nightlife

Valletta by night can resemble something of a ghost town. There are no discos or clubs here and few bars open late. The exceptions are **Café Jubilee** (▶ 70), **Labyrinth**, 44 Strait Street and **Eddie's Café Regina**, on Republic Square. The latter only stays opens until 10 pm, though it has live music most summer evenings. It's a lovely place to sit outdoors on a balmy summer evening when it has a much calmer atmosphere than during the day.

Dance, Ballet, Opera, Concerts

If you get a chance to attend any of the performances at the **Manoel Theatre** (▶ 63) then seize it. It is one of Europe's oldest and most beautiful little theatres, and although it does not attract too many international names these days, Sir Yehudi Menuhin, Segovia, the Ballet Rambert and the Bolshoi Ballet are just some of the many names who have graced its boards.

Dance, ballet, opera and concerts are staged here, as well as the occa-sional play, though rarely in English. A free concert is held on Wednesday at 12:30 pm in the recital room. Note that the theatre season runs from October to May and it is closed June to September.

Malta's newest performing arts venue is the **St James Cavalier Centre for Creativity** (▶ 66), set in the beautifully restored space of the St James Cavalier fortification by the main City Gate. It stages art exhibitions, classical concerts and recitals, dance, foreign and art house cinema and plays, mostly of the fringe or experimental kind. To find out what's on, pick up a copy of the bi-monthly programme from the tourist office or email them at info@stjamescav.org

More experimental and fringe theatre is produced by the **YMCA Valletta**, whose annual festival takes place in July with productions at St James Cavalier and Labyrinth. The latter is a large, run-down, rambling old labyrinthine house, home to a café, an antiques shop

(with some truly ancient books) and a basement gallery where temporary art exhibitions are staged. A pianist plays jazz on Wednesday and Friday evenings.

Strait Street was the red-light district during the days when the British fleet were here in force. There are still some pretty seedy looking places along here and prostitutes still occasionally solicit.

Another small arts venue is the hall of **Le Meridien Phoenicia Hotel** (▶ 67), which stages its Monday Ovations series on the first Monday night of each month (October–June). The series includes piano, instrumental and vocal recitals, orchestras, ballet and choir presentations.

Films and Audio-Visual Shows

Fans of foreign films might like to know that French films (with English subtitles) are screened free on Wednesday (October–June) at 7 pm at the **Alliance Française**, St Thomas Street, Floriana.

The **Embassy Shopping Complex** (St Lucia Street; ▶ 76) has six screens that are devoted mainly to showing Hollywood blockbusters.

During the day these screens are the dedicated venue for two of Malta's historical audio-visual shows, **The Valletta Experience** and **Malta George Cross; The Wartime Experience** (▶ panel, opposite).

Casino

The island's newest and smartest casino, the **Casino de Venezia**, opened in 2001 on the waterfront on Vittoriosa. It attracts a wealthy clientele whose super yachts are often moored directly outside the front entrance.

SLIEMA

Sliema, somewhat surprisingly, has little in the way of organised nightlife. But that doesn't mean it is quiet. The main event here each summer evening is the traditional *passeggiata*, or promenade, along Tower Road (▶ 61). The Malta Tourism Authority also does its bit to entertain the strolling families with brass bands, singers and rock musicians.

There's also usually plenty of noise and music coming from the lidos, restaurants and bars along Tower Road and a lively café-bar scene on the Strand by Sliema Ferries.

If you're looking for a disco, try **Frenchies**, part of the Crowne Plaza Hotel (▶ 67), on the Tigne promontory.

Popular watering holes include **Black Gold** on the Strand, **Snoopy's** at 265 Tower Road (both open all day) and **Simon's Pub** at 115 Depiro Street (closed Monday and in the middle of the day), tucked away in the residential area (ask any local for directions).

Many young revellers simply make the short hop to **Paceville** (▶ opposite).

Multimedia Shows

Valletta has several audio-visual shows using slide and cinematic technology to portray island history. The best of these is **The Malta Experience** in the Mediterranean Conference Centre (▶ 65; shows Mon–Fri 11 am, noon, 1 pm, 2 pm, 3 pm and 4 pm, Sat and Sun 11 am, noon and 1 pm).

Also worth seeing is **Malta George Cross; The Wartime Experience**, highlighting the 1940–43 siege.

This alternates with **The Valletta Experience**, at the Embassy Mall in St Lucia Street (Mon–Sat 10 am, 11 am, and noon), which depicts how Valletta was built and later developed.

Sacred Island, next to Upper Barrakka Gardens, focuses on religious aspects of island history (shows Mon–Fri 10 am, 11.30 am, 1 pm, 2.30 pm and 4 pm, Sat 10 am, 11.30 am and 1 pm, Sun 10 am and 11.30 am).

Nightlife

There is no doubt where Malta's nightlife centre lies – just follow the noise to **Paceville** (pronounced *par-chay ville*) in St Julian's.

This small area, just behind Spinola Bay, is Malta's answer to San Antonio in Ibiza or Agia Napa in Cyprus. Come here any evening during summer, or weekends in winter, and you'll witness a heaving mass of Italian, Maltese and British late teens and 20-somethings, weaving unsteadily from bar to bar, en route to giant discos and nightclubs. A line of traffic – sonic boom boxes on wheels – parades along the St Julian's seafront and through the streets of Paceville. It is not a place for the faint-hearted.

To find out what's on, see the newspapers, listen to Island Sound radio (FM 101.8), or ask around and pick up flyers in the bars.

Unless you're aged between 16 and 25, most of the drinking, eating and karaoke venues in Paceville are to be avoided. They are really just loud, poor-quality pick-up and refuelling centres whose only real function is to act as a warm-up for the clubs. These are usually discernable from the bars by an admission charge and are considerably more sophisticated, with state-of-the art sound systems and lighting. They are generally licensed until 4 am. The music is also up-to-the-minute, presented by DJs specially flown in from all over Europe and beyond.

The biggest, most popular and longest-established club is **Axis** (Friday, Saturday from 10:30 pm to the early hours; www.axis.com.mt). Look out for one-off special club nights and parties in the summer months, usually advertised on posters, flyers and local radio.

Wilga Street is one of the best places for its selection of bars and clubs. Latino fans should salsa on down to **El Barrio Latino** at No 7. Their *fajitas* are good too.

The **Alley**, also on Wilga Street, serves mostly no-nonsense rock, with occasional performances by live bands.

Coconut Grove, as passé as the name suggests, is teen-orientated. **Lady Godiva** is one of Malta's few gay bars, with a very camp atmosphere.

Around the corner, on Paceville Avenue, **Misfits** is more sophisticated than most, attracting a more discerning class of club goer, who come for the classy décor and good music with dancing at weekends. Art-house films are shown on Tuesdays at 8:30 pm and there's a very good restaurant (▶74) with no cover charge.

Another good place to chill out is **BJ's Nightclub and Piano Bar** on Ball Street. It claims to be Malta's only real piano bar and hosts bands on some weekend nights.

Two other venues that regularly host live bands are the **Rock Café** on St George's Street (including some big names from the UK) and **Muddy Waters**, 56 Main Street (rock and blues).

On St George's Bay, **Fuego** is the island's most popular salsa bar, offering free classes Monday and Tuesday 8:30–10:30 pm. You'll find crowds here almost every day of the year.

There's no shortage of pubs in St Julian's. **Ryan's**, the inevitable Irish pub, right on Spinola Bay, is one of the best. Most bars are licensed until 1 am.

Younger teens are also catered for in Paceville with early evening alcohol-free discos hosted in some of the venues.

Bay Street Mall

If the throbbing central streets of Paceville are too young and loud for you, look in at the **Bay Street Mall** (▶76). Mostly dedicated to shopping, it stages a wide range of exhibitions and entertainment most nights, with activities as diverse as line-dancing, talent shows, sword-fighting and karate demonstrations. There's a concert every Saturday night, from choral to classical to soft rock, and Sunday night is devoted to local musicians (nearly always free). To find out what's on, pick up a copy of the Bay Street monthly calendar of events at the mall, or visit their website, www.baystreet.com.mt

A branch of the famous **Hard Rock Café** chain attracts live bands of the louder variety, and **Hacienda**, on Level 3 of the Mall, is a bar/club with thumping hip-hop and garage sounds.

Films and Audio-Visual Shows

Eden Century Cinemas (tel: 21 376401), in St Julian's, is the island's premier multiplex, with up to 16 different films being screened per day. It also includes a new 3-D IMAX theatre. For details visit their website, www.imax.com.mt

Other St Julian's Activities

Ten-pin bowling is very popular in Malta, and the multi-lane **Eden**

Super Bowl (St George's Bay, tel: 21 387398) is an excellent facility.

The **Eden Ice Arena** (St George's Bay, www.edenleisure.com/icearena) opened in 2001 and claims to be the only ice-rink in the Mediterranean, so while it's a sweltering 35°C outside, you can chill inside at a cool 15°C. For skaters with rhythm there's a weekend disco.

Also part of the Eden company is the state-of-the-art **Cynergi Health and Leisure Centre** (St George's Bay, tel: 21 376500 or 371900, www.edenleisure.com/cynergi), with squash courts and virtual mountain climbing.

Casinos

The **Dragonara Palace casino** is set in the former villa of a wealthy banker, at the tip of the promontory now occupied by the plush Westin Dragonara Resort (▶ 69). It offers the usual casino games and also has a restaurant. You must be 18 or over to enter the gaming room and you will also need your passport.

Annual Events In and Around Valletta

For further information log on to www.visitmalta.com/events

February/Early March

The **Carnival Week** celebrations (always the week immediately preceding Lent) may not be quite as exuberant in Malta as in other Latin countries, but this is still a lively time to visit. Decorated floats with dancing troupes and giant grotesque masked characters fill the streets. The festivities are island-wide, though the main events take place in Valletta.

April

1st week: Valletta: **History and Elegance** presents pageantry, folklore, music and dance.

Good Friday pageants are held at around 5 pm in 14 different towns and villages. Life-sized statues depicting scenes from the life and death of Christ are carried shoulder high in procession along the main street and locals dress as biblical characters to complete the scene.

On **Easter Sunday** there are early morning processions with statues of the Risen Christ. If you can, attend one of these in Vittoriosa, Senglea or Cospicua, where the bearers actually run through the streets with the statue aloft. Children along the route have their special Easter *figola* (almond cake) blessed by the effigy of the Risen Christ.

The **Valletta Festival** celebrates the Knights of St John, with parades, re-enactments, concerts and other events at various venues.

May

Festival ta'l-Ghana, the **National Folk Singing Festival**, is held at Argotti Gardens, Floriana, just outside Valletta main gate.

July

Mid- to late July: The **Malta Jazz Festival**, one of the highlights of Malta's social calendar, takes place at the quayside in Valletta. Top international musicians play.

Late July–August: The **Farsons International Food and Beer Festival**.

October

The **Maltese Theatre** season begins and continues until May, including top-class opera in Valletta.

November

The **Malta International Choir Festival** is held in Valletta and features choirs from all over Europe.

December

Second week: **Christmas Arts and Crafts Fair** in Valletta.

13 December: **Republic Day** celebrations include a special day of horse-racing at Marsa racecourse.

The South

Getting Your Bearings

Almost every other Mediterranean holiday island has developed its sunnier southern shores, but with high cliffs lining much of the south of Malta and with the temperature often soaring above the 30s Centigrade, this has been neither desirable nor necessary. In fact the island's only resort south of Sliema is Marsaskala, which compared to St Julian's and Buġibba hardly registers a blip on the tourism scale. However, a growing number of visitors are discovering its charms.

Lack of tourist development unfortunately does not mean that the south is unspoiled. Industry, quarries and two airports (Luqa and the disused military base of Ħal Far) fill much of the landscape. Heavy traffic goes all the way from Valletta to Żejtun, while the huge Delimara power station competes with Marsaxlokk Bay.

The good news is that Marsaxlokk is still a picturesque fishing village, the famous Blue Grotto and unsung Dingli

Previous page: Blue, yellow and green are the favoured colours for painting *luzzu*

Cliffs remain largely unsullied, and if you want to cool off there's no better place than Peter's Pool or Għar Lapsi, near the cool Blue Grotto.

The south is also home to the island's great temples – the Ħal Saflieni Hypogeum, Tarxien, Mnajdra and Ħaġar Qim. It's best to visit the Hypogeum first as it is a truly world-class archaeological site, with a visitor interpretation centre to match. Armed with information gleaned from a tour of the Hypogeum, you can march on confidently and explore the island's other famous antiquities.

Left: A porthole door cut through the stone at Ħaġar Qim

Above: Traditional fishing boats gather at Marsaxlokk

Right: Arches and sea caves stretch above azure waters at the Blue Grotto

This tour of temples and cobalt blue waters will show you the quintessential Malta.

The South in Two Days

Day One

Morning

Make an early start from Valletta and follow the signs to Paola and the ❶ **Hal Saflieni Hypogeum** (➤ 86–88). Note: all visits must be booked in advance. It's a five-minute walk from the Hypogeum to the ❷ **Tarxien Temples** (➤ 89–90). Once you have had a look round both of these, return to your car and head towards ❺ **Marsaskala** (➤ 94), via Żejtun. Keep your eyes open as signposting is poor.

Lunch

Stop in Marsaskala and have lunch at Grabiel (➤ 97). Pick up a bottle of water and perhaps a snack for later.

Afternoon

Follow the road back towards Żejtun; turn left and pick up the road towards Delimara Point. Look to your left to see ❻ **Peter's Pool** (right, ➤ 94); stop here to swim and sunbathe. Continue back along the Delimara road and turn left to ❸ **Marsaxlokk** (below, ➤ 91–92).

Evening

Round off the day with a fish supper on the quayside at Marsaxlokk.

Day Two

Morning

It's vital that the sun is shining and that you make an early start so you not only beat the crowds but also see the water of the Blue Grotto at its best. From Marsaxlokk, take the road towards Żebbug, then to Siġġiewi and Żurrieq. A dusty road leads to Wied-iz Żurrieq, where boats leave for the **4 Blue Grotto** (left, ► 93). After your 25-minute boat journey, drive back up the hill and turn left to the temples of **7 Mnajdra and Ħaġar Qim** (► 94–95). They are within a short walk of each other, and both are served by the same car-park, where there is a bar and restaurant.

Lunch

Visit Ħaġar Qim (above) first, have lunch, then walk down to Mnajdra.

Afternoon

Go back towards Siġġiewi and take the road left past the Inquisitor's Palace to **8 Dingli Cliffs and Buskett Gardens** (► 95).

Evening

Enjoy the views from Dingli Cliffs (right) and either stay on the clifftop road for dinner at Bobbyland restaurant (► 97; note it's closed Monday), or if you want to head back towards "civilisation" take the road to Rabat and Mdina, where there are plenty of choices for a meal (► 111–113).

Ħal Saflieni Hypogeum

The Ħal Saflieni Hypogeum, or "underground chamber", is by far the finest of Malta's temples – a spectacular and complex arrangement of passageways, chambers, halls and niches spread over three levels. Its subterranean location has not only protected and preserved it over some 5,000 years, but also gives it real atmosphere.

The Ħal Saflieni Hypogeum, named after the suburb of Paola in which it is located, descends to a depth of 12m. In places tall people have to bend almost double. It is beautifully lit by soft, glowing lights that replicate the conditions in which it would have been viewed by the fortunate few allowed to come here.

The introductory video and the guided tour give the best possible idea of what went on here – as far as anything is certain about this mysterious age.

The temple lay undisturbed until builders working above accidentally broke through its roof in 1902. Realising that building would be stopped if the authorities should learn about it, they kept their discovery a secret and used it to dispose of rubble. Word did not get out about its existence until three years later.

The temple was cut from solid rock some 4,000–5,000 years ago, using tools made from flint, bone and hard rock. It was built using the same architectural features of the temples above ground.

Because it is underground, it is worth noting that the Hypogeum's roof is intact, which helps visitors to imagine what the now roofless above-ground temples might once have looked like.

It was not only used for

Cool It

The video presentation and display boards you see before entering the temple have a vital secondary function. In the time it takes to see these, the air-conditioning system assures that bodies cool down to the ambient temperature and humidity before entering the temple proper, thus preserving the state of the fragile stone.

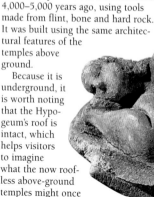

Go underground and learn some of the tricks of the trade used by Malta's temple builders

The *Sleeping Lady* – just one of the vault's many secrets

worship, but also as a place of burial, as attested to by the remains of around 7,000 people found on the highest (oldest) level. This level dates to around 3000 BC. Red ochre was found daubed on their bones, perhaps in a symbolic attempt to restore life. Red represented the colour of blood, sacrifice and death.

On the middle level there are intricately carved pillars with spirals and hexagons, probably created around 2500 BC. In the main altar chamber, known as the **Holy of Holies**, parts of the ceiling and walls are covered in red ochre. It was in the middle chambers that the ***Sleeping Lady*** statuette, now in the National Museum of Archaeology in Valletta (➤ 62), was discovered.

The guide will demonstrate the echoing acoustic properties of the **Oracle Chamber**, which impressively, and almost

Better Safe Than Sorry

For much of the 1990s Malta's most famous temple was closed to the public. Indeed, it was feared at one time that visitors might never be re-admitted. The problem was that the very breath, body heat and humidity of the large numbers of visitors were inadvertently destroying this fragile complex. But protective work and new visiting arrangements were completed in 2000, and the Hypogeum was re-opened.

Today visitor numbers are restricted to 100 per day, and their effects on the atmosphere are being strictly monitored. If it turns out that the Hypogeum is suffering then numbers will be reduced.

supernaturally, deepen and magnify the voice. This device was probably used by the chief priest for his conversations with the gods, a sure way to impress his followers and underscore his own powers.

The third (lowest) level is enigmatically empty. It is thought that this had only just been completed when the temple age came to an end. Why that happened, nobody knows.

Red-ochre spirals on the ceiling of the Hypogeum's inner sanctum symbolised a belief in life continuity

TAKING A BREAK

There are no refreshments available at the temple nor restaurants worth recommending near by. However, turn left out of the entrance, then left again, and almost opposite the church is a basic **café**.

✛ 181 E2 ✉ Cemetery Street, Paola ☎ 21 825579 🕐 Daily 9–4 (admission by guided timed tour only; tour time will be specified when you book) 💷 Moderate

---

HAL SAFLIENI HYPOGEUM: INSIDE INFO

Top tips To prepare for your visit here, go to the **National Museum of Archaeology** in Valletta (► 62) where there are helpful models of the site and explanatory notes.

• There may not be any **written information** at the Hypogeum itself so it makes sense to read up beforehand.

2 Tarxien Temples

The above-ground Tarxien Temples (pronounced *tar-sheen*) is the largest temple complex from the "Copper Age" on Malta. It was the last of its kind to be built (*c* 3000–2500 BC) and is the most elaborately decorated. It remained untouched for thousands of years until eminent Maltese archaeologist Sir Themistocles Zammit (who also led the excavations at the Hal Saflieni Hypogeum) started his excavations in 1915.

An altar stone with spiral patterns, typical of the Tarxien Temples

The Tarxien Temples complex is only a few hundred metres from the Hal Saflieni Hypogeum. There are three temples and a fourth in ruins, each a rich repository of prehistoric art.

The **South Temple** is the first temple after the entrance, with a central paved square in the midst of which was probably a ritual fire. Visitors are greeted by a statue of the lower half of a **"Fat Lady"** (▶ panel below). The original statue, along with other important finds from the site (such as altars and friezes), are in the National Museum of Archaeology in Valletta (▶ 62).

Next to the statue is a characteristic "square-window" altar niche with spiral carvings. A flint-bladed sacrificial knife was found here, and elsewhere in the temple you can see holes in the ground which were used to drain away the blood of sacrificial animals. In the apse to the left are friezes of the animals whose burned bones were found here. Many of the decorations in the temple have worn away over time and those you see here are mostly replicas of originals that are now in Valletta's National Museum of Archaeology.

The Giant Goddess

In his book *Malta: An Archaeological Guide*, Dr Trump describes the Giant Goddess statue (right), which is thought to have represented a fertility goddess: "When complete she stood about 2.75m high, but time, weather and above all the local farmers have reduced her to waist height...She wears a very full pleated skirt. It would be ungentlemanly to quote her hip measurements, and her calves are in proportion. She is supported, however, on small, elegant, but seriously overworked feet."

The **Central Temple** is later (*c* 2400 BC) and larger than the South Temple, though in the same classic "butterfly" pattern – the "wings" are set at an equal distance either side of a narrow entrance. It has three chambers, or apses. In the first one, to the left, is a giant decorated bowl, carved from a single piece of solid rock. Its use can only be guessed at – "for the stewing of missionaries, it has been suggested", writes Dr Trump, former curator of the National Museum of Archaeology, with tongue firmly in cheek. He suggests it was for burning aromatic herbs. There are more carvings, too, of two bulls and a sow suckling 13 piglets, representative of virility and fertility.

The third and oldest section, the **East Temple**, is in poor condition. It has the remains of an oracle chamber where the acoustics are exceptional – you can speak in a low voice through the niche and be heard through the temple and beyond. This was perhaps where oracles were spoken.

TAKING A BREAK

There are no refreshments available at the temples, nor restaurants worth recommending near by. It's a five-minute walk into **Paola** where you will find cafés and basic eating places.

➕ 181 E2 ✉ Neolithic Temples Street, Tarxien ☎ 21 695578 🕐 Mon–Fri 7:45–2, mid-Jun–Sep; Mon–Sat 8:15–5, Sun 8:15–4:15, rest of year 💶 Inexpensive

Above: In the temple complex

Far right: The watchful Eye of Osiris looks out from the prow of a *luzzu* fishing boat

Right: Marsaxlokk harbour – for the perfect catch

TARXIEN TEMPLES: INSIDE INFO

Top tips You have to know what you are looking at, and (for example, with the missing roof) what you are *not* looking at to make sense of the Tarxien Temples. The best way to find this out is to visit the **Hal Saflieni Hypogeum** (➤ 86–88) immediately beforehand (it's a five-minute walk away). Then simply apply what you have seen there to this site.

• There is also an essential section on the Tarxien Temples in the **National Museum of Archaeology** in Valletta (➤ 62), with an artist's impression of what they once looked like.

• Don't count on being able to get any **information** at the Tarxien Temples complex itself.

3 Marsaxlokk Bay

Marsaxlokk Bay, one of the largest and best-protected inlets on Malta, is full of history, from prehistoric caves to 20th-century industry. In 1565 the Ottoman Turks disembarked here to begin the Great Siege; in 1798 Napoleon did likewise for his more successful sortie upon the island that ended the Knights' rule; and in 1989 presidents Bush and Gorbachev met here to pronounce the official end to the Cold War.

Today Marsaxlokk Bay is most famous for its fishing village, **Marsaxlokk** (pronounced *marsa-shlock*), the largest of its type on the island. It gets its name from the Arabic *marsa*, meaning "harbour" and *xlokk*, the local name for the hot dry sirocco wind which blows in from the Sahara. Marsaxlokk draws visitors from all over Malta, who come to sample the fish, buy lace at the daily market and take pictures of the colourful boats. The harbourside market is biggest on Sunday, but in truth there is little to see here, and lace aside, nothing for the serious shopper.

    Luzzus – colourful Maltese boats which provide the transport for the island's largest fishing fleet – are the big attraction here (➤ 92). Make time to eat here, too; fierce competition means that this is one of the least expensive places for fish, and there are plenty of options.
    Further west around the headland is the **cave of Għar Dalam** or "Cave of Darkness".

MARSAXLOKK BAY: INSIDE INFO

Top tip Peter's Pool (➤ 94) is the best known of three bathing spots on the Delimara peninsula. The others are **Long Bay** to the south of Peter's Pool and **Island Bay** to the north. Island Bay (signposted Xrobb L-Ghagin) is the nicer of the two and features a naturally eroded arch.

One to miss The **Bronze Age Village** at Borġ-in-Nadur is hard to find and turns out to be little more than ankle-high remains of a fortified settlement.

The cave stretches for over 200m into the limestone, although only 80m is illuminated and open to the public. Explanations along the way tell you what you're looking at. Neolithic man lived here around 5000 BC, but it is the animal remains that are the most remarkable. Among the bones of some 7,000 animals stranded here are dwarf elephant and dwarf hippotami, which died out 180,000 years ago, as well as red deer, bears, wolves and giant swans. All the animal remains seem to be European, suggesting that Malta may once have been joined to mainland Europe, but not to Africa. A museum at the entrance displays some of the animal skeletons found here and a reconstruction of a dwarf elephant.

Further around the coast signposts point alluringly to **Pretty Bay** and the promise of a sandy beach. The beach is quite large by Maltese standards, but Pretty Bay is now something of a misnomer since it has been spoiled by the **Malta Freeport**, a profitable but ugly tax-free container port.

Luzzus

A *luzzu* is a traditional Maltese fishing boat, painted in dazzling hues of red, blue, green and yellow. The design of its characteristic high prow dates back to Phoenician days,. though the boats are still very much in use today. The eye, carved out and painted on either side of the prow, is the eye of Osiris, a good luck charm intended to ward off the devil.

TAKING A BREAK

Marsaxlokk has many **fish restaurants** on the quayside. Best are **Ir-Rizzu** (open daily) and **Pisces** (closed Mon), but neither has tables outside. Some places trade on price at the expense of quality. Have a look at what other diners are eating before you sit down.

➕ 181 E1
Għar Dalam Cave and Museum
➕ 181 E1 ✉ 1km north of Birżebbuġa ⏲ Mon–Fri 7:45–2, mid-Jun–Sep; Mon–Sat 8:15–5, Sun 8:15–4:15, rest of year
💷 Inexpensive

4 Blue Grotto

A trip to the Blue Grotto is on most itineraries, and with good reason. The sea caves, with their cobalt blue waters, are very appealing. The caves are iridescent with green, purple and orange according to the various minerals present. If you want to see the colours at their sparkling best (and to avoid the crowds), come early when the water is calmest.

Above and inset: Speeding towards the caves and aquamarine waters

Left: Picking over the bones of the past at Għar Dalam

To really see the caves at their best make the trip on a bright morning, and preferably before 11 am so the sun is still low enough to illuminate them. Boats depart from the pretty fishing village of **Wied iz-Żurrieq**. The maximum number in a boat is supposed to be eight, but the fishermen try and cram in as many people as possible. On the 25-minute tour you'll see cliffs eroded into strange shapes by the sea and a series of six caves, including the Blue Grotto. The deep blue that gives the cave its name is created from the sky reflected off the white sand bottom.

If it's a warm summer day you'll probably be longing to get into the water yourself. The best place near by is **Għar Lapsi**, 6km west of Ħaġar Qim and Mnajdra, a natural lido with handrails in the rocks to allow easy access to the water. The unprepossessing Lapsi Seaview restaurant makes a decent job of serving rabbit, swordfish and other local favourites.

TAKING A BREAK

It's best to go to **Għar Lapsi**, though it can get crowded.

🔢 181 D1   ✉ Wied iz-Żurrieq   ☎ 21 829925   🕐 9–4 (weather permitting)   💷 Expensive

At Your Leisure

5 Marsaskala

The south's only resort, Marsaskala is in a picturesque location, clustered around a horseshoe bay with *luzzus* and other craft at anchor and a large Venetian-style campanile dominating the far end of the bay. It is well known to Maltese families, and in recent years increasing numbers of foreign visitors have discovered it. There's just one large hotel and a handful of good restaurants.

The promenade is lined with bars, cafés, restaurants and fast-food outlets. On a summer night it comes alive with locals and Maltese holiday-makers taking part in the *passegiata*.

Around the bay, next to the Jerma Palace Hotel, is **St Thomas Tower**, a sturdy, well-preserved four-square fort dating from the early 17th century. It is currently being renovated as an historic attraction.

Continue past the hotel, round to the left and you will come to St Thomas Bay, a rather scruffy locals' beach with a tiny stretch of sand. If the water is calm, it's better to swim off the rocks on the far side of the bay. Better still, carry on to Peter's Pool (► below).

🕂 181 F2

6 Peter's Pool

This beautiful, calm, natural pool, halfway along the Delimara penin-sula, is formed by a small deep inlet

Four Good Places for a Picnic
- Buskett Gardens (► 95)
- Peter's Pool (► below)
- The cliffs beside Mnajdra looking out to Filfla (► 27)
- Għar Lapsi (► 93)

and is by far the nicest place to take the waters in the south of the island. Large, flat rocks provide comfortable sunbathing slabs, and there is easy access to the water for everyone, or you can leap off the higher ledges.

It is best to avoid Peter's Pool on summer weekends as it can get really crowded and noisy and there is little space for car parking. Beware too that thieves are sometime at large here. Leave nothing of value inside your car, even in the boot.

🕂 181 F1

7 Ħaġar Qim and Mnajdra

Ħaġar Qim (pronounced *ha-jah eem*) means "standing stones", an appro-priate description of the most imp-ressive feature of this weather-beaten megalithic temple. One stone alone measures a giant 7m by 3m. Too close for its own good to wind and wave, its battered appearance is due to the fact that it was built from soft globigerina limestone. However, its powerful façade, with giant sturdy square lintels and capstones, is relatively well preserved and visitors are free to wander inside. Two important finds from here, now in the National Museum of

Archaeology in Valletta (➤ 62) are the *Venus of Malta* and a decorated free-standing altarpiece.

A five-minute walk down the cliffs towards the sea is **Mnajdra** (pronounced *im-na-ee-dra*), the most dramatically sited of Malta's temples, with just the sea and grassy cliffs as its backdrop (➤ 6–8).

It was constructed of coralline limestone, a harder stone than that used for Ħaġar Qim, so has survived the millennia in much better shape. It is fenced off to protect it against vandalism.

The small island lying 5km out to sea is **Filfla** (➤ 27).

➕ 180 C1 ✉ 1.5km southwest of Qrendi 🕐 Mon–Fri 7:45–2, mid-Jun–Sep; Mon–Sat 8:15–5, Sun 8:15–4:15, rest of year 💰 Moderate (combined entrance to Ħaġar Qim and Mnajdra)

🎱 Dingli Cliffs and Buskett Gardens

The most spectacular section of Malta's coastline, Dingli Cliffs drop steeply into the Mediterranean from a height of over 250m. The village of Dingli is the highest in Malta (253m above sea level) and the cliffs offer breathtaking views over the sea. This is one of Malta's favourite beauty spots, particularly among local people. On a summer evening you'll see couples, dog walkers and families out strolling.

Just inland from the cliffs is **Buskett Gardens**, a charming area created in the 17th century with a diverse selection of trees including pine, oak and cypress as well as orange and olive groves. The gardens are particularly delightful in spring, and in the summer provide welcome shade from the heat. The name comes from the word *boschetto*, which means "little wood". In June, Buskett Gardens is the venue for the Mnarja Festival (➤ 98).

Also close by are the enigmatic "cart ruts" at Clapham Junction (➤ 28).

➕ 180 B2/C2

Left: An altar at Ħaġar Qim, with a replica of a decorated altarpiece discovered here

Below: The dramatic clifftop setting of Mnajdra

Where to... Stay

Prices
Expect to pay per double room per night
£ under LM15   ££ LM15-30   £££ LM31-50   ££££ over LM50

MARSASKALA

Alison's £

If you want to do Malta on the cheap and get to know the locals at the same time, then this friendly, first-class guest-house may be the answer. It's just off the main promenade in Marsaskala, just a stone's throw from the centre of town and a possibility of watching the *passeggiata*. All rooms have their own shower and toilet and there is a bar and small family pool. The helpful family owners will be happy to advise you on all matters.

🞧 181 F2   ✉ Vajrita Street
☎ 21 639814; fax: 21 687593;
www.mol.net.mt/alisons

Charian Hotel £

This friendly, family-owned hotel has a smart and fresh feel. All 25 rooms are doubles and have en-suite shower and toilet. The hotel is located on a quieter part of the main promenade, two minutes' walk from the centre of town. To minimise being disturbed from any noise, ask for a room on the top floor, with a sea view. Many visitors pay just a little more for half board to enjoy the good home-cooking. The rooftop garden offers a heated Jacuzzi and breathtaking views over Marsaskala and the bay.

🞧 181 F2   ✉ Salini Road
☎ 21 636392; fax: 21 636391;
www.mol.net.mt/charian

Corinthia Jerma Palace ££££

The south's only major hotel, the luxury Jerma is a modern five-storey complex that occupies the southern tip of Marsaskala Bay. Rooms are comfortable and well equipped and there is a good coffee-shop and bar. Dining options are mostly restricted to the "international" category. The sunbathing area is attractive, and the swimming pool, almost at the water's edge, is designed to blend seamlessly into the sea's horizon. Several watersports – water-skiing, jetskiing, inflatables, paragliding – are available and there's also an indoor swimming pool, tennis court, gym and sauna. It's an easy 10- to 15-minute walk to the centre of Marsaskala.

🞧 181 F2   ✉ Dawret it-Torri
☎ 21 633222;
www.corinthiahotels.com

Emma Apartment £-££

This modern seafront apartment is in a quiet elevated position at the side of Marsaskala Bay. From the balcony there are good sea views. There's a spacious living area, an open-plan kitchen with a washing machine, three double bedrooms, a bathroom and utility room. There is also a one-bedroom apartment available.

🞧 181 F2   ✉ Sir Thomas Ashby Street   ☎ 21 826108;
www.mol.net.mt/emma

Etvan Hotel and Apartments £

High on the hill directly overlooking Marsaskala Bay, this small, well-equipped accommodation is in an excellent location, just five minutes' walk from the centre of town. In addition to 55 attractive and comfortable hotel rooms there are 14 apartments, which offer a very inexpensive family holiday. The swimming pool faces towards the bay. If you don't need all the international trimmings this is excellent value. Ask for a room with a sea view.

🞧 181 F2   ✉ Bahhara Street
☎ 21 632323; www.etvan.com

Where to...
Eat and Drink

Prices

Prices indicate what you should pay per person for a three-course meal, excluding drinks and service charge.

£ under LM8   **££** LM8–12   **£££** over LM12

MARSASKALA

Café Ximo £

This tiny café-restaurant spills out on to the pavement across the road from the Marsaskala promenade. If there isn't a seat, the friendly and helpful staff will endeavour to bring one out to you. The short menu is mostly Maltese favourites with fresh fish specialities. Make room for a dessert by Fontanella, the famous tea-rooms in Mdina (▶ 112).

➕ 181 F2 ✉ Marina Promenade
☎ 21 633299 ⏰ 10 am–midnight/
1 am Jul, Sep–Oct; 6 pm–midnight/
1 am, Aug; 10 am–4/5 pm, Nov–Jun

Fishermen's Rest £

If your idea of a good fish supper is to rub shoulders with locals and fishermen in basic surroundings, then this large shack, opposite the beach, is for you. Try the catch of the day or perhaps a seafood platter. Service here can be slow so it's best not to be in a hurry.

➕ 181 F2 ✉ St Thomas Bay
☎ 21 632049 ⏰ Wed–Sat dinner,
Sun lunch (closed most of Jan)

Grabiel £££

Don't worry about its unprepossessing location and exterior, inside Grabiel is light and elegant, and you will soon realise why it is regarded as the best fish restaurant in the south, and one of the finest in the archipelago. The menu is based almost completely on fish and seafood, all perfectly cooked and beautifully presented. The staff are friendly and will advise on any types of fish you may be unsure of.

➕ 181 F2 ✉ Mifsud Bonnici Street
☎ 21 616336 ⏰ Mon–Sat lunch and
dinner (closed last two weeks Aug)

Sottovoce £££

The romantic, pastel-washed Sottovoce is Marsaskala's prettiest restaurant and offers a range of pasta dishes and steaks, though fish is the speciality: try swordfish with pinenuts and sultanas, or your own choice of fish, cooked al cartoccio (in paper) or in wine and garlic.

➕ 181 F2 ✉ 29 Marina Promenade
☎ 21 632669 ⏰ Tue–Sun dinner

Tal Familja ££–£££

If you want to sample some of the most interesting dishes in the south of Malta, then this is the place to come. Start with Gozo fried cheese, and follow with filet ta familja (fillet steak stuffed with scallops, spinach and oysters) or chicken San Paolo (stuffed with crabmeat, spinach and salmon). Book a seat on its pretty front terrace and don't be in a hurry as service can be very slow.

➕ 181 F2 ✉ Triq il-Gardiel ☎ 21
632161 ⏰ Tue–Sun lunch and dinner

DINGLI CLIFFS

Bobbyland £–££

Famous for its views and food, Bobbyland is a south Malta institution. It is best avoided at weekends when it is gets really busy. The house speciality is fenek (rabbit). Book a table outside to enjoy the wonderful views over Dingli Cliffs.

➕ 180 B2 ✉ Triq l-Irdum ☎ 21
452895 ⏰ Tue–Sun lunch and dinner
(closed Christmas and most of Jan)

Where to... Shop

The south of Malta is not exactly stacked with shopping opportunities.

The best option is to check out the local markets. **Marsaxlokk Open-Air Market** every Sunday attracts people from all over the island. Basically a fish market, the variety of shapes and colours of the Mediterranean fish here can be surprising.

There is also a daily market in Marsaxlokk which sells a little bit of everything, but nothing of any great quality.

Another option is **Ta' Qali Crafts Village** (▶ 114), which is only 17km from Marsaskala. You'll find most souvenir goods here, at reasonable prices: silver and gold filigree, pottery, wood, wool and metal. Most shops are open Mon–Fri 8–6 and Sat 8–12:30.

Where to... Be Entertained

NIGHTLIFE

On a warm summer night Marsaskala is really the place to be, with everyone doing the *passegiata* around the bay.

If you want something more dynamic, try **Cine Palais** or the roof garden of the Speakeasy Bar, and at weekends, **Generation X** nightclub (both on Triq il-Gardie) – just follow the lasers. Most people are happy to have a meal, a couple of drinks and watch the world go by. This is a good place to do it.

WATERSPORTS

The south is very good for diving, with four popular sites. On Marsaskala Bay, **Zonqor Point** features a remarkably well-preserved World War II Blenheim bomber at a depth of 42m. At **Delimara Point** there are vertical cliffs and caverns with varied colourful flora and fauna. **Wied iż-Żurrieq** is a submerged valley with a labyrinth of gloriously coloured caves. **Għar Lapsi** is shallow, but varied. The dive school at the Corinthia Jerma Palace Hotel (▶ 96) can arrange trips.

HELICOPTER TOURS

There's no better way of seeing Malta than from a helicopter. Particularly impressive are Valletta, the "Three Cities" and their harbours, the huge parish churches standing out from their tiny villages, the dramatic cliffs of the south and the aquamarine waters of Comino's Blue Lagoon. You also get a very good view of the layouts of the ancient temple complexes.

Flights depart from Luqa Airport. You can try 20 minutes (just Malta) or 40 minutes (the whole archipelago). Contact **Malta Air Charters** for flight details (tel: 22 999138, www.airmalta.com; expensive).

MNARJA

At the end of June, one of the island's biggest festivals, **Mnarja** (pronounced *eem-nar-ya*), is held at Buskett Gardens (▶ 95). The term Mnarja is derived from *luminarja* ("illuminations"), from a time when bonfires illuminated the proceedings. The feast celebrates the summer harvest and festivities begin on 28 June with folk-singing and other open-air musical activities. Maltese dishes, particularly *fenek* (rabbit), are served. On 29 June there are agricultural shows, marching bands, and in the afternoon bareback horse-, donkey- and mule-racing takes place in Rabat.

Central Malta

Getting Your Bearings

As urban sprawl blurs the lines between Valletta, Birkikara and Attard, and as Mosta and Naxxar blend into almost one single conurbation, so also blurs the character of Malta's central towns and villages. The famous "Three Villages" – Attard, Balzan and Lija – can no longer even be recognised as such and only the local postman knows where one ends and the others begin. Standing out above this confusion is Mdina, the ancient capital of Malta and still a symbol of the island.

Like Valletta there is a tangible sense of history in Mdina, though unlike Valletta this is a city built by the Maltese – not the multi-national Knights. Its boundaries and character remain distinct and discrete, in no small measure thanks to the sturdy city walls which insulate it from the noise and pollution that engulfs much of the island.

This isolation has its plus and minus points. Mdina's fans talk of a civic self-respect not found elsewhere in Malta, its critics liken it to a theme-park village preserved in its own historical aspic. Both have a point. For a dose of everyday life you have to step outside the walls into workaday Rabat and don't leave without stepping underground too. Rabat's catacombs are just as fascinating as Mdina's passageways.

The bastion terrace of Mdina is the best place for surveying the island (unless you are in a helicopter) and gives a particularly good panorama of the centre of Malta. Below, to the left (northeast), is the great dome of Mosta, straight ahead (east) are the floodlights of the Ta' Qali national sports stadium, and beyond the "Three Villages" and Valletta.

Previous page: St Paul's Cathedral dome dominating Mdina and the countryside around

Mtarfa

Mdina ➊

Rabat ➋

★ Don't Miss

At Your Leisure

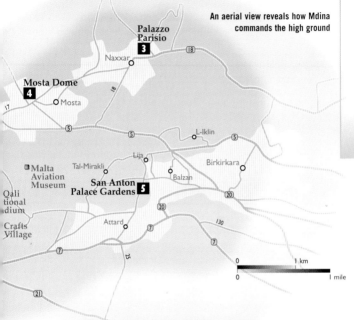

An aerial view reveals how Mdina commands the high ground

Palazzo
Parisio
3

Naxxar

Mosta Dome
4

Mosta

L-Iklin

Lija

Tal-Mirakli

Birkirkara

Balzan

Malta
Aviation
Museum

San Anton
Palace Gardens **5**

Qali
tional
dium

Crafts
Village

Attard

0   1 km

0   1 mile

Left: Carved
details in the
soft sandstone
of a mansion
in Mdina

Right: The
stunning dome
of St Paul's
Cathedral in
Mdina

Heritage and architecture are the main themes, from the inky darkness of Rabat's catacombs via Mdina's honey-coloured stones to Mosta's mighty dome and Naxxar's stately home.

Central Malta in Two Days

Day One

Morning/Lunch
Make an early start and park outside the main gate of **1 Mdina** (left, ► 104–106). Perhaps take the suggested walking tour (► 160–162). Have lunch with a view at Ciappetti (► 111).

Afternoon
Step outside Mdina into **2 Rabat** (► 107–109). Visit the Roman Villa Museum, St Paul's Cave and, if you have time, both the catacombs (bottom). If you only have time for one, choose St Agatha's, right. It may sound like an ambitious itinerary, but all are within a short walk of each other and none demand more than 20–30 minutes.

Evening
Walk back into Mdina for a drink or a meal at the Xara Palace Hotel, inside the main gate. There's a choice of two excellent restaurants (► 112).

Day Two

Morning/Lunch

Drive from Mdina to Naxxar and park as close as possible to its grand parish church. Opposite is the **3 Palazzo Parisio** (➤ 110). A tour will take around 30 minutes. Have a coffee in the palazzo's own café area or with the locals, opposite. Retrace your route to **4 Mosta** (➤ 110) where once again the imposing church, and in particular its dome, is the landmark. After visiting the church (below) take the main road back towards Msida and Valletta. Turn off at Balzan and make your way to **5 San Anton Palace Gardens** at Attard (bottom, ➤ 110). You can either picnic at the San Anton Palace Gardens or treat yourself to a leisurely lunch at the Pool Garden restaurant (➤ 113) in the Corinthia Palace Hotel opposite the gardens.

Afternoon

After a leisurely stroll in the Palace Gardens (a maximum of around 30 minutes) return to your car and head off in the direction of Mdina. Take the turn off to **Ta' Qali** (➤ 114). You can watch the glassblowers, and flying enthusiasts might enjoy the **Malta Aviation Museum** (➤ 110).

Evening

Continue the short distance to Mdina and Rabat and end the day with a meal at family-friendly Il-Veduta (➤ 112) in Rabat, or Bacchus (➤ 111) or The Medina (➤ 112) in Mdina.

⬤ Mdina

Perched high on a hill and commanding a huge sweep of the Maltese landscape, Mdina is one of Europe's finest medieval walled cities. The dynamic cathedral dome and ancient walls rise above the plains of Central Malta. It is the jewel in Malta's crown, with a palpable sense of history and atmosphere, and is a must for any visitor.

Rise and Fall

Mdina (pronounced *im-deena*) means "walled city". It was named by the Arabs, who occupied Malta from 870 to 1090. The city flourished as the seat of Malta's most noble families and many beautiful palaces were built. Most of these are on

or just off **Triq Villegaignon** (Villegaignon Street).

The beginning of Mdina's decline came with the Knights of St John. After the Great Siege of 1565 they built up its impregnable bastion walls to their present appearance, but they also built Valletta, which they made their capital. They rechristened Mdina Città Vecchia (Old City) to distinguish it from their new capital, to which many nobles now flocked. In 1693 a great earthquake reduced much of Mdina to rubble, including the old cathedral. But less than ten years after its destruction a new baroque church was built – the city's crowning joy.

For many years Mdina has been depopulating and has now become known as **"The Silent City"**. Today it has just 400

Above: The approach road to "The Silent City"

Inset: Great views from the Bastion Walls

permanent residents. By day visitors break the silence, though with its streets (virtually) free of traffic, Mdina is still the quietest and most relaxing place for an urban stroll.

Palazzo Falzon

A visit to the Palazzo Falzon, built in the early 16th century and now a museum, is an opportunity to see inside one of the aristocratic palaces. It is a fine example of its age with a beautiful inner courtyard and period antiques and paintings.

St Paul's Cathedral

The exuberant **baroque interior** of St Paul's Cathedral is one of the finest in Malta. It was designed by the Maltese architect, Lorenzo Gafà, and built between 1697 and 1702. Its lantern **dome** has become a landmark for miles around.

The plain exterior (left) of St Paul's Cathedral belies its ornate interior (right) – note the macabre tomb slabs

The Great Bluff

In 1565 the Ottoman Sultan decided to withdraw some of his troops from the Great Siege (► 10) and attack Mdina. The city was vulnerable as it had sent most of its defenders to reinforce the Knights at Birgu (Vittoriosa) – leaving it mostly occupied by peasants and their women – and it was woefully short of powder and shot. Fortunately Mdina's commander received word of the impending attack and decided on a show of strength. He dressed the peasants and women in soldiers' uniforms and sent them, and all available guns, up to the ramparts. When the Turks attacked they were met with so many uniforms and such a volley of cannon fire that they decided Mdina was perhaps a tougher opponent than they had thought. Cursing, they withdrew. The garrison heaved a massive sigh of relief at the success of their bluff and a thanksgiving service was immediately convened.

MDINA: INSIDE INFO

Top tips There are four separate **"heritage" attractions** (Mdina Experience, Knights of Malta, Medieval Times and Tales of the Silent City), all of which re-create local and island history. The Knights of Malta is the best.
• If you want a good potted **history** of just Mdina, the best is the audio-visual Mdina Experience.

Hidden gems Search out works by **Goya and Dürer** in the Cathedral Museum.
• Stay on **after dark** and take an atmospheric stroll through the quiet lantern-lit streets.

The colourful **marble tombs** set into the floor recall those in Valletta's St John's Co-Cathedral (▶ 52), though here they are devoted to clerics, not knights. There are paintings and gilded carvings all around, including Mattia Preti's mural of *The Shipwreck of St Paul*, which was saved from the original cathedral. In the sacristy note the superb Irish bog-oak door, also saved from the original Norman cathedral.

Cathedral Museum

Try out some time travel at one of Malta's many audio-visual shows

Often overlooked is the Cathedral Museum, displaying items of interest rescued from the original building and a valuable art bequest, including the works of some Old Masters. Particularly worth a look are the woodcuts by Dürer, engravings by Rembrandt and works by Goya.

TAKING A BREAK

Try **Ciappetti** (▶ 111) for modern Maltese-Mediterranean, **Palazzo Notabile** (▶ 112) for a quick coffe and pastry, or pizza and pasta, or **Bacchus** (▶ 111) for more chic French/Maltese cuisine and a romantic atmosphere.

✚ 180 C3
Palazzo Falzon
✉ Triq Villegaignon ☎ 21 454512 🕐 Mon–Fri 10:30–1, 2–5 (subject to staff availability) 💷 Free but donation requested

St Paul's Cathedral and Museum

Top right: Bernini's marble statue of St Paul

✉ St Paul's Square ☎ Cathedral: 21 454136; Museum: 21 454697 🕐 Cathedral: Mon–Sat 9–1, 2–4:30 (Sun mass only); Museum: Mon–Fri 9–4:30, Sat 9–2 💷 Inexpenisve

Mdina Experience

Right: St Paul's Church, Rabat, and the grotto beneath, where the saint briefly sojourned

✉ Mesquita Square ☎ 21 454322 🕐 Mon–Fri 10:30–4, Sat 10:30–2 💷 Moderate

Knights of Malta
✉ 14–19 Magazine Street ☎ 21 451342 🕐 Mon–Fri 10:30–4 💷 Moderate

② Rabat

Sitting on Mdina's doorstep, Rabat is something of a poor relation, merely "the suburb" (the meaning of its name) to "the walled city". It was named by the Arabs who dug the ditch that separated the two. However, it has a history that stretches far back beyond the Arabic invasion of 870, as well as some of the island's most unusual attractions.

Under the Romans, present-day Rabat and Mdina were one town, called *Melita*. Remains of a Roman town house were uncovered here in 1881, though only its impressive mosaics survive, in particular the floor. Around this has been built the **Museum of Roman Antiquities**, featuring statuary, busts, amphorae, an olive press and other Roman items that were discovered else-where on the island.

St Paul's Church and Grotto

Malta was actually of little importance to the Romans, but it was during this period that the Apostle Paul was shipwrecked on the island (► 126). Local lore maintains that he made his way to Rabat, where he cured the gover-nor's father of a fever, converted the governor (Publius) to

Christianity and ordained him as the island's first bishop. Paul preached and lived in the cave now known as **St Paul's Grotto**. With its marble statue of St Paul, sculpted by Bernini, it has become an important place of pilgrimage. Pope John Paul II prayed here in 1990. The present **St Paul's Church**, built above the grotto, dates from the end of the 17th century.

The Catacombs

Unlike the Romans, Jews and early Christians did not believe in cremation and, where possible, buried their dead. However, due to the shortage of topsoil in Malta this was (and still is) problematic. The alternative was to build underground chambers, or catacombs. The features of the catacombs are fairly standard: there are tombs cut from rock (which resemble shallow baths), niches for infants, and round, slab-like tables (known as *agape* tables) with benches around them where mourning relatives would come and pay tribute to the dearly departed with a funeral feast. In times of persecution the catacombs were also used as a refuge. So far 3sq km of catacombs have been discovered beneath the streets of Rabat, but it is thought that there are many more undiscovered tunnels, both in Rabat and elsewhere on the island.

Beneath the main street are two complexes of 4th-century catacombs. Both are open to visitors, in part at least. The first is **St Paul's Catacombs**, a labyrinthine 1,700-year-old underground graveyard. Buy the rather scant map, on

RABAT: INSIDE INFO

Top tips If you plan to explore St Paul's Catacombs take along a **torch**!
• The catacombs may be a bit too scary for **small children**, and they also aren't recommended if you are claustrophobic.

The altar and colourful frescoes at St Agatha's Catacombs

sale at the entrance, which shows the layout. The 1,400 or so bodies that lay here were removed long ago, although wandering around in the semi-darkness is still pretty eerie.

Further along the street, knowledgeable guides (admission is by tour only) and bright electric lighting make **St Agatha's Catacombs** a less scary proposition. Apparently St Agatha hid here to escape Roman persecution in the 3rd century, although she later died a martyr's death in Sicily. The principal feature of this complex is its 32 brightly coloured frescoes. Most of them date from between 1200 and 1480, though some go back to the 4th century. Sadly they have all been damaged and defaced (quite literally) by Muslim corsairs.

TAKING A BREAK

Try the **Grapes** in Catacombs Street (traditional Maltese food), the **Peristyle** opposite the Museum of Roman Antiquities (pizza, burgers, some local dishes) and the **Cuckoo's Nest Tavern**, St Paul's Street (Maltese dishes). See also 112–113.

✚ 180 B2
Museum of Roman Antiquities
✉ Wesgha Tal-Muzew
☎ 21 454125 🕐 Mon–Fri 7:45–2, mid-Jun–Sep; Mon–Sat 8:15–5, Sun 8:15–4:15, rest of year
💷 Inexpensive

St Paul's Church and Grotto
✉ Parish Square ☎ 21 454467
🕐 Daily 9:15–1, 2–5 💷 Free

St Paul's Catacombs
✉ St Agatha Street ☎ 21 454125
🕐 Mon–Fri 7:45–2, mid-Jun–Sep; Mon–Sat 8:15–5, Sun 8:15–4:15, rest of year 💷 Inexpensive

St Agatha's Catacombs
✉ St Agatha Street 🕐 Mon–Fri 9–4:30, Sat 9–12:30, Jul–Sep; Mon–Fri 9–12:30, 1–4:30, Sat 9–12:30, rest of year 💷 Moderate

At Your Leisure

🛐 Palazzo Parisio, Naxxar

Malta's finest stately home sits rather incongruously right in the busy centre of Naxxar (pronounced *nash-ar*) opposite the church. Built between 1898 and 1906, its materials and craftsmanship set new standards on Malta. The inspired stuccowork, painted ceilings, Lombardy furniture and marble make it the finest non-ecclesiatical building on the island outside Valletta.

➕ 180 C3 ✉ Victory Square, Naxxar
☎ 21 412461; www.palazzoparisio.com
🕐 Mon–Fri 9–1 (by guided tour only, on the hour) 💷 Expensive

🛐 Mosta Dome

This imposing church was built between 1833 and 1860 and its remarkable dome, completely self-supporting, was erected without the use of scaffolding by notching each course to the one below. Measuring 37m in diameter, it is one of the largest church domes in Europe and is visible from almost every vantage point in Malta. In 1942, when the church was packed with worshippers, the dome was hit by three bombs. Two bounced off and a third went through the dome but failed to explode. A replica of the "miraculous" 200kg bomb can be seen in the vestry.

➕ 180 C3 ✉ 8.5km west of Valletta
☎ 21 433826 🕐 Daily 9–noon, 3–5
💷 Free

🛐 San Anton Palace Gardens

The president's official residence is San Anton Palace. The palace is closed to the public, but you can get a look at the rear, via the subtropical gardens that back on to the palace. This small splash of green has some very mature trees, including impressive palms and a splendid old ficus.

➕ 180 C3 ✉ Attard 🕐 Daily dawn–dusk 💷 Free

Take a break from the heat in shady San Anton Palace Gardens

Boyzone

The themes of Central Malta's attractions are mostly architecture and history. The **Malta Aviation Museum** at Ta' Qali, with its small, colourful collection of fighter and civilian aircraft, might provide light relief for some while others go shopping at the adjacent **Crafts Village** (➤ 114).

Where to... Stay

Prices
Expect to pay per double room per night
£ under LM15   ££ LM15–30   £££ LM31–50   ££££ over LM50

MDINA

Xara Palace Hotel ££££

The magnificent Xara (pronounced *shah-ruh*) Palace occupies one of the most beautiful 17th-century palaces in Mdina. Major features such as the atrium, piano nobile and façade have been totally rebuilt as close to the original as possible. Accommodation is in 17 luxury suites. Some of these rooms were originally an astonishing 6m high and have had a mezzanine floor inserted. The hotel has its own gym, sauna, an attractive bar and two restaurants (▶ 112).

➕ 180 C3 ⊠ Misrah il-Kuncill ☎ 21 450560, www.xarapalace.com.mt

ATTARD

Corinthia Palace Hotel ££££

The long-established Corinthia Palace oozes old-world charm and calm, though it has also undergone major refurbishment. The most conspicuous addition is its state-of-the-art Atheneum spa complex. The public rooms and (most) bedrooms are very impressive, but its pride and joy are the landscaped gardens and magnificent outdoor swimming pool, with large but private sun terraces. The hotel restaurants are top class (▶ 113) and attract non-residents from all over the island.

➕ 180 C3 ⊠ De Paule Avenue ☎ 21 440301, www.corinthiahotels.com

Where to... Eat and Drink

Prices
Prices indicate what you should pay per person for a three-course meal, excluding drinks and service charge.
£ under LM8   ££ LM8–12   £££ over LM12

MDINA

Bacchus £££

Something of an Mdina institution, Bacchus was once the 17th-century gunpowder magazine for "The Silent City". Now it's a vaulted restaurant serving an ambitious French/Maltese/international menu. Try the delicious almond soup with julienne of chicken, fillet steak served with a wine and brandy sauce, or duck with Chartreuse and shallots. There's no doubting the quality. There are also outside tables on the bastion from where you can enjoy fine views.

➕ 180 C3 ⊠ 1 Inguanez Street ☎ 21 454981 ⊙ Daily lunch and dinner

Ciappetti £££

Ciappetti has evolved from a tea-room to become one of the finest restaurants in "The Silent City". Headed by an experienced international chef, the best way to describe the menu is modern Maltese-Mediterranean, with dishes such as five-spiced Dingli pork bely on chive mash, braised lamb shank in mild curry sauce on pear chutney, and yellowfin tuna sealed in soy and sesame seed oil on seaweed. Ciappetti also serves a vast range of tea, coffee, latte and other drinks, though their bastion terrace is only open to diners. The beautiful downstairs courtyard is a pretty good consolation setting if you just want a drink.

🗺 180 C3 🗹 5 St Agatha's Esplanade ☎ 21 459987
🕒 Daily 10 am–late

De Mondion Roof Garden £££

Dining rooms with a view are fairly common in Mdina, but this one, on top of the 17th-century Xara Palace Hotel (▶ 111) is probably the most elegant of all. Of course it is also the most expensive. The décor, with exposed beams and rustic, colour-washed walls, reflects the northern Italian and Mediterranean cuisine. But there the simplicity ends. Dishes such as yellowfin tuna with Tuscany green

lentils and veal jus, or porcini risotto with oyster mushrooms in a silky chive *velouté* indicate how seriously cooking is treated here. Finish off with orange crème brûlée, served with apricot compôte and Italian-style biscotti.

🗺 180 C3 🗹 Xara Palace Hotel, Misrah il-Kuncill ☎ 21 450560
🕒 Daily dinner; Sun lunch and afternoon tea, winter only

Fontanella Tea Rooms £

It's often overcrowded, frequently overrated and all too often – whether its busy or not – the service is just plain awful. But if you can get a seat on the front row of their flower-festooned terrace, with a view that stretches over a third of the island, choose the right cake (many people rave about the chocolate cake) and if you're lucky with the service, then you'll find out why Fontanella still has so many fans. It's particularly pretty when the bastion walls are illuminated at night.

🗺 180 C3 🗹 Bastion Square
☎ 21 454264 🕒 Daily 10 am–11 pm, summer; 10 am–7 pm, winter

Il-Veduta £–££

Immediately outside the walls of Mdina, Il-Veduta enjoys a fine view to the south of the island. Mdina's most famous views look north, and in most other ways too this is the opposite of a typical Mdina restaurant. Service is excellent, the staff are very friendly, there are good facilities for children, and the food (most Maltese favourites plus various pizzas and pasta dishes) is very reasonably priced.

🗺 180 C3 🗹 Saqqajja Square
☎ 21 454666 🕒 Daily 11:30–11

The Medina £££

The Medina, a long-established favourite in Mdina, is an old Norman house with a series of rough stone arched rooms and, in the winter, two roaring fires. In summer, dining is in an open-air

courtyard under vines next to a pink oleander tree. Either way it is ideal for a romantic candlelit rendezvous. The food is a mix of French, international and Maltese.

🗺 180 C3 🗹 7 Holy Cross Street
☎ 21 454004 🕒 Mon–Sat dinner only

Palazzo Notabile £–££

Half way along Mdina's main street, this converted 17th-century *palazzo* is something of a tourist trap. But for all that its courtyard is still a charming place for a coffee and pastry or a traditional Maltese snack. They also do pasta, pizza, grills and seafood.

🗺 180 C3 🗹 Villegaignon Street
☎ 21 454625 🕒 Mon–Sat 10–4:30, Sat also 7–11 pm

Stazzjon ££

Stazzjon – the name means "station" – is a reminder that some 70 years ago a train service huffed and puffed its way between Mdina and Valletta. Drinks are ordered at the former ticket window and the dining-area occupies what was once the waiting rooms and part of the platform. The international and Maltese menu is reasonably priced and the setting is unique.

➕ 180 C3 🚇 Museum Station ☎ 21 451717 🕐 Tue–Sun dinner only

Trattoria AD 1530 ££

Just off the main street, literally and figuratively, the relaxed Trattoria AD 1530 (part of the Xara Palace Hotel, ▶ 111) stands out from the tourist-swamped venues in Mdina. It is a perfect place for a light meal or just a drink, with some inventive home-made pasta dishes and salads on the menu. Take a look inside the attractive bar and note too the façade, reconstructed as near as possible to its 17th-century glory, particularly beautiful when floodlit by night.

➕ 180 C3 🚇 Xara Palace Hotel, Misrah il-Kuncill ☎ 21 450560 🕐 Daily 11–6, 7–11

ATTARD

Corinthia Room £££

Dress to impress at the top dining room of the luxury Corinthia Palace Hotel (▶ 111). As you enter this grand candle-lit space, you feel almost as if you have walked on to the location of a film set in the the 19th century. This was formerly the home of one of the island's wealthiest families, and today bankers, businessmen and Malta's *glitterati* meet here to wine and dine each other. The menu changes every three months and is a mixture of Mediterranean and Maltese flavours with a French influence. Expect unlikely but winning partnerships such as Galway Bay salmon and local shellfish, or Aberdeen Angus fillet of beef and *ġbejnet* (peppered goat's cheese from Gozo). Splash out on a special occasion, and don't forget your gold credit card.

➕ 180 C3 🚇 Corinthia Palace Hotel, De Paule Avenue ☎ 21 440301 🕐 Daily dinner only

Pizza Pasta Basta £–££

The gardens of the Corinthia Palace Hotel (▶ 111) are transformed with the use of soft lighting into an enchanted woodland at night. This not only attracts couples looking for a romantic setting, but large family groups, too. (If you are the former book a table well away from the children's mini-playground!) The menu is obvious from the name – it means pizza and pasta will do nicely – and the service is generally good.

➕ 180 C3 🚇 Alongside Corinthia Palace Hotel, Birbal Street ☎ 21 440301 🕐 Daily dinner

Pool Garden Restaurant ££

At this delightful poolside restaurant, part of the Corinthia Palace Hotel (▶ 111), you can relax in beautiful landscaped grounds, disturbed only by the most delicate of splashes and the gentle rustle of paperback pages being slowly turned. The food, international and Maltese snacks and light meals, is

almost incidental, but high quality. Choose from the specials on the blackboard.

➕ 180 C3 🚇 Corinthia Palace Hotel, De Paule Avenue ☎ 21 440301 🕐 Daily lunch, Jul–Sep

Rickshaw £££

Probably the best Eastern food on the island (see also the Blue Elephant, ▶ 73) is served in this sumptuous, Asian-themed restaurant in the Corinthia Palace Hotel (▶ 111). You can eat your way round India, Thailand, Malaysia, Singapore, Indonesia and China. Take the stress out of ordering by starting with a Rickshaw Platter and moving on to a Rickshaw Sizzler. Both combine the taste of many Far Eastern lands. This is a popular place with affluent older couples and business people on expense accounts. The service, of course, is impeccable.

➕ 180 C3 🚇 Corinthia Palace Hotel, De Paule Avenue ☎ 21 440301 🕐 Mon–Sat dinner

Where to...
Shop

TA' QALI CRAFTS VILLAGE

Ta' Qali Crafts Village is a group of around 20 World War II nissan huts scattered around a former airfield site. It is scruffy and uncared for and at first sight you will probably wonder if you have come to the right place. It's worth persevering with, though, as here you will find most of the goods that the island is famed for, at reasonable prices: silver and gold filigree, pottery, wood, wool and metal. Most of the shops open Mon–Fri 8–6 and Sat 8–12.30.

By far the best looking, most entertaining and most popular outlet is **Phoenician Glassblowers.** Watch them blowing, forming, shaping and generally waving molten glass about in a fashion that might give health and safety officers

palpitations. The end product, however, is rarely less than impressive. The workshop runs Mon–Fri 7:30–4, Sat 7:30–noon.

MDINA, RABAT AND AROUND

Mdina's shops sell mostly souvenirs, and ironically the biggest and best outlet in the immediate vicinity is in the high street of its more residential neighbour, Rabat.

The **Empire Crafts Centre** sells all the usual stuff, while craftspeople make lace, silver and gold filigree, and blow glass. You can taste wine here.

Rabat also hosts an **open-air market** on Saturday morning (opposite St Paul's Church).

The prosperous "Three Villages" (Attard, Lija and Balzan) are the place for serious art, antiques and bric-a-brac. **Melitensia** (Transfiguration Avenue, Lija) is one of the island's best art galleries, while **Ceramica Saracina** (St Anthony Street, Attard) is also worth a look.

Where to...
Be Entertained

SPORT

Tucked away in an industrial suburb, 4km south of Valletta, the **Marsa Sports Club** is Malta's biggest sports centre (Mon–Fri 9–9, Sat–Sun 9–5, tel: 21 233851, www.maltaweb.com/ sports). It has five squash courts, 18 tennis courts, two billiards halls, a gym, sauna, open-air pool, minigolf and Malta's only public golf course, the **Royal Malta Golf Club.** Visitors can buy a day membership.

Next to the Marsa Sports Club is the **horse-racing stadium**. In Malta horse-racing means trotting, with jockeys seated behind the horse in a two-wheeled racing trap. Meetings take place every Sunday in summer with around 12 races per day. It's very popular, drawing large crowds. Admission is inexpensive.

The **national sports stadium** is at Ta' Qali (▶ opposite). The Maltese national football team play here. Don't expect to see any household names limbering up, indeed some play on a semi-professional basis only, and the team is ranked low in the world ratings. On the plus side, however, it is inexpensive to watch matches, even qualifying games of major tournaments (such as Euro 2004) against top-class opposition. See the local paper for further details.

NIGHTLIFE

There is little nightlife in this area, but you are only a 20-minute drive from St Julian's, where there is plenty of choice (▶78), so there's no need to tuck up early.

The North

Getting Your Bearings

For most visitors the north of Malta is all about sun, sea and sand. With the exception of St Paul Bay's, and a handful of watch-towers built by the Knights, its tangible history is much less conspicuous than in other parts of the island.

The north's greatest attraction is its concentration of sandy beaches – in fact all of the sandy beaches on the island. It's interesting therefore that the two major purpose-built holiday centres, Buġibba (pronounced *boo-gee-bah*) and Qawra (pronounced *ow-rah*) don't have a grain of sand between them. By contrast, the village of Mellieħa (pronounced *mell-ear*) and Mellieħa Bay

Previous page: Have a day of fun at Popeye Village

Right: Making a splash at Mellieħa Bay

Right inset: About to take the plunge at Paradise Bay

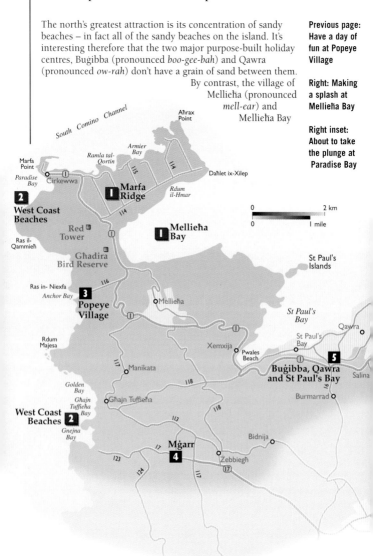

Għallis Rocks

Ras il- Qrejten

Baħar iċ-Cagħaq (White Rocks)

6

121

Baħar iċ-Cagħaq

between them offer an original village and the biggest sandy beach on Malta.

Around 200 years ago the north was more or less uninhabited. Modern tourism has since brought jobs and people, but none the less, venture away from the concrete jungle around St Paul's Bay, and the ratio of people and buildings to open countryside is still quite low. Here, ancient countryside staples such as drystone walls, neat fields, wild fennel and caper bushes can still be seen. Perhaps the most pleasant surprise of all is that, despite attracting huge weekend crowds, the small golden beaches of the west coast, with their dramatic craggy headlands, remain largely undeveloped.

North of Mellieħa is Marfa Ridge – the tail of fish-shaped Malta. On the rocky, high part of the ridge, hunters are the only inhabitants and there is an almost world's end feel. On the northern side of the ridge, down by the sea, a handful of houses cluster around small sandy bays. Visitors rarely venture here, but Maltese families come in the summer to take their holidays.

The north of Malta may have been developed with visitors in mind, but, as this tour reveals, it is possible to escape the crowded beaches and tourist complexes.

The North in Two Days

Day One

Morning/Lunch

From Buġibba, follow the coast road north through Xemxija and Mistra Village and, just before you start to descend to Mellieħa village, by a roundabout is the Belleview Bakery (► 122). Stop here to buy some provisions for a snack or picnic lunch. Park by the church in **❶ Mellieħa** (right, ► 121), take a look inside, then drive down to **Mellieħa Bay** and the beach.

Afternoon

After you've had enough sun, sea and sand, continue past the beach up the steep hill to **❷ Marfa Ridge** (► 121–122). Halfway up, take the sharp left to see the Red Tower (► 121) and enjoy the views down to Mellieħa Bay (below). Drive on along the rough road to the end of the promontory for sweeping sea views. Head back to the main road and cross straight over to explore the northern side of Marfa Ridge. Take the fourth left (signposted Little Armier) to find the prettiest and quietest of the three bays here. Come back down the hill past Mellieħa Bay and if you have time, or perhaps children with you, turn right, following the signs to **❸ Popeye Village** (top right, ► 125; note that it closes at 5 pm Oct–Mar).

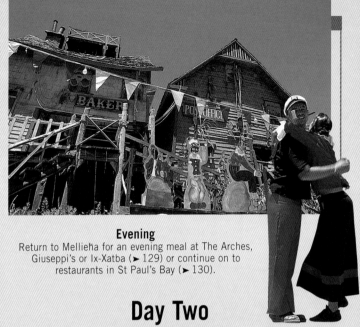

Evening

Return to Mellieħa for an evening meal at The Arches, Giuseppi's or Ix-Xatba (► 129) or continue on to restaurants in St Paul's Bay (► 130).

Day Two

Morning/Lunch

Follow the road inland to Bur Marrad and Mosta and 2km south of here you will come to part of the curious **Victoria Lines fortifications** (► 16). Pick up the signs to Żebbieħ and Mġarr and stop in the square at **4 Mġarr** (► 125) for a coffee and a peek at the church. Then take the signs for **2 Gnejna Bay** (► 123) where you can spend a couple of hours swimming or sunbathing. Return to Mġarr for lunch. Charles il-Barri (► 129) on the village square is a good spot.

Afternoon

After lunch take the road to **2 Għajn Tuffieħa Bay** (► 123) and **2 Golden Bay** (above, ► 123). To get a different perspective on the surrounding countryside, go horse-riding with Golden Bay Horse Riding (► 132).

Evening

The road from Golden Bay cuts straight through St Paul's Valley and is less than 5km back to **5 Buġibba** (► 125). Grapevine (► 131) is a good place for dinner, or carry on a bit further to **5 Qawra** (► 125) and dine out in style at Savini (► 131). If you are staying in Mellieħa, return via Manikata. The Arches (► 129) is a Maltese dining institution, or try Giuseppi's (► 129). Either way, go for the one you didn't try on Day One!

Mellieħa and Marfa Ridge

Mellieħa is famous for its beach, the biggest stretch of golden sand on the islands. It's a lovely place out of season, in the early morning and late in the day in summer. At other times it's too popular for its own good. Just the other side of Marfa Ridge are more sandy beaches, less familiar to tourists, but well known to the Maltese.

Mellieħa Bay

Mellieħa Bay is the largest bay in the archipelago. The 750m sandy shore, officially known as Għadira Beach, draws families and beach lovers from all over the island. Bars with disco music cater for teens, while young children and families can safely wade far out into the shallow water. It's not a good place for serious swimming, but there are lots of watersports – windsurfing, water-skiing, jetskiing, parasailing and inflatables. The best place to view this colourful scene is from the **Red Tower** on Marfa Ridge (► opposite). Behind the north end of

Above: Serried ranks of sunseekers at Mellieħa Bay

Right: The startling hues of the Red Tower at Marfa Ridge

Blood Sport

Have you ever wondered why there are no seabirds on Malta and so little, if any, birdsong to be heard? It is because the Maltese shoot birds. The organisation Bird Life Malta estimates that each year over a million finches, thrushes, swallows, turtle doves, golden orioles and various birds of prey are killed. This also includes thousands of internationally protected birds on migratory routes. Marfa Ridge is one of the hunters' sites.

the beach, protected by tall padlocked gates, is the **Għadira Bird Reserve** (Sat and Sun only 9–noon, 2–4, summer, tel: 21 347646).

Mellieħa Village

Above the beach is the old village of Mellieħa. It retains a traditional atmosphere with small everyday shops, an old-fashioned bakery and some good restaurants aimed at the tourist trade.

Its pride and joy is the huge 15th-century **church**, devoted to Our Lady of Victories. In a small, cave-like chapel is a fresco of the Virgin, supposedly painted by St Luke. In 1990 Pope John Paul prayed here.

Marfa Ridge

Although it overlooks Mellieħa Bay, the remote character and atmosphere of this rocky, windswept ridge is very different from the holiday resort below.

The western half of the "tail" rises to 122m above sea level. Gaunt, weather-beaten Fort St Agatha, better known as the **Red Tower**, was built in the mid-17th century by Grand Master Lascaris to guard against pirate raids and the ever-possible return of the Turks. It is closed to the public.

The western tip of the ridge offers a superb view over the busy channel to south Comino. From here you can see the ferry from Gozo to Comino shuttling back and forth, and alongside, a whole armada of pleasure boats on their way to and from the Blue Lagoon on Comino (► 143).

The eastern tip of the ridge is marked by a tiny chapel and a lonely Madonna statue,

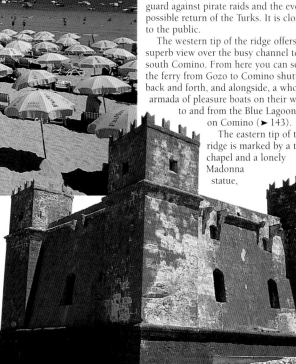

though the view from here is not as interesting as the one to the west.

Running off the eastern spinal route across the ridge are four well-signed straight roads leading to the soft, golden beaches of **Armier Bay** and **Little Armier Bay**. In high season these become pretty busy. A couple of restaurant-bars provide refreshments and watersports are available. In low season everything is closed and it is almost deserted.

Armier Bay, delightful from afar, but packed solid on summer weekends

TAKING A BREAK

Avoid the bars and cafés on the beach and eat in Mellieħa. There is a choice of inexpensive restaurants such as **Atlantil Bay**, 61 Georg Borg Olivier (grills, salads, Maltese dishes) or take away some snacks from the **Bellevue Bakery** – freshly baked sweet and savoury pastries, cakes and bread.

Right: Golden Bay is one of the island's most popular beaches

🔲 180 B4 Mellieħa Bay   🔲 180 A5 Marfa Ridge

MELLIEĦA AND MARFA RIDGE: INSIDE INFO

Top tips Keep away from Mellieħa Bay on **summer weekends**. The queues of traffic heading south from here on a Sunday evening are legendary.
• Because of hunters (➤ 121), it's best to **avoid walking on Marfa Ridge** during the bird migratory seasons (March–May, September–November), particularly early morning and in the evening.

Hidden gems Dotted about Marfa Ridge are the remains of several *girnas*, igloo-like stone hut dwellings of Bronze Age man. Don't confuse these with the many shelters and hides cobbled together by modern-day hunters on the ridge.
• If Mellieħa Bay and Armier Bay are too busy, check out the charming little cove of **Rdum il-Ħmar**, a short walk east of Little Armier Bay. It is often quiet.

2 West Coast Beaches

The west coast of the island has by far the best concentration of beaches – golden sandy bays separated by rugged headlands and cliffs providing good walks. The following beaches, which are all easily accessible, have three things in common – soft sand, sheltered swimming and popularity at weekends.

Golden Bay

This is the most popular of the three bays of Għajn Tuffieħa, which also includes Għajn Tuffieħa Bay and Ġnejna Bay. Sandwiched between two headlands, the sands here go back a fair way, making the water shallow and good for families (but take note if the warning flags are flying). Try your hand at water-skiing or windsurfing, or take a speedboat to Comino's Blue Lagoon (► 143).

Għajn Tuffieħa Bay

The largest and most beautiful of the three bays of Għajn Tuffieħa (it's pronounced *ein tuff-ear* and means "eye [underground spring] of the apple"), Għajn Tuffieħa Bay is also Malta's least crowded sandy beach. It's a long walk up and down the steps, which deters many beachgoers. There are limited watersports available, but no cafés.

Ġnejna Bay

Easily acessible by car and very popular, Ġnejna (pronounced *juh-nay-nuh*) Bay has shingle as well as sand. But if the beach becomes too crowded, there are always the large rock slabs to the north which are also good for sunbathing. There are watersports and a couple of vans offering basic refreshments. Fishermen's huts built into the rock and the presence of local families give Ġnejna Bay a down-to-earth feel.

WEST COAST BEACHES: INSIDE INFO

Top tips It's quite common to see people trying to **walk the short distance** across the ridges between Għajn Tuffieħa and Ġnejna Bay. Be aware, however, that it involves a precarious scramble up and down steep slopes of loose earth. If you want to attempt it, wear footwear and clothing that will cope with the climb and also give you the option of paddling or swimming around a flooded headland. Take a first-aid kit with you, too!
• In rough weather there's a **dangerous undertow** at Golden Bay and Għajn Tuffieħa. Do not swim at these times.

Anchor Bay

This idyllic tiny sandy bay is overlooked by **Popeye Village** (▶ opposite), which sits immediately above it. Still, very few Popeye visitors actually use Anchor Bay, so bring along your swimming gear and take full advantage.

Paradise Bay

Just around the corner from the Ċirkewwa ferry terminal, with views of the busy South Comino Channel, this small protected beach is a paradise scene of golden sand and turquoise waters backed by lush greenery. All watersports are available and new hotels and restaurants are being built close by.

Below: It's definitely worth the trek to Għajn Tuffieħa beach

TAKING A BREAK

Overlooking Golden Bay, the terrace of the **Apple's Eye** is a pleasant place for a snack and a drink. Mġarr or Mellieħa (▶ 129) are the nearest places for good food.

➕ 180 A4 Golden Bay
➕ 180 A4 Għajn Tuffieħa
➕ 180 A3 Ġnejna Bay
➕ 180 A4 Anchor Bay
➕ 180 A5 Paradise Bay

At Your Leisure

🄱 Popeye Village

Built as the set in 1980 for a film of the cartoon strongman *Popeye* (that both its star, Robin Williams, and audiences labelled a turkey), the Newfoundland-style Popeye, or Sweethaven, Village has not only stood for over 20 years, but has also established itself as one of Malta's most visited attractions. It comprises some 17 ramshackle buildings and is undeniably picturesque, though there is little attempt to engage the visitor and few facilities on site.

Malta in the movies: on the set of *Popeye* at Popeye Village

🏠 180 A4 ✉ Anchor Bay
☎ 21 572430 🕐 Daily 9–7, Apr–Sep; 9–5, rest of year 💰 Moderate

🄳 Mġarr

This typical Maltese village is famous for its handsome "Egg Church", built during the 1930s on the proceeds of village produce, of which the largest part was poultry and eggs. In tribute the great silver dome is egg-shaped!

Open to the public is the **Mġarr Shelter** (Tue–Sat 9–2, Sun 9–11:30), one of Malta's deepest and largest World War II shelters, preserved in its original state. Visitors can also see a multimedia show of Malta at war.

For details contact the Charles il-Barri restaurant; tel: 21 573235.
🏠 180 B3

🄵 Buġibba, Qawra and St Paul's Bay

Buġibba was built in the 1980s as a home-from-home for the British on package holidays, and it is probably the least expensive place to stay on the island. The emphasis here is on pubs, restaurants and discos. There are watersports from the promenade and boat trips to Comino and Gozo.

Buġibba's neighbour, **Qawra**, merges almost seamlessly with Buġibba. Qawra is more up-market and a bit quieter, but also caters only for package tourists. There are lots of restaurants and bars and plenty of choice for those keen on watersports.

The straggling settlement of **St Paul's Bay** (San Pawl il-Baħar), immediately west of Buġibba, is distinguishable from the holiday enclave by the local Maltese shops and houses. There are tourist restaurants and hotels here, but more subtle and local in flavour than those of its neighbours. Near to the

St Paul and St Luke
According to the Acts of the Apostles, in AD 60 St Paul and St Luke were ship-wrecked off *Melita* (Malta) on their way from the Holy Land to stand trial in Rome. They were treated well by the Maltese and Paul reciprocated with a "miracle". As he was building a fire a poisonous snake bit him, but he cast it into the fire and survived. The Church of St Paul (Our Lady of Sorrows), in St Paul's Bay, marks the spot where the event took place. Paul and Luke stayed for three months, preaching to the Maltese. Whatever the truth of the legends, it is clear from 2nd-century Christian catacombs that Christianity took hold early in Malta.

bay, **Wignacourt Tower**, one of few reminders of the days of the Knights, was built in 1610. It houses a small museum devoted to Malta's rich military architectural heritage.

Aside from lying on the beach, the principal tourist activity here is a boat tour; a popular excursion is St Paul's Bay, where the main landmark is St Paul's Island, the spot where the apostles St Paul and St Luke were shipwrecked in AD 60 (► above).

➕ 180 C4
Wignacourt Tower
✉ St Paul's Bay 🕐 Mon–Sat 9–1, Jul–Sep; Mon–Fri 9:30–4, Sat–Sun 10–noon, rest of year 🎟 Free

6 Baħar iċ-Cagħaq (White Rocks)
Families with children should go to White Rocks if only for the opportunity to swim with the dolphins at a bargain price. Swimming with the dolphins (summer only) is restricted to ten people per day and must be pre-booked. Of the three attractions here, **Mediterraneo Marine Park** is the main one. It is small but enjoy-

Excursion boats head out into the bay from Buġibba

able, and spectators get very close to the dolphins and sea lions.

Adjacent is a small, very popular waterpark, **Splash and Fun**, with four water chutes. There is also a small play area with funfair rides, mainly for younger children.

➕ 181 D4
Mediterraneo Marine Park
✉ Baħar iċ-Cagħaq ☎ 21 372218 🕐 Daily, 10:30–4:30, summer; call for winter timetable 🎟 Expensive (combined ticket available with Splash and Fun)

Splash and Fun
✉ Baħar iċ-Cagħaq ☎ 21 374283 🕐 Daily, 9:30–5, summer only 🎟 Expensive (► above)

Where to... Stay

Prices
Expect to pay per double room per night
£ under LM15 ££ LM15–30 £££ LM31–50 ££££ over LM50

MELLIEĦA AND MELLIEĦA BAY

Grand Hotel Mercure Selmun Palace ££££
If you're bored with bland high-rise hotels and their lookalike neighbours lining a crowded seafront, the Selmun Palace will make a refreshing change. This imposing castle-palace, built in the 18th century as a fortified country house, stands in splendid isolation on top of a hill overlooking the sea. It is now the frontage for a very smart hotel with 150 rooms and a discerning pan-European clientele. A rocky beach is within walking distance and Mellieħa Bay is a five-minute courtesy bus drive away. Most guests, however, seem to prefer the attractive pool area. Other facilities include two tennis courts, volleyball, archery, children's club, indoor pool and sauna. Half board is compulsory but the food here is good.

➕ 180 B4 ⊠ Selmun ☎ 21 521040; www.accorhotels.com

Note that most hotels in this area are block booked in advance by package tour operators.

Mellieħa Holiday Centre ££
Back in the 1970s, the setting up of this Danish-run complex was promoted by the controversial Maltese socialist prime minister, Dom Mintoff, as an exercise in social welfare offering cheap holidays to Danish communist workers. Since then it's been smartened up and is now occupied by families with an eye for a bargain. Each of its 150 self-catering bungalows has two bedrooms and if you don't want to cross the road to the beach there's a large swimming pool and gardens. Other facilities include a restaurant, bar and playground.

➕ 180 A4 ⊠ Mellieħa Bay ☎ 21 573900, fax: 21 575452

Pergola Club Hotel £££
Occupying a quiet corner of the old village with views down to the sea (1.5km away), this small but attractive apartment/hotel complex offers a choice of 25 hotel rooms or 54 self-catering apartments. There are two outdoor swimming pools, an indoor pool, gym, Jacuzzi and sauna. It's a good choice for families who want comfort and some facilities but not all the trappings of a large resort.

➕ 180 B4 ⊠ New Bridge Street, Mellieħa ☎ 21 523912, fax: 21 521436

GOLDEN BAY

Golden Sands ££
This large, 1960s-style hotel is rather old-fashioned and overdue for refurbishment, but if top of your wish list is overlooking a sandy beach (and you don't like the more crowded atmosphere of Mellieħa Bay), then this is the one for you. The hotel also has its own private beach area with a range of watersports, and if that gets too busy there are outdoor and indoor swimming pools. Golden Bay is relatively isolated, with no bars, restaurants or nightlife, though the hotel stages entertainment and has its own nightclub. Half board is compulsory, though rates are inexpensive.

➕ 180 A4 ⊠ Golden Bay ☎ 21 573961; fax: 21 580875

GHAJN TUFFIEHA

Hal Ferh Holiday Village £

If all you want is sea, sand and sun at a bargain price then book a cheap flight and flop down in this ex-British barrack house, now converted into a no-frills holiday home complex of rooms (fans and shared bathrooms) and apartments (double beds with kitchen area). The location is very quiet at night and the sandy beaches of Golden Bay and Ghajn Tuffieha are just a couple of hundred metres away.

✚ 180 A4 ☒ Ghajn Tuffieha
☎ 21 573883, fax: 21 573888

ST PAUL'S BAY

Corinthia Mistra Village ££££

Part of the Corinthia hotel group, the Mistra Village is the most luxurious holiday village on the island. It's very popular with families with young children. Accommodation is low rise and full of character, and the main pool area is very attrac-

tive. Facilities include a sports centre with gym and sauna, squash courts and tennis court, though there is a charge to use all of these. All apartments are self-catering and there is a mini-market on site, but there are restaurants, too. The location, a steep hill on a busy road, is not conducive for walking out, though the apartments are set well back from road noise, and a courtesy bus runs to most places of interest. Staff are friendly and helpful, running crèches and clubs for small children and also organising the occasional guided walk for parents.

✚ 180 B4 ☒ Xemxija Hill, Xemxija ☎ 21 580481; www.corinthiahotels.com

Gillieru Harbour £££

Small and secluded, the chic, 50-room Gillieru enjoys an enviable position overlooking St Paul's Bay. The views from the (small) rooftop swimming pool are outstanding. Facilities are limited, though having

one of Malta's best fish restaurants on the premises (▶ 130) might convince some people to stay here.

✚ 180 C4 ☒ Church Street, St Paul's Bay ☎ 21 572723; fax: 21 572745

QAWRA

New Dolmen Hotel ££££

Probably the best hotel in the St Paul's Bay area, the name refers to neolithic remains which were found near by and which have been tastefully incorporated into the grounds of this luxury property. Facilities are anything but Stone Age, with a gym, private lido, three freeform swimming pools and attractive landscaped gardens. The on-site Oracle Casino and Black Sea dance club (▶ 132) mean you don't even have to stray for some of the area's best nightlife. La Sibylle restaurant (▶ 131) provides dining in style. Some self-catering rooms are also available.

✚ 180 C4 ☒ Qawra ☎ 21 581510; www.dolmen.com.mt

Santana ££££

This attractive luxury hotel exudes that touch of class missing from many hotels in the Qawra/Bugibba area. Rooms, restaurants and the public areas are tastefully furnished and although Santana is not acutally on the seafront it still enjoys excellent views out to sea, and over open countryside to the south. Facilities include a indoor heated swimming pool, Jacuzzi sauna and fitness room.

✚ 180 C4 ☒ Gozo Road
☎ 21 583451; fax: 21 583450

SunCrest ££££

If you like your hotels state-of-the-art, big, brassy and with plenty of action and facilities, you'll like this 433-room chic seafront palace. It has a very good lido, a health and leisure centre, tennis court, speciality restaurants, and, of course, a nightclub. You can also hire diving equipment here.

✚ 180 C4 ☒ Qawra Coast Road
☎ 21 577101; fax: 21 575478

Where to...
Eat and Drink

Prices
Prices indicate what you should pay per person for a three-course meal, excluding drinks and service charge.

£ under LM8   ££ LM8–12   £££ over LM12

MELLIEHA AND MELLIEHA BAY

The Arches £££

The Arches has been a Maltese culinary institution for 30 years, constantly lauded for the quality of its food and impeccable service. You make a grand entrance up a sweeping staircase into the first-floor dining room decked out crisply in pink and white table linen. The menu is continental; traditional with a modern touch, and with a passing nod to local dishes. Try Chateubriand, *tournedos* glazed with Stilton and cider, Barbary duckling caramelised with lemon, honey and peppercorns, medallions of grouper and fillets of sea bass wrapped in a crispy potato crust. The wine list is said to be the best on the island.

➕ 180 B4 ⊠ 113 Georg Borg Olivier Street ☎ 21 523460 🕑 Mon–Sat dinner (closed mid-Jan–mid-Feb)

Giuseppi's £££

Long regarded as one of the finest restaurants on Malta, Giuseppi's has been serving informal romantic meals for 15 years. The setting is a lovely old house, paved with flagstones, decorated in dark terracotta with flashes of blue and yellow, and dotted about with antique wine paraphernalia. The menu, modern Mediterranean/Maltese, changes regularly, but retains two favourite starters; chestnut mushrooms with garlic, basil, tomatoes and parsley, and deep-fried goats' cheese with salad leaves and a tomato and garlic sauce. Look out too for quail, rabbit with a bitter chocolate twist, thyme- scented lamb and duckling marinated in ginger, lemon grass, apple juice and Calvados. Brulée is the house dessert speciality.

➕ 180 B4 ⊠ Georg Borg Olivier Street ☎ 21 574882 🕑 Tue–Sat dinner

Ix-Xatba ££

This small, cosy restaurant, the pick of the bunch along the Mellieha Bay/Marfa road, has views back up to the village and church. Bamboo canes against bare stone walls and pillars, old prints and simple drawings give a nice rustic feel. There's also an outside patio area The food is well-cooked Maltese/international dishes – fish, seafood, grills, with lamb and *fenek* (rabbit) the house specialities.

➕ 180 A4 ⊠ Marfa Road, Mellieha Bay ☎ 21 521753 🕑 Wed–Mon dinner (closed mid-Jan–mid-Feb)

MGARR

Charles il-Barri £–££

In a sleepy traditional village like Mgarr you may not expect to find the main restaurant decked out in chrome, purple and black. But try not to let the 1970s interior put you off, as Charles il-Barri (also known as Charlie's) is one of the places on the island for a tasty *fenkata* (rabbit feast, ➤ 22). Book for Sunday lunch and follow the locals' example.

➕ 180 B3 ⊠ Mgarr village square ☎ 21 573235 🕑 Tue–Sat noon–2, 7–10.30 (closed Mon)

ST PAUL'S BAY

The Admiral ££

This tiny restaurant, run by a very friendly husband and wife team, gives a good name to "international cooking", with dishes ranging from fillets of Norwegian salmon to fillet steak in truffle sauce with walnut, cream and Calvados or tenderloin of Irish beef "as you like it" (as long as it is not "well done"!). There are some tasty dishes for vegetarians too, such as Blue Ilchester Stilton and broccoli flan. Booking at weekends is essential. Service is good and attentive.

➕ 180 C4 ⌧ 285 Main Street
☎ 21 571360 🕙 Mon–Sat dinner

Cafeteria Capriccio £

In an area where good-quality snack bars are thin on the ground, this simple but friendly little café just down the hill from St Paul's Church is definitely worth knowing about. Look out for the toasted *focaccias* and home-made pies, savoury and sweet; try the spinach, ham and cheese, or chicken.

➕ 180 C4 ⌧ Church Street
🕙 Daily 9–6

Da Rosi £££

If you're in the mood for top-quality fresh fish and seafood, you have the choice of Gillieru (▶ below) or, just across the street, this friendly family-run establishment. In many ways, this small, cosy and informal place is the opposite of its famous neighbour. However, dining here is inside so there's no sea view. Try *risotto da Rosi* (with mushrooms, prawns, caviar and cream) then perhaps push the boat out with a (half) lobster Thermidor. Friday night is all-out fish night with a special fixed-price menu. It's not all seafood, however, Da Rosi also serve a good pepper steak, and a house special chicken.

➕ 180 C4 ⌧ 45 Church Street
☎ 21 571411 🕙 Tue–Sun dinner; also open Sun lunch, winter (closed two weeks Feb)

Don Vito ££–£££

This popular restaurant is situated right at the top of the hill overlooking St Paul's Bay and the views are spectacular. The food's good too, with mostly Italian and local dishes. Try the steaks, chicken, fish and pasta Don Vito (with mushrooms, ham, garlic, brandy and cream). If you have a healthy appetite come along on Friday night when it's all you can eat and drink for a single price.

➕ 180 C4 ⌧ Luigi Preziozi Street
☎ 21 585755 🕙 Daily dinner only, summer; lunch and dinner, winter

Gillieru £££

Serious fish lovers should float along to this long-established favourite overlooking St Paul's Bay. It is large, modern and quite formal, and popular with business types. The emphasis is on the food rather than the atmosphere. The best time to come is for lunch or on a warm summer evening when you can sit outside on the balcony enjoying the sea views. The menu offers fishy favourites like lobster bisque, spaghetti vongole (with clams), prawns, salmon and fresh oysters.

➕ 180 C4 ⌧ Church Street
☎ 21 573480 🕙 Daily lunch and dinner

XEMXIJA

Mange Tout £££

Mange Tout arrived on the Maltese restaurant scene with a bang, winning several awards, including National Chef of the Year and highest rated restaurant in *The Definitively Good Guide to Restaurants in Malta and Gozo* (▶ 37). It is owned and run by a husband and wife team who cook up some serious French/ Mediterranean food: fettuccini with prawns, cannelloni of salmon and crab, confit loin of pork and stuffed saddle of rabbit, to name just a few. Vegetable accompaniments are carefully considered; carrot *bavarois* with ginger mustard sauce, cauliflower *pavé*, parsnip puree. Ask for a window seat over-looking the bay.

➕ 180 B4 ⊠ 356 St Paul's Street
☎ 21 572121 🕒 Mon–Sat dinner

Wild Thyme £££

Wild Thyme is a chic, family-run Italian trattoria, decorated in pastel colours with gentle opera music creating a very civilised atmosphere. Start with marinated swordfish, then choose sea bass in a salt crust, or one of the house speciality pasta dishes. It's slightly off the beaten track and a little hard to find – but why not order a taxi so you can have an extra glass of wine or *grappa*. They are open late and last orders are not usually until 11 pm.

➕ 180 B4 ⊠ Piscopo Macedonia Street, Xemxija Heights ☎ 21 572202 🕒 Tue–Sun lunch and dinner

BUĠIBBA

Da Michele £££

Locals and holidaymakers in the know travel from all over the island to this shrine of modern gourmet cuisine, incongruously sited in the heart of the island's package tourist capital. The menu – mostly French/international – changes at least twice a year, but expect dishes such as ravioli of wood pigeon, fillet of beef over carrot pureé with red wine and garlic sauce, and locally inspired items such as stuffed rabbit. The dining room is tastefully decorated with modern art but most eyes are on the open-plan kitchen where the internationally trained chefs cook up a storm.

➕ 180 C4 ⊠ Turisti Street ☎ 21 582131 🕒 Daily dinner only

Grapevine ££–£££

Pioneer Road in Bugibba is associated more with beers and burgers than good places to eat, so all credit to Grapevine owner/chef Jason Sultana for bringing his talents here. The décor is trendy Med with bright primary colours, wooden beams and a terracotta floor. There's a pretty outdoor terrace, too. The food is mostly Italian and Mediterranean; penne Chef (with spinach, parma ham and cream), fillet steak stuffed with Stilton and walnuts and flam-beed in brandy, duck breast with brandy, honey and orange. Look on the board for Maltese specials. Considering the quality, the prices are very reasonable.

➕ 180 C4 ⊠ Pioneer Road ☎ 21 580625 🕒 Daily dinner, Sun also lunch (closed last two weeks Feb)

QAWRA

Savini £££

This beautifully converted 300-year-old farmhouse, completely at odds with the modern outskirts of Qawra, is well worth seeking out. In summer you can sit outside with views over open countryside, and in winter the upstairs dining room is very cosy. Run by four brothers, the restaurant offers a menu that is modern and varied, with some unusual dishes. Start with *won ton mille feuille* or mascarpone terrine, progress to piccata cf pork coated with sage and onion, pan-fried and served with port *jus*, or try the breast of duck with spicy risotto and apricot and pear chut-ney. Finish off with home-made ice-cream.

➕ 180 C4 ⊠ Qawra Road ☎ 21 576927 🕒 Mon–Sat dinner (occasionally open Sun lunch)

La Sibylle £££

The premier dining room of the New Dolmen Hotel (▶ 128), this is a good place for that special end of holiday blow-out, or to spend any winnings from the hotel casino. There's a rich type of fusion cooking on offer here. Begin with terrine of sea bass and red mullet, or shallot soup with truffle oil and apple wafers, continue with sesame coated magret of duck or tea-steamed salmon, and finish off with vodka parfait and cassis sherbe:. Ask about the popular theme nights, too.

➕ 180 C4 ⊠ New Dolmen Hotel ☎ 21 581510 🕒 Mon–Sat dinner

Where to... Shop

The north of the island has little in the way of shopping opportunities. The St Paul's Bay resorts only really sell cheap tourist souvenirs and there are very few shops of any kind in Mellieha.

Stockhouse (Islets Promenade, Bugibba, tel: 21 571554, Mon–Sat 9–10, Sun 9–1), a popular and inexpensive tourist shop, has souvenirs galore plus gifts. There are also knitted woollen garments on sale for those who can overcome the psychological barrier of contemplating them when the island's heat is ferocious.

Ta' Qali Crafts Village (▶ 114) is the nearest place with a good selection of shops and is only 15–20 minutes away.

Where to... Be Entertained

NIGHTLIFE

Nightlife in the resorts revolves around music bars and discos with names like Goodfellows, Little Waster, Screamers and Bonkers. Two of the better venues are **The Abyss** in Bugibba, and the open-air **Fuego Salsa Bar** in Qawra.

The **SunCrest** and **New Dolmen** hotels in Qawra (▶ 128) have their own nightclubs and often stage shows from folk evenings to Las Vegas-style reviews. The New Dolmen Hotel has both the **Black Rose** dance club and the **Oracle Casino**. On Thursdays the latter is host to a Carnival-style review, while every night you can play roulette, blackjack, craps, the slot machines and more. Overseas guests must be over 18 and produce their passport.

The **Empire Cinema complex** in Bugibba has seven screens showing the latest Hollywood blockbusters.

WATERSPORTS

The shallow waters of Mellieha Bay are great for learning how to **windsurf**, but in the late afternoon when the crowds thin and the wind gets up watch the pros take over.

Diving

The north of the island is excellent for diving with sites catering for all levels of experience. The principal sites are: **Tugboat Rozi**, a tug deliberately sunk just north of Marfa Point; **Marfa Point**, a great site with caves, reefs, promontories and tunnels at depths of 15–30m; **Cirkewwa Arch**, with underwater walls and a magnificent arch where you can find different fish; **L-Ahrax Point**, shallow but spectacular, with an impressive drop-off and rich marine life: **St Paul's Islands**, with a reef wall which drops 34m to a sandy bottom; and **Anchor Bay**, with many caves and passageways.

Experienced divers should check out the unspoiled bays of Fomm-ir-Rih and Ras ir-Raheb, both a little south of Gnejna Bay.

For a drier glimpse beneath the waves, try **Captain Morgan's Underwater Safari Boat** (Bugibba Harbour, tel: 21 343373) with its special glass hull. It tours round St Paul's Bay.

HORSE-RIDING

Golden Bay Horse Riding (Golden Bay, tel: 573360) offers a one-hour trek along the coastal path or a two-hour trek to Anchor Bay. No experience is necessary and children are welcome. There is a 15-stone weight limit on riders.

Gozo and Comino

Getting Your Bearings

Gozo is a tiny island, measuring 15km by 7km at the widest points. It is 6km from Malta and its area is only a third of Malta's. You're never more than 10–15 minutes' drive from the capital Victoria (Rabat).

Getting around is relatively easy by car, although all main roads go through Victoria (Rabat) Consequently, places on the coast that are only a couple of kilometres apart as the crow flies are separated by a journey of perhaps 20–30 minutes, in to and out of Victoria (Rabat).

Popular myth has it that Gozo is like Malta was 30 or 40 years ago, and while this is true in some respects, it also does the island a disservice. The most obvious difference between the two, as far as visitors are concerned, is that Gozo has not been developed to cater for mass-market packaged tourism, and this therefore gives it a completely different atmosphere.

Although for years Gozitans were considered "country cousins", these days they are often better off than their Maltese counterparts, not only financially but in terms of quality of life. The ratio of green fields to concrete, fresh air to car fumes and people and buildings per square kilometre are all more favourable here.

Independence

Although Napoleon ousted the Knights of St John from Malta in June 1798, it appears that the Gozitans were made of sterner stuff. In September the people rebelled and succeeded in incarcerating the French within the Citadel in Victoria. At the end of October the French surrendered and left the island. And so for nearly two years, until the British arrived in September 1800, Gozo was an independent country, declaring itself La Nazione Gozitana (Nation of Gozo).

★ Don't Miss

At Your Leisure

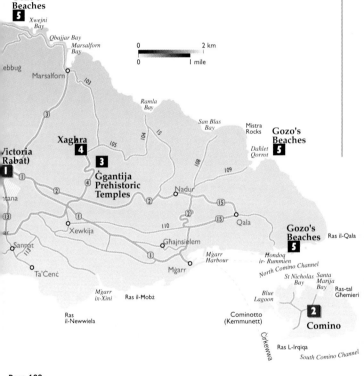

Page 133:
Comino's Blue Lagoon

Left: The oldest man-made structure on earth, Ġgantija

Most people come to Gozo for the day, but there is much more to see than you can cram into just one day. The beaches of Ramla Bay and San Blas Bay provide relief from the sun; Ġgantija Prehistoric Temples are testament to its long history; the Citadel at Victoria proves how it was considered an important post; the fishing villages of Xlendi and Marsalforn continue ancient traditions; and the tiny island of Comino is a place for escape.

As well as the tours to Comino, steep yourself in history at Victoria's Citadel and relax on the sandy beaches on the northern shores of Gozo.

Gozo and Comino in Four Days

Day One

Morning/Lunch

From the ferry at Mġarr make your way to ❶ **Victoria** (► 138–141) and find out some of the history of the island with the audio-visual show Gozo 360 Degrees. Take a look at the morning market on Pjazza Indipendenza, have a coffee and then explore the **Citadel** in Victoria on a walking tour (► 169–170). After the tour, have lunch at Ta' Rikardo (► 150).

Afternoon

Follow the **Gozo Tour** (► 165–168) which goes from Victoria to Għasri, then via the saltpans (right) near Qbajjar to Marsalforn and back to Victoria.

Evening

End the day with a meal at Il-Kartell (► 151) in Marsalforn, at Ta' Frenc (► 151) on the road back to Victoria, or back in Victoria itself at Brookies (► 150).

Day Two

Morning/Lunch

To beat the heat and coach tours arrive at ❸ **Ġgantija Prehistoric Temples** (► 144) at 8:30 am. Close by are the Ta' Kola Windmill and the Museum of Toys in ❹ **Xagħra** (left, ► 144). Have lunch at Oleander (► 151).

Afternoon

Choose from ❺ **Ramla Bay** or ❺ **San Blas Bay** (► 145) for sunbathing and swimming. To get here turn left outside Xagħra. Take the road back towards Nadur, then Għajnsielem, enjoying the views over Mġarr Harbour (above right) and towards Comino.

Evening

Go down to Mġarr Harbour (above), have a drink at the Gleneagles Bar (10 Victory Street) and dinner at Manoel's or the L-Imġarr Hotel (▶ 150).

Day Three

Morning/Lunch

Head west from Victoria and visit the church at **6 Ta' Pinu** (▶ 146; note dress code). Return to the main road and continue west. Carry on to **7 Għarb** and its Folklore Museum (▶ 147). Try Salvina's (to the right of the church) in Għarb for lunch.

Afternoon

Return to the main road and continue towards San Lawrenz. There's more shopping at the Ta' Dbieġi Craft Village (▶ 152). Carry on to **8 Dwejra Point** (▶ 148) to see the Azure Window, Fungus Rock and the Inland Sea. If the weather is calm hop aboard a boat and see Gozo's "blue grottoes".

Evening

Finish off the day with a meal at It-Tmun (▶ 151) in Xlendi, or head for the nightclubs of La Grotta or Paradiso (▶ 152). All are only a 10-minute drive from Victoria. Or stay in Victoria and take in an opera at one of the two opera houses, the Aurora or the Astra (▶ 140 and 152).

Day Four

Take the ferry from Mġarr to the tiny island of **2 Comino** (▶ 143). Day-trips are organised, but if you want to stay there is the charming Hotel Comino (right, ▶ 149).

❶ Victoria (Rabat)

Gozo's capital may be small, but it has plenty of character and an imposing Citadel with great views over the island. The town was given its official name in 1897 to commemorate 60 years of Queen Victoria's reign, but the locals have never really taken to this British imposition and continue to call it by their name, Rabat.

Around Victoria

The pretty central square where the morning market and many a coffee meeting takes place under the neatly trimmed ficus trees is officially called Pjazza d'Indipendenza (Independence Square). To the locals, however, it's simply known as **It-Tokk** – meaning "main square" or "meeting place". This stubborn regard for tradition says a lot about the character of the Gozitan people.

Just off the square is **Gozo 360 Degrees**, an entertaining audio-visual introduction to the island. You'll learn about the culture, sights and history of the island, the blackest moment being in 1551 when Turkish corsairs carried off most of the 5,000-strong population into slavery. Only 300 escaped.

Triq ir-Repubblika (Republic Street) runs east from the Citadel to **Rundle Gardens**, a welcome patch of greenery and a good place for a picnic.

The Citadel

The Citadel took its present shape in the 17th century, but each and every invader who has occupied the island has made their headquarters here. The earliest traces go back to the

Top right: Take a helicopter ride to see Victoria at its very best

Right: Bygone crafts in the Citadel's Folklore Museum

Below: Pjazza d'Indipendenza, where everyone meets in the morning

Carthaginians, who left behind a Punic inscription relating to temples they built during the 3rd century BC. Then came the Romans, the Arabs and finally the Knights of St John.

When first built, the Citadel must have been awesome, with its sheer rock faces, mighty curtain walls and bastions dominating the countryside for miles around. Indeed it still is a fine sight from most directions, particularly the north. The best view is by helicopter tour (► 32).

With the Turks driven far from Malta, the Citadel was never again to be tested in battle and its importance was fleeting. Until 1637, as a precaution against invasion, all islanders were required by law to sleep within its confines, but with the relaxing of this restriction the Citadel depopulated and in 1693 an earthquake reduced many of its fine buildings to ruins. Restoration is still going on today.

There are four museums within the Citadel walls: the **Museum of Archaeology**, the **Folklore Museum**, the **Cathedral Museum** and the **Natural History Museum**. Details of all of these are in the walking tour of the Citadel (► 169–170).

What's In a Name?

Rabat is an Arabic name meaning "suburb", which may seem inappropriate as Victoria is the island capital. In fact it refers strictly to that part of the city outside the Citadel walls.

St George's Basilica and the Cathedral

It's well worth wandering through the narrow alleyways around Pjazza d'Indipendenza (Independence Square), if only to browse the little old-fashioned shops.

St George's Basilica, dominating Pjazza San Gorg (St George's Square) a few yards behind the main square, was built in its present form between 1672 and 1678, though it has been much extended since. Step inside and you will see why it bills itself as "The Golden

Healthy Competition

If it comes as a surprise to learn that tiny Victoria (population around 5,000) has its own fully fledged opera house, then it is nothing less than astonishing to learn that there is a second one almost within singing distance. The **Aurora** (seating 1,500) came first, built in 1976 by the marching band of St George's Basilica. A few streets away, their rivals, the marching band of Gozo Cathedral, not to be outdone, decided to build their own opera house, the **Astra** (► 152). This opened in 1978 with seating for 1,200. Both houses enjoy capacity crowds, with the music provided by the Malta National Orchestra and top-class Italian soloists.

All that glitters at St George's Basilica

VICTORIA (RABAT): INSIDE INFO

Top tip It's best to visit Victoria **in the morning** to experience the hustle and bustle of the daily fruit and vegetable/household goods market on Pjazza d'Indipendenza. There's a buzzing atmosphere, but by early afternoon everything is packed away and most people have gone.

Basilica". With its lavishly gilded interior it is Victoria's hidden gem. The striking canopied altarpiece is a copy of Bernini's masterpiece in St Peter's, Rome.

The **Cathedral**, within the Citadel walls, was designed by Lorenzo Gafà and built between 1697 and 1711. It is a fine example of baroque vernacular architecture and was the Knights' own conventual church on Gozo. The inside is very ornate, with tombstones covering the floor. Its main attraction is the *trompe l'oeil* ceiling painting which makes you think that the roof is dome-shaped, although if you go outside and take a look you will see that it is flat.

You might think that in a small place like Victoria there wouldn't be enough room for two major churches and certainly there is no love lost between the Cathedral and the Basilica. This is most manifest in their marching band clubs and respective opera houses, the Astra and Aurora (➤ panel opposite).

TAKING A BREAK

Sopos, a characterful, down-to-earth café/bar on Pjazza d'Indipendenza (Independence Square) is a good place to rub shoulders with locals and fellow tourists. Come early when the market is on. Or you could try **Ta' Rikardo** (➤ 150) for a simple traditional Maltese lunch.

🖫 186 B2
Gozo 360 Degrees
✉ Citadel Theatre, Castle Hill ☎ 21 559955 🕓 Mon–Sat 10:30–3:30 tours every 30 minutes, Sun and public holidays 10:30–1 every 30 minutes 💷 Moderate

St George's Basilica
✉ St George's Square ☎ 21 556377 🕓 Daily 4:30 am–1 pm, 3:30–7 💷 Free

Museum of Archaeology
✉ Triq Il-Habs (Prison Street) ☎ 21 556144 🕓 Mon–Sat 8:30–6:30/7, Apr–Sep; Mon–Sat 8:30–4:30, rest of year; Sun 8:30–3, all year 💷 Moderate (one ticket allows access to all the Citadel museums)

Folklore Museum
✉ Triq Bernardo de Opuo ☎ 21 556144 🕓 Mon–Sat 8:30–6:30/7, Apr–Sep; Mon–Sat 8:30–4:30, rest of year; Sun 8:30–3, all year 💷 Moderate (one ticket allows access to all the Citadel museums)

Cathedral Museum
✉ Triq il-Fosos (Fosse Street) ☎ 21 556087 🕓 Mon–Sat 10–4:30 💷 Moderate (one ticket allows access to all the Citadel museums)

Natural History Museum
✉ Triq il-Kwartieri (Quarters Street) ☎ 21 558153 🕓 Mon–Sat 8:30–6:30/7, Apr–Sep; Mon–Sat 8:30–4:30, rest of year; Sun 8:30–3, all year 💷 Moderate (one ticket allows access to all the Citadel museums)

2 Comino

Tiny Comino, bare of foliage and almost devoid of people, lures a daily armada of excursion boats to bask in its Caribbean-like Blue Lagoon, the beautiful stretch of limpid turquoise water between Comino and its islet, Cominotto. But if you also want to sample the peace and quiet that the island has to offer you can stay overnight (▶ 149).

Visit in spring to see, and smell, Comino at its best. Wild thyme and clumps of cumin (from which the island takes its name) assail the eyes and nostrils. By summer the island is barren and almost unbearably hot. There's not a scrap of shade and even a simple five-minute walk seems the equivalent of a desert trek. There's only one thing to do and that's to cool off with a swim.

There are three tiny sandy **beaches**, the **Blue Lagoon**, which is always very busy, the private beach of the **Hotel Comino**, and **Santa Marija Bay**, which is always busy but only overcrowded at peak times.

Very few visitors come to Comino for its history, but to the south of the island, set dramatically on the clifftop, is **St Mary's Tower**, built by the Knights of St John in 1714, and recently restored to its former glory. You can't go in, but it's a fine sight from a passing boat.

Left: Into the blue – the waters around Comino (☐ 186 D1/E1) are some of the most beautiful in the Mediterranean

TAKING A BREAK
The only refreshments available on the island are at the **Hotel Comino** (▶ 149).

COMINO: INSIDE INFO

Top tips Avoid the Blue Lagoon at **summer weekends** when it is very busy.
• Some **excursions** to the Blue Lagoon aboard larger boats anchor too far away for you to swim to the little sandy beach. Check before booking if this is the case.
• Bring along plenty of **suncream** and a **parasol** if you are going to land on Comino.
• Take the **Oki-Koki** speedboat excursion (they will pull along-side your excursion boat in the Blue Lagoon). It's great fun and shows you some of the island's best caves.

At Your Leisure

🔳 Ġgantija Prehistoric Temples

The temple complex at Ġgantija (pronunced *juh-gant-ear*) is not only Malta's oldest such example, but also the world's oldest freestanding structure. Built around 3,600 BC, it well deserves the gigantic name with its largest stones standing some 6m tall and weighing up to 20 tons.

You can walk right into the temples, but as with Malta's other ancient remains there is no on-site interpretation and it will mean little to you unless you have read up on the subject and/or have visited the Ħal Saflieni Hypogeum (➤ 86–88) and the National Museum of Archaeology (➤ 62).

🔳 186 C2 ✉ Xagħra ☎ 21 553194
🕐 Mon–Sat 8:30–6:30/7, Apr–Sep;
Mon–Sat 8:30–4:30, rest of year; Sun
8:30–3, all year 💶 Inexpensive; also
valid for Ta' Kola Windmill Museum

🔳 Xagħra

This little village (pronounced *shah-ruh*) has one of the archipelago's classic village squares, including the

Lost for Words

As well as being a famous poet, Englishman Edward Lear was also a very well-travelled landscape painter. He came to Malta many times and in 1866 visited Gozo for a week. "I drew every bit if it, walking fifteen to twenty miles a day. Its coast scenery may truly be called Pomskizillious and Gromphibberous, being as no other words can describe its magnificence."

quaint **Coronation Stores** shop, a red telephone kiosk and post box, pink oleander trees and a fine church. It also offes four unusual visitor attractions just a few minutes' walk away. Two of these, **Ninu's Grotto** and the larger **Xerri's Grotto**, are small caves – with stalactites and stalagmites – beneath private houses.

A few metres beyond the church is the **Pomskizillious Museum of Toys**. This is an enjoyable collection for adults as well as children, with some exhibits dating back to the 1790s. But what makes it that bit special is its association with Edward Lear, the famous English writer of nonsense verse (➤ panel above). A full-sized wax model of Lear has pride of place alongside some of his wacky writing.

On the Ġgantija side of the village is the **Ta' Kola Windmill Museum**, a beautifully restored flour mill, dating from 1725, now housing various Gozitan rural bygones.

🔳 186 C2
Ninu's Grotto
✉ 17 Windmill Street, Xagħra ☎ 21
556863 🕐 Mon–Sat 8:30–6, Sun by
appointment only 💶 Inexpensive

Agricultural heritage at the Ta' Kola Windmill Museum

Ramla Bay can be viewed from a cleft in Calypso's Cave near Xagħra

Xerri's Grotto

✉ Gnien Imrik Street, Xagħra ☎ 21 560572 🕐 Daily 9–6 💷 Inexpensive

Ta' Kola Windmill Museum

✉ Ġgantija, Xagħra ☎ 21 560820 🕐 Mon–Sat 8:30–6:30/7, Apr–Sep; Mon–Sat 8:30–4:30, rest of year; Sun 8:30–3, all year 💷 Inexpensive (also valid for Ġgantija Prehistoric Temples)

Pomskizillious Museum of Toys

✉ 10 Gnien Xibla Street, Xagħra ☎ 21 562489 🕐 Thu–Sat 10–1, Apr; 10–12, 3–6, May–mid-Oct; Sat 11–1, mid-Oct–Mar 💷 Inexpensive

5 Gozo's Beaches

Gozo's beaches are less crowded than those on Malta, but at weekends and during summer holidays you will still be sharing with a lot of other bodies. Here is a round up, moving clockwise from north to south.

Ramla Bay: This is by far the biggest of Gozo's beaches, with some 200m of reddish-golden sand that goes back a fair distance, too. There are a couple of snack bars set back but otherwise it is pleasantly

Resort Beaches

Marsalforn and Xlendi (pronounced *sh-len-dee*) each have their own tiny sand and pebble beaches. Marsalforn is not worth a special trip, though nearby Qbajjar Bay and Xwieni Bay are lovely spots for swimming. Xlendi is attractively located at the head of a fiord-like bay, which is good for swimming.

uncommercialised. Don't swim in rough conditions as there are reefs and dangerous currents.

San Blas: Lovers of small intimate coves should make the effort to get to this charming little sandy beach. The road diminishes to a narrow track and you will have to park and walk the vertiginously steep final approach. There is a ramshackle sandwich bar where the friendly owners slumber in a hammock.

Dahlet Qorrot: There's little foreshore here but the quay is a

Calypso's Cave

Some 2km north of Xagħra, apparently off the beaten track, but very popular with coach tours, is Calypso's Cave. This tiny, dark, claustrophobic cleft in the rock is supposedly where Odysseus (or Ulysees) spent seven years with the sea siren, Calypso. In its defence, a rock fall prevents you from seeing the "original" cave, though there is a great view down to Ramla Bay from inside the cleft – but you can enjoy the view almost equally well from outside the cave. There's no formal opening times or admission charge, but if you do go inside, tip the boys with the candles who light your way (or take your own torch with you!).

popular place for swimming. The boat-houses cut back into the rocks make it quite a picturesque spot, too. A small kiosk provides basic refreshments.

Hondoq ir-Rummien: This small patch of golden sand, next to a concrete quayside, has great views over the Gozo Channel, and from a

Right: Thanks be to God: ex-voto offerings at the Basilica of Ta' Pinu

Below: The basilica is the national shrine and a highly venerated place

viewpoint just above the beach Comino's Blue Lagoon can be seen quite clearly. A ferry shuttles to and from here, while other motorboats provide water-skiing and inflatable rides. Avoid weekends when the locals descend en masse. Bring sandwiches or go to the snack bar.

Mġarr-ix-xini (pronounced *im-jar ee zee-nee*): This narrow, fiord-like inlet is one of the nicest places on the island for swimming. Sunbathers should note that the shore is pebbly here. There is a small, friendly café-bar under the trees.

Ramla Bay ✚ 186 C3
San Blas Bay ✚ 186 D2
Dahlet Qorrot ✚ 186 D2
Hondoq ir-Rummien ✚ 186 D1
Mgarr-ix-xini ✚ 186 C1

6 Ta' Pinu

Ta' Pinu is not just the holiest church on Gozo, it is the national shrine and the most venerated place in the archipelago. It all began in 1883 when the voice of Jesus was supposedly heard by a local lady called Carmela Ghrima. Several miraculous events

Anglo-Maltese influences are apparent in picturesque Għarb, a truly traditional Maltese village

+ 186 B3
Ta' Pinu Church
Near Għarb ☎ 21 556992 ⏰ Mon–Sat 6:30 am–12:30, 1:30–7, Sun 5:45 am–12:30, 1:30–7 💷 Free (men must wear long trousers – long shorts are not acceptable – and women must cover their shoulders and wear a long skirt, which can be loaned from the church)

7 Għarb

With its blue police lamp, red telephone box and golden sandstone buildings, the classic Maltese village square of Għarb has graced many a postcard.

Its parish **church**, begun in 1699, is particularly striking, and notable for its unusual concave façade.

Also on the square, a handsome 18th-century stone house is now home to the **Għarb Folklore Museum**. This is the archipelago's finest collection of bygones and memorabilia, with 28 rooms crammed full of interesting, well-captioned exhibits, giving an insight into island life in the 19th and early 20th century.

+ 186 B3
Folklore Museum
99 Church Square ☎ 21 561929 ⏰ Mon–Sat 9–4, Sun 9–1 💷 Inexpensive

happened and the small church attracted thousands of pilgrims. To cope with them the present huge basilica was built between 1920 and 1931. It encloses part of the original church and includes the tomb of Carmela Ghrima. Look into the side chapel where discarded plaster casts, leg braces and crutches, plus crash helmets, a lifejacket, pictures of cars marooned on cliff edges and so on, are touching testaments to miracle cures and narrow escapes. (Note the dress restriction for entering the church, ► below).

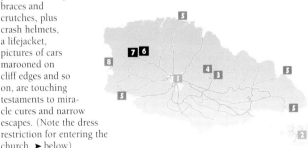

Three Romantic Spots for Outdoor Summer Dining
• Ta' Cenc Hotel, Sannat (➤ 149)
• L-Imgarr Hotel, Mġarr (➤ 150)
• Brookies, Victoria (➤ 150)

8 Dwejra Point

Dwejra Point is famous for its naturally formed giant rock arch known as the **Azure Window**, one of the most photographed images on the island. It is on the itinerary of every tour company and attracts large crowds. The most spectacular time to come is at sunset.

Just behind the ice-cream vans is a small lagoon known as Il-Qawra, the **Inland Sea**, fed by a narrow fissure which emerges just around the corner from the Azure Window. Fishermen's boats offer trips which pass through the cleft in the limestone rock and venture into the sea caves on the other side. It's worth jumping aboard as the colours match those of the more

Sea and wind have created the perfect "Azure Window" at Dwejra Point

famous Blue Grotto on Malta (➤ 93).

Opposite the Azure Window is a huge monolith known as **Fungus Rock**, home to a rare kind of parasitic plant. In the days of the Knights this was thought to be a cure for blood diseases and dysentery and was used to staunch the flow of blood from wounds. A primitive funicular system using boxes and pulleys was set up to harvest it. The Knights sent the plant as a present to heads of state, and anyone caught attempting to steal it was sentenced to three years in the slave galleys (a virtual death sentence). Alas, modern scientific tests have pronounced it of no medical use whatsoever!

✚ 186 A2

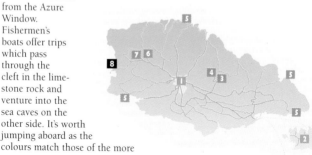

Where to... Stay

Prices
Expect to pay per double room per night
£ under LM15 ££ LM15–30 £££ LM31–50 ££££ over LM50

COMINO

Hotel Comino £££

This is the only choice if you want to stay overnight on Comino. The facilities of this well-equipped hotel are good, though the rooms are rather basic. If you really want to get away from it all, stay in one of the 45 bungalows. The sports facilities are excellent.

📍 186 D1 ✉ Comino ☎ 21 529821, www.cominohotels.com

XAGHRA

Cornucopia £££

Set just outside Xaghra, the Cornucopia is a small atmospheric hotel,

converted from a farmhouse to accommodate 50 rooms, two outdoor pools, a children's pool and other facilities. The rooms are fairly plain but with all mod cons. Across the road, under the same management, are 11 self-catering, two-bedroom bungalows sharing two more swimming pools.

📍 186 C2 ✉ 10 Gnien Imrik Street ☎ 21 556486; www.vjborg.com

MGARR

L-Imgarr ££££

High on the hill above Mgarr Harbour, this luxury hotel enjoys a wonderful view. Its 74 luxurious modern rooms have more than a

touch of Gozitan farmhouse style about them, with good use of wood and stone. There's a sauna, gym and two outdoor pools. Its well-regarded terrace restaurant is a wonderful setting for a romantic evening meal (▶ 150).

📍 186 D1 ✉ Mgarr ☎ 21 560455

XLENDI

St Patrick's ££

Set right on the front of Xlendi Bay, this well-equipped hotel is far and away the best accommodation in the resort. St Patrick's is owned by the proprietors of the Ta' Cenc Hotel (▶ below); much use is made of bare stone and potted plants, and the whole hotel is built around a covered central courtyard. There is a small splash pool on the roof overlooking the pretty, fjord-like bay. Prices are very reasonable and as long as peace and quiet aren't too high on your agenda this is a good choice. Rooms are nicely furnished, though be sure to specify a sea view

and consider an upgrade to the attractive superior rooms.

📍 186 B2 ✉ Xlendi ☎ 21 562951; www.vjborg.com

SANNAT

Ta' Cenc ££££

This superb, away-from-it-all luxury hotel is reckoned by most island critics to be the best in the archipelago. Its style is harmonious with the island; single storey, natural golden stone, beautifully landscaped, with drystone walls and luxuriant vegetation enclosing a peaceful "village" of around 85 small apartments and rooms. The most sought after are the completely round *trullos*. Inside they are cosy and very romantic. There are two swimming pools (one for adults only), two tennis courts, a private beach (2km away, reached by shuttle bus) and a very pretty outdoor restaurant Il-Carruba (▶ 150).

📍 186 B1 ✉ Sannat ☎ 21 561522; www.vjborg.com

Where to...
Eat and Drink

Prices
Prices indicate what you should pay per person for a three-course meal, excluding drinks and service charge.
£ under LM8 ££ LM8-12 £££ over LM12

VICTORIA (RABAT)

Brookies £££
Brookies is set in a beautifully converted 300-year-old farmhouse on the outskirts of Victoria. It is run by two professionally trained brothers who put a modern international touch to local dishes, such as stuffed quail in a red wine sauce. The pasta is good but fish is the speciality and portions are generous. In summer book a table on its romantic terrace.

🚩 186 B2 🖂 1-2 Wied Sara Street ☎ 21 559524 🕲 Wed–Mon dinner only

Ta' Rikardo £–££
Set in one of the Citadel's narrow lanes, there's no name outside, just a large wooden barrel with various comestibles on top. Downstairs in this old refurbished house is an attractive shop selling preserved foodstuffs, while upstairs is a rusticised dining room serving simple meals of bread, tomatoes, pickles, onion, Maltese cheese, cold meats and sausage, all washed down with local wine. It's an enjoyable and very apt place for a break while sightseeing in the Citadel (in fact, it is the only place!), but for what is

basically "peasant fayre", the bill is somewhat patrician.

🚩 186 B2 🖂 4 Triq il-Fosos ☎ 21 555953 🕲 Mon–Sat lunch only

MĠARR

L-Imġarr £££
On a warm summer night a seat on the candle-lit terrace of the chic Hotel L-Imġarr (▶ 149), looking out over Mġarr Bay and the distant lights of Malta is one of the nicest, most romantic places in the archipelago. The food – mostly Italian – is pretty good too; veal Milanese, roulade of turkey with aubergines and tomatoes, fish al Cartoccio, plus many flambée specialities.

🚩 186 D1 🖂 Mġarr ☎ 21 560455 🕲 Daily lunch and dinner

Manoel's ££
There are a number of attractive restaurants by the harbour in Mġarr, but with its handsome setting, in the 18th-century Custom House, and its unusual dishes, Manoel's is probably the pick of the bunch. Its owners are also renowned veterans of the island's restaurant scene. Start with creamed crab ramekin (gratiné of crab in a bechamel sauce), then choose the fish of the day or lamb fillets in a tangy caper sauce, and finish with walnut cheesecake. There is plenty of seating with views out over the harbour.

🚩 186 D1 🖂 27 Manoel de Vilhena Street ☎ 21 560721 🕲 Daily dinner only (closed Nov–Apr)

SANNAT

Il-Carruba £££
If you want a cast-iron guarantee of romance in the air, great service and a meal you won't forget in a hurry, bring along your gold credit card to the renowned Ta' Ċenc Hotel (▶ 149) on a summer's evening. Dining is intimate, al fresco on different levels, next to a sail-less windmill, under pergolas or a 150-year-old carob tree, surrounded by drystone walls and a profusion of

plants. Why not add to the theatricality by ordering dishes that are specially cooked at the table: "pasta springtime", fillet steak with cognac and pepper sauce, and of course crêpe flambée.

🚹 186 B1 🖾 Hotel Ta' Cenc 🖀 21 561522 🕓 Daily lunch and dinner

MARSALFORN

Il-Kartell ££–£££

Enjoying a perfect setting on the corner of Marsalforn Bay, Il-Kartell is one of Malta's best fish-without-fuss restaurants. Seating is outside under an awning, and is usually accompanied by music (sometimes live). A complimentary starter of lightly pickled tuna with a hint of chilli sets the tone. Choose a whole fish (you can always share) and have it simply barbecued. Finish off with a flambéed crêpe and cinnamon ice-cream.

🚹 186 C3 🖾 Marina Street 🖀 21 556918 🕓 Tue–Sun lunch and dinner; Fri–Sun only, Nov–Feb

Otters £–££

You won't find gourmet food at Otters, but if you're looking for a good-quality, reasonably priced pizza, pasta or steak, right on the seafront, at any time of day or night, this is a good place to come. Sports fans (or anti-sports fans) might like to know there are big TV screens here.

🚹 186 C3 🖾 St Mary Street 🖀 21 562473 🕓 Daily dinner only (reduced hours Jan–Feb)

Ta' Frenc £££

If you want to impress someone, or enjoy a romantic meal, Ta' Frenc is renowned as one of Gozo's more formal heavyweight hitters, offering a blend of French and Maltese cooking that makes liberal use of rich sauces. In chillier weather, diners retreat into the converted farmhouse interior. Start with chunky fish soup Ta' Frenc style, or perhaps seafood gratiné. Move on to lamb fillet fried with onion and tarragon, then simmered in red wine, or push

the boat out by going for lobster – as many as five different variations might be on offer. Finish off with trifle Maltese or a crêpe flambée. Service is efficient if a little wooden at times.

🚹 186 C3 🖾 Marsalforn Road (just south of Marsalforn) 🖀 21 553888 🕓 Daily lunch and dinner (closed Jan–Mar)

XLENDI

It-Tmun £££

Among foodies and the *cognoscenti*, "the Helmsman" is currently the place to eat on Gozo. Set just back from the seafront at Xlendi, and therefore avoiding the hustle and bustle, its calm, ordered terrace exudes style. It is run by a husband and wife team who put an international and Mediterranean spin on local produce. It's a good place for oysters as they're flown in daily.

🚹 186 B2 🖾 3 Mount Carmel Street 🖀 21 551571 🕓 Wed–Mon lunch and dinner

GHARB

Jeffrey's ££

A converted farmhouse with a delightful garden is the setting for this traditional, welcoming Gozitan restaurant. Start with the local salad, *insalata Gharbese* (tomatoes and fresh sheep's cheese) then tuck into rabbit in wine and garlic.

🚹 186 B3 🖾 10 Gharb Road 🖀 21 561006 🕓 Mon–Sat dinner only (closed Nov–Mar)

XAGHRA

Oleander £–££

The Oleander is probably the quintessential Gozo restaurant. It serves typical Maltese home-made dishes, such as *aljotta* (fish soup), *bragioli* (▶ 23), *ravjul* (ravioli) and stuffed chicken breast. In winter you can sit inside the cosy little dining room, decorated with works by local artists.

🚹 186 C2 🖾 Victory Square 🖀 21 557230 🕓 Tue–Sun lunch and dinner

Where to...
Shop

The choice of goods on Gozo is basically the same as on Malta, though there are fewer outlets.

Victoria has a small number of souvenir and craft shops, the biggest being **Citadella**, at the foot of the Citadel, while **Ta' Dbiegi Craft Village** is a smaller version of Malta's Ta' Qali (➤ 114).

The **daily market** in Victoria sells fruit and vegetables, beach towels, baseball caps, leather belts and various household items. It's colourful and worth a visit to see a slice of Gozitan life, but doesn't have many souvenirs.

Good places for gifts are the **Fontana Cottage Industry shop**, on the road from Victoria to Xlendi, and **Gozo Glass**, Gharb Street, just outside Gharb (tel: 21 561974, Mon–Sat 9–6, Sun 10–4), where you can watch glass being blown.

LOCAL PRODUCTS

The three main island products, as far as visitors are concerned, are **gbejna**, small rounds of goat's cheese (*gbejniet* is the peppered variety), **thick woollen jumpers** and **lace**. The cheese is ubiquitous, woollen jumpers, usually at very reasonable prices, can be found in Victoria and elsewhere, while the best place to find lace is in Sannat.

In the square behind the village church in Sannat is the **Old Lace House** where Queen Elizabeth II visited as a princess in 1951. There is no shop as such here, but you may still be able to buy direct. Knock on the door and ask. Real hand-made Gozitan lace is very expensive, reflecting the many hours of painstaking labour; cheap lace will almost certainly have been made elsewhere, and/or by machine.

Where to...
Be Entertained

ENTERTAINMENT

If you're a lover of **opera**, make enquiries (preferably well ahead of your trip) about the dates of the next performances in Victoria's two famous theatres (➤ 140), the **Aurora** (tel: 21 562974) and the **Astra** (tel: 21 556277), both on Republic Street. Failing that, you can always visit these venues to see the latest film releases.

The island's best nightclub is **il-Grotta**, partly located in a cave, and partly open-air. It's just outside Xlendi on the road to Victoria. Next door is **Paradiso**. Both nightclubs open for the summer season and draw large crowds.

Other good places to go are **Black Jack** in Victoria or **Ir-Rook** in Marsalforn.

SPORT

Gozo is a superb place for diving, with a dozen popular dive sites clustered around Xlendi, Dwejra and the northwest corner. They cater for all levels of experience (there are no wreck dives).

San Dimitri Point near Dwejra is exceptional for offering visibility that can exceed 50m. Not surprisingly, the limpid turquoise waters of **Comino** are also very popular. Reputable dive operators include **St Andrew's Divers** at Xlendi (tel: 21 551301). You could also contact the **Gozo Diving Centre** at Xewkija (tel: 21 551315). The same company operates boat cruises.

On Comino there is **Tony's Diving** at the Hotel Comino (tel: 21 529822).

Walks and Tours

1 VALLETTA

Walk

DISTANCE approx 2–3km
TIME 1–2 hours
START/END POINT City Gate ✚ 182 B3

Valletta, Malta's one true city, is tiny by modern city standards, and with its numerous steps and narrow streets, which are closed to, or unsuitable for motor vehicles, can only be explored on foot. Aside from its considerable weight of history, there are colourful local vignettes around most corners. This walk stays away from the central area where most of the attractions are found, but at any point you are only about three minutes from the main artery of Republic Street.

1–2

Once inside the City Gate, turn immediately right, past the tourist office and **St James Cavalier Centre for Creativity** (▶ 66), with the ruins of the Opera House in front of you. Keep right, passing the Church of Our Lady of Victory, to Misraħ Kastilja (Castile Place), where on your left is the splendid façade of the **Auberge de Castile** (▶ 50), one of the *auberges* (inns) of the Knights of St John.

Continue straight ahead to **Upper Barrakka Gardens** – the old Garrison Church on the right is now Malta's Stock Exchange – and enjoy the marvellous views from here over **Grand Harbour** (▶ 46–48).

2–3

Exit the Upper Barrakka Gardens to the right on to St Ursula Street, turn immediately right then left into Batterija (Battery) Street and keep straight on. You are now passing **St Barbara's Bastion**, possibly the nicest residential part of Valletta. The houses here are very well tended and enjoy fabulous views over Grand Harbour. Continue to **Lower Barrakka Gardens**. The battered Doric Temple memorial is dedicated to Sir Alexander Ball, the first British governor of Malta. Immediately below you is the Fish Market. The huge **Siege Bell** (▶ 47) is opposite.

The Siege Bell commemorates the victims of the Second Great Siege (1940–1943)

3–4

Continue along Irish Street/Mediterranean Street, passing the **Mediterranean Conference Centre** to the left (▶ 65) and the **Malta Experience** (▶ 78) to the right. Continue on and the road bends left. You have now reached the tip of the promontory, **Fort St Elmo** (▶ 58–59), scene of the bloodiest battle of the Great Siege of 1565 (▶ 10). Note the protuberances resembling manhole covers in front of the fort. These were underground granaries. Continue past the main entrance to the fort, and past the **National War Museum** (▶ 58–59).

Taking a Break

Gunpost Snack Bar
➕ 182 B4/C4 ⊠ Marsamxett Street ⏰ Daily lunch and dinner

Café Diva
➕ 182 C4 ⊠ Manoel Theatre; ▶ 70

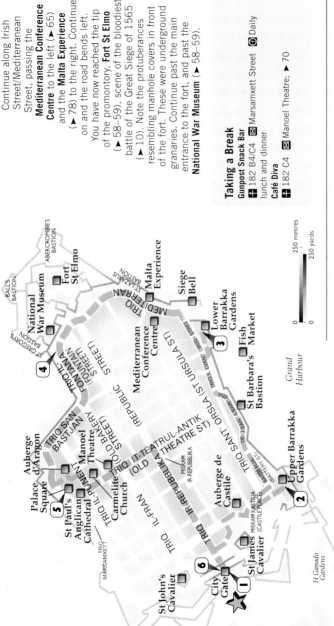

Marsamxett Harbour

Grand Harbour

```
0        250 metres
0        250 yards
```

The airy interior of the landmark
Carmelite Church

4–5

Head up Fountain Street, and bear right into St Sebastian Street. On the corner of here and West Street is one of the old *auberges* (inns) of the Knights (➤ 50–51), the **Auberge d'Angleterre et Baviere**, once shared by English and Bavarian knights. It is now a government office. Continue around the main perimeter road into Marsamxett Street. You are now on the other side of Valletta's promontory. Take a break at the unusual Gunpost Snack Bar, and enjoy the views of Marsamxett Harbour. Down below is the ferry that goes from Sliema to Valletta.

After another 100m turn left up the steps into **Palace Square**, dominated by the statue of the Maltese patriot, Dun Mikiel Xerri who, along with 33 companions, was executed by the occupying French forces in 1799 for plotting to open the city gates to the Maltese rebels. Across the square is the former **Auberge d'Aragon** (➤ 50), which is now also a government office.

5–6

Head right (with your back to the sea) out of the square, along West Street, passing **St Paul's Anglican Cathedral**. Its slender spire, usually seen from afar next to the great dome

of the Carmelite Church, is a Valletta landmark. Inside it is very modest. Further along, the **Auberge d'Allemagne** was demolished in 1838 to make way for the church.

Just past here, on the junction with Old Theatre Street, on the right hand side by the steps, is a plaque commemorating the brief sojourn of Sir Walter Scott at the Beverly Hotel on this site in 1831.

Turn left up Old Theatre Street and on the left is the entrance to the **Carmelite Church**. Badly bombed during World War II, its light, airy interior was completely rebuilt and is well worth a look inside.

A little further up the street, on the corner with Old Bakery Street, is the **Manoel Theatre** (➤ 63), one of Valletta's hidden gems and also an excellent spot for a break – coffee or lunch.

From here Old Bakery Street heads directly back

to St John's Cavalier and City Gate, or you can walk two more blocks, passing Strait Street to bustling Republic Street, which also runs directly back to City Gate.

Strait Street has been Valletta's most infamous street since the days of the Knights. They would come here to duel, though it was strictly forbidden and risked severe punishment. In the 20th century it became Valletta's red-light area, attracting British servicemen (who nicknamed it "The Gut").

2 VITTORIOSA

Walk

DISTANCE 2–3km
TIME 1–2 hours
START/END POINT The Three Gates ⊞ 181 E2

Vittoriosa, or Birgu as it used to be called, was the seat of the Knights of St John from 1530 onwards, and had its greatest moment in 1565 when it held out as their last refuge against the Ottoman invasion (►10). After their victory, the Knights moved their headquarters to Valletta, but their galleys and arsenals remained here. Today it's all very quiet and mostly residential, though this walk will pick up the Knights' trail and show you some of their former haunts.

1–2

Although it's difficult to picture the fortifications of Vittoriosa as they stand today, the best entrance is through **The Three Gates**, comprising the Advanced Gate (rebuilt 1722), the Couvre Port and the Main Gate.

The Couvre Port is also home to Café Bccaccio, the best restaurant in Vittoriosa (►70). Book a meal here for when you finish the walk.

The Three Gates entrance zigzags its way through to the main street, Triq il-Mina L-Kbira, emerging almost opposite another fortification, St John's Cavalier. Turn left, pass the Church of the Annunciation on your left, and a little further on, right, is the **Inquisitor's Palace** (►51).

After visiting here continue to the main square, the **Piazza Vittoriosa** (Victory Square).

2–3

There are a number of interesting features in Piazza Vittoriosa, including the **Victory Monument**, built in 1705 in memory of the Great Siege of 1565, and the intricate façade of the **St Lawrence Band Club building**, giving an insight into how the Maltese prize this aspect of island life.

To the left, note the small stone bollard marked with the letter "C". It stands for

The Victory Monument, dedicated to the heroes of the Great Siege of 1565

Collachio del Ordine and was one of the boundary markers of the private area of the Order of the Knights.

One of the Knights' inns, or *auberges* (➤ 50–51), the Auberge d'Allemagne, stood right on the square, to the left of here, before it was destroyed in 1942. A marble tablet commemorates it.

Keep on this side of the square and look up at the small stone crucifix relief high on the building on the corner with **Triq Hilda Tabone** (Britannic Street). It marks the place where public executions were held prior to the 16th century.

Cottonera

While in this area you may well hear, or see signposted, the name Cottonera or Cottonera Lines. These were a series of defensive fortifications built by Grand Master Cottoner in the 1670s to protect Vittoriosa, Senglea and Cospicua, and the name became a synonym for this area. It is also known as "The Three Cities".

3–4

Triq Hilda Tabone was the main street for the Knights in Birgu in the early 16th century. The *auberges* of France, Castile, Portugal, Auvergne and Provence once graced this street, but now only name plaques remain.

A few metres on the right turn into Triq Majjistral (Mistral Street) where the English Knights' **Auberge d'Angleterre** survives. It is now a public library (open Mon–Sat 7:30–1:30, summer; Mon–Sat 8:30–4:30, winter). Adjoining this is the house of Sir Oliver Starkey, secretary and friend to Grand Master La Valette (➤ 54).

Go back to Triq Hilda Tabone, continue for a short way and turn right into Triq-it-Tramuntana, where at No 11 you will find

0 — 250 metres
0 — 250 yards

the **Norman House** in Vittoriosa, dating from the 11th century; note its fine Siculo-Norman window. In Malta, Norman or Siculo-Norman covers the period from around 1070 (the arrival of the Normans) to 1530 (the arrival of the Knights.

4–5

Return to the main square, go straight across and leave it by the street on the left, passing on the left the **Church of St Lawrence** (➤ 49) and its Oratory of St Joseph. In front of here is the **Freedom Monument** commemorating independence from

The plaque high on the corner of Triq Hilda Tabone and Piazza Vittoriosa shows that executions once took place here

Kalkara Cr...

5 Fort St Angelo

Map labels:
VITTORIOSA (BIRGU)
Casinò di (BIRGU)
Casinò di Venezia
St Lawrence Band Club
Norman House
Auberge d'Angleterre
Inquisitor's Palace
Piazza Vittoriosa
Church of St Lawrence
Maritime Museum
Freedom Monument
The Three Gates
TRIQ IL MINA IL-KBIRA
TRIQ BOFFA
TRIQ SAN LAWRENZ
TRIQ HILDA TABONE
SENGLEA
kyard Creek

Fort St Angelo, headquarters for both Great Sieges

Britain. In 1799 Lord Nelson's representative landed here to govern Malta, and from here the last British military contingent left the island in 1979.

Continue along the waterfront, where you can visit the **Maritime Museum** (➤ 49) and on the tip of the promontory **Fort St Angelo** (➤ 50). In between, the **Casinò de Venezia** (➤ 49 and 78) occupies the former residence of the Captain General of the Galleys.

5–6
Walk back along the waterfront and up the ramp to return to the Three Gates.

Taking a Break
Café Boccaccio
➕ 181 E2 ⊠ Couvre Porte ☎ 21 675757
🕐 Sun–Fri 11:30–3, Sat–Sun 7–10:30

3 MDINA
Walk

DISTANCE approx 2km
TIME 1–2 hours
START/END POINT The Main Gate ✚ 180 C3

Mdina (▶104–106), known as "The Silent City", seems inappropriately named at the height of summer when crowds of visitors tramp along Villegaignon Street. Mdina is so small that it's hard to get too far off the beaten track. However, this short walk will try to show you a few of its less obvious corners.

1–2

Immediately inside the Main Gate the building to the left is the **Torre dello Standardo**, built as a watch-tower in 1750. A beacon fire here would alert the population to invaders. Today, it's a police station. Opposite is the **Palazzo Vilhena**, originally built in 1730 as the seat of the city's Università (governing body). The main body of the palace houses the Natural History Museum. Part of it served as the law courts and its basement has been converted to the grisly **Mdina Dungeons**, a graphic portrayal of some of the darker episodes in Malta's history.

Turn left at the end of this square and just on the corner with Villegaignon Street, locked but visible behind a grille, is the **Chapel of St Agatha**, rebuilt in 1694. It contains a graphic image of Agatha, one of Malta's three patron saints, being mutilated. It is thought she took refuge in the catacombs in Rabat (▶109) before meeting a grisly end in Sicily in AD 251. Almost opposite, at No 6, is the 1370 **Casa Inguanez**, the palace of one of the oldest families in Malta and still in their hands.

2–3

Continue up Villegaignon Street a short way to Mesquita Street. Note the "Gilders" workshop of **Joe Farrugia & Son** and peer into the window to see religious statues being re-gilded. Next door is the 17th-century **Casa Viani**, which got its 15 seconds of fame in 1798 when the French Commander was thrown off

The Midas Touch of the Farrugia family brings new life to important statues in "The Silent City"

its balcony. The people of Mdina were furious that he was selling off tapestries from the looted Carmelite church (further along the street) and it was this incident that sparked the beginning of the uprising against the French occupation. Opposite is another historic noble house, the **Casa Testaferrata** (the building with the red doors).

Turn left into Mesquita Street and in Mesquita Square is **The Mdina Experience** audio-visual show (▶ 106), housed in a medieval patrician building.

Continue through the square to Magazine Street and the **West Gate** to the city. There is a fine view looking down on to the surrounding countryside.

3–4

Retrace your steps and turn left back into Villegaignon Street, passing various aristocratic palaces now converted into tourist attractions. On the corner of Holy Cross Street, the **Palazzo Santa Sophia** is said to be the oldest house in the city, with its ground floor dating from the 13th century.

A little further along, across the street, is the best-preserved of all Mdina's many *palazzi*, the **Palazzo Falzon** (▶ 105).

4–5

Villegaignon Street ends at **Bastion Square**, famous for its views. In less peaceful times it was a gun position. If it's time for a coffee or a lunch break at this point, don't follow the crowds to the **Fontanella Tea Rooms** (▶ 112), but turn left to **Ciappetti** (▶ 111) instead.

Map labels:
0 100 metres
0 100 yards

West Gate
Greek Gate
Palazzo Falzon
PIAZZA TAS-SUR
SANTU ROKKU
St Paul's Cathedral
Bishop's Palace
Cathedral Museum
MISRAH SAN PAWL
TRIQ TAS-SUR
VILLEGAIGNON
(MAGAZINE STREET)
The Mdina Experience
Palazzo Santa Sophia
Casa Testaferrata
SAN NIKOLA
MISRAH MESQUITA
TRIQ L-IMRAZEN
TRIQ L-IMRAZEN
MISRAH TAL-MINA TAL-GRIEGI
Casa Viani
Casa Inguanez
TRIQ MESQUITA
Nunnery of St Benedict
Xara Palace Hotel
Chapel of St Agatha
Palazzo Vilhena
Torre dello Standardo
Main Gate
TRIQ IL-MINA L-IMDINA
Mdina Dungeons
Howard Gardens

5–6

From Bastion Square turn right and follow the street round. Turn right into Triq Santu Rokku (St Roque Street) and left into St Paul's Square where you'll find **St Paul's Cathedral**

St Paul's Cathedral Square provides Mdina's only large open space

6–7

Go round the back of the Archbishop's Palace into Triq San Pawl (St Paul's Street). On the right notice the **Nunnery of St Benedict**, a medieval hospital for women which took its present shape in 1625. Today around 20 nuns live in here, adhering to strict rules that have changed little over the centuries. The nuns are never allowed to leave the building; even after death they are buried in the vaults. They spend their days in prayer and tending their small garden.

St Paul's Street ends in a charming little square graced by the **Xara Palace Hotel** (➤ 111). Its informal café/restaurant, **Trattoria AD 1530** (➤ 112), is the perfect place to take a break at the end of your walk. Just around the corner is the Main Gate.

(➤ 105–106). According to early Christian lore it was built on the site where St Paul converted the Roman governor, Publius to Christianity. On the other side of the cathedral is the 1722 **Bishop's Palace** and the **Cathedral Museum** (➤ 106), originally a seminary, built in 1733. It contains a fine collection of art and many interesting religious objects.

Taking a Break
Ciappetti
➕ 180 C3 ✉ 5 St Agatha's Esplanade
☎ 21 459987 🕐 Daily 10 am–late

Trattoria AD 1530
➕ 180 C3 ✉ Xara Palace Hotel, Misraħ il-Kunċill ☎ 21 450560 🕐 Daily 11–6, 7–11

4 DINGLI CLIFFS
Drive

DISTANCE approx 12km
TIME Driving 30 minutes, plus walking 30 minutes
START/END POINT Mdina ✚ 180 C3

Peace and quiet are pretty rare commodities in Malta, so it's well worth making the short trip to Dingli Cliffs, one of the island's best beauty spots. At the height of summer the cooling breezes are particularly welcome. If you're lucky, you may even hear the occasional bird singing (but avoid coming here during the hunting season; ➤ 121, and particularly in the early morning and in the evening).

1–2

From Mdina take the main road south for 3km, following the signs to **Dingli** and bypassing the centre of the village. At the **Mater Dolorosa Church** fork left and continue until you reach the cliffs. Ahead is a large abandoned building, which was formerly an Armed Forces Post.

At this point you turn left (if you turn right here, after another kilometre you'll find the area's most popular restaurant, Bobbyland, ➤ 97).

2–3

This area has long been popular with the security forces and after another 300m is a large **"golfball" tracking station**. It's worth stopping and getting out of the car for the views. The clifftop road is not quite as precarious as it first appears, but resist the temptation to venture down as the descent is dangerous and even if you make it down in one piece there are no proper paths and the land here is all privately owned.

After another 500m you will come to the **Madalena Chapel.** Away to the left the sandcastle-like building is the **Verdala Palace**, built in 1586 for Grand Master Fra Huges de Verdale. Today it is the summer residence of the president.

3–4

Just set back from the cliffs is the cluster of ancient "cart ruts" known as **Clapham Junction** (➤ 28). To get there turn off the cliff road left towards Buskett Gardens and Clapham Junction is signposted.

Some of the ruts continue and actually disappear over the cliff edge, for example, at Ghar Zerrieq (though you will need an expert

Ancient stones and 20th-century technology happily co-exist

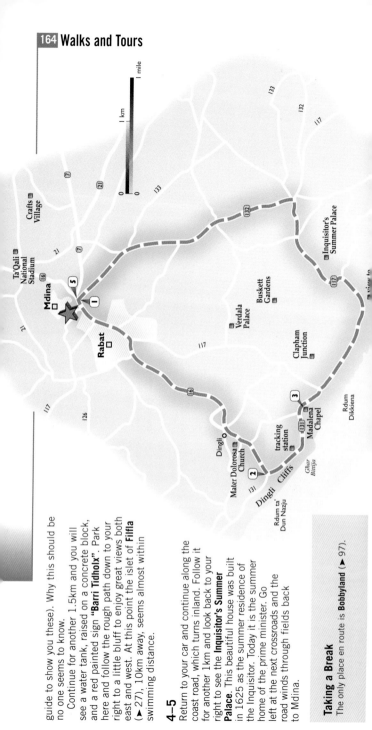

guide to show you these). Why this should be no one seems to know.

Continue for another 1.5km and you will see a water tank, raised on a concrete block, and a red painted sign **"Barri Tidholx"**. Park here and follow the rough path down to your right to a little bluff to enjoy great views both east and west. At this point the islet of **Filfla** (➤ 27), 10km away, seems almost within swimming distance.

4–5

Return to your car and continue along the coast road, which turns inland. Follow it for another 1km and look back to your right to see the **Inquisitor's Summer Palace**. This beautiful house was built in 1625 as the summer residence of the Inquisitor. Today it is the summer home of the prime minister. Go left at the next crossroads and the road winds through fields back to Mdina.

Taking a Break

The only place en route is **Bobbyland** (➤ 97).

5 GOZO
Walk/Drive/Cycle

DISTANCE 11.5km **TIME** Total route: driving 30 minutes; cycling 45 minutes; walking 2–2.5 hours; Ghasri-Marsalforn walking 1.5 hours
START POINT Victoria/Ghasri ✚ 186 B2/B3 **END POINT** Marsalforn/Victoria ✚ 186 C3/B2

This diverse route takes you along a valley full of colourful wild flowers in spring and early summer, to saltpans that have a fascinating folk history, a beautiful little bay and one of Gozo's finest natural sights.

1–2

From Victoria (Rabat) head west towards Gharb. After just over 1km, turn right to **Ghasri** (signposted) to the church square. With the church behind you, leave the square by the top left corner. After 100m turn left (signposted to **Wied l-Ghasri**) and keep straight ahead, following the Wied l-Ghasri signs. Just past the last of the houses you will pass a chapel. After another 200m the road becomes a dirt track. Look to your left to see the *wied* (valley) running down to the sea. In the height

The cone-shaped formation on the headland has been formed by saltpans, which still produce large amounts of salt each year

of summer it is dry and scorched, but from spring to early summer it is a riot of colourful wild flowers and herbs. Continue straight on and just past a farmhouse the dirt track becomes a surfaced road again. After another 500m look left to see the **Ta' Gordan lighthouse**, while high on the hill to your right is the village of Żebbuġ.

After another 400m the road dips sharply (cyclists beware). There is a small fork to the left after 100m but ignore this and carry straight on.

2–3
After another 400m you will see the sea and the first of the **saltpans** (▶ 168). These have been in use since Roman times and still produce many tons each year. As you round the corner and come to a proper tarmac road, ahead in the distance are weird eroded sandstone shapes, the most prominent being

the small volcano-like formation. Behind it are the remains of a castle. The road gets more picturesque as you continue, with the

sea reflecting back from the saltpans below and soft, rounded sandstone walls coming right down to the edge of the road. Pause and look down to the plateau of salt-pans. The cave-like holes in the back of the rock face are used for drying the salt.

3–4
The road continues for another 1km, ending in picturesque little **Xweini Bay** (pronounced *sh-way-nee*) where local people

Taking a Break

Horizon Bar/Restaurant
🏠 186 C3 ⊠ Qbajjar Bay

Il Kartell
🏠 186 C3 ⊠ Marina Street, Marsalforn 🕿 21
556918 🕐 Tue–Sun lunch and dinner; Fri–Sun only, Nov–Feb

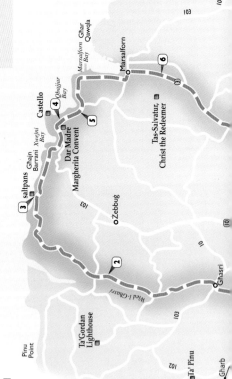

swim and fish. The crystal-clear waters are excellent for swimming and snorkelling, and there are handrails to get help you in and out of the water.

Continue around the bay until you are opposite the castle promontory. Note on the right the **Dar Madre Margherita Convent**. This is a summer home used by

By Foot, by Bus, by Bike

If you want to walk this route, but don't fancy the idea of the busy main roads linking Victoria to Ghasri or Marsalforn to Victoria, catch bus No 10 or 91 from Victoria to Ghasri and bus No 21 from Marsalforn to Victoria. In summer No 21 also goes to Qbajjar Bay. Bikes can be hired in Victoria or Marsalforn – enquire at the tourist office in Victoria (➤ 33). You don't have to be an experienced cyclist to tackle this route, but a mountain bike is recommended on any of the dirt roads.

Kerċem

Fontana○

Victoria (Rabat)

①
②
⑩ ⑫ ⑬
★
¼

Maltese nuns and you may see them sitting outside in their white summer habits, sewing or knitting, or swimming in the sea, still in their habits.

4–5
If you are driving, park your car here and walk down the small incline to enter **Qbajjar Bay** (pronounced "ch" [glottal stop]-buy-yar) on the other side of the castle.

Sit and enjoy peaceful views from the Horizon bar/restaurant at Qbajjar Bay

Here, hidden away from the main road, is the appropriately named **Horizon bar/ restaurant**. Take a seat on its terrace and you've found one of the finest spots in the archipelago for a coffee or cold drink. The food here is pretty good, too, although service can be a bit too much on the laid-back side.

In the foreground local children splash in the water and a fishing boat occasionally draws in and out. Beyond, a calm blue sea stretches to the horizon.

5–6

Follow the road around the coast until you reach the beginnings of **Marsalforn**, a pretty, traditional fishing village. A sharp left will take you to the front, passing the **Il-Kartell restaurant** (➤151), the best fish restaurant on Gozo.

Go over a small bridge and turn right to head back towards Victoria. Turn right again and then straight on. After 500m or so look to your right to see the small **statue of Tas-Salvatur, Christ the Redeemer**, modelled on the famous statue in Brazil.

Continue back to Victoria.

Malta's (smaller) version of the famous Christ the Redeemer statue in Brazil, Tas-Salvatur

Tragic Saltworks

"It is about thirteen to fourteen years ago from the present day, 1788, that a clockmaker from Malta had the bright idea of constructing a salt-works by cutting out shallow salt pans and filling them with sea water. He flattered himself that the sun's heat would evaporate the water and that it would deposit salt, which would cost him practically nothing and would bring him a nice profit…Imagine his surprise when he discovered that the water was disappearing not because it evaporated, but because it was being absorbed by the porous rock…and he [had] collected only a thick sludge…Waves driven by the gusts piled up in this cave…formed a spectacular geyser…It fell inundating the land for more than a mile with an abundant salty rain which destroyed the vegetation and terribly ravaged the fields that had been cultivated with great care…the Gozitans brought charges against [him], and demanded of him such enormous sums in compensation that he [couldn't] pay; these demands so aggravated his grief and his malady that he died of them."

Voyage Pittoresque des Isles de Sicile, de Lipari et de Malte, Jean Houel, 1788

6 VICTORIA (RABAT) CITADEL, GOZO
Walk

DISTANCE 1–2km
TIME Walking 30–45 minutes, sightseeing 1 hour
START/END POINT Cathedral Square, Victoria (Rabat) ✚ 186 B2

It's easy enough to see Victoria's Citadel without a guide, and small enough that you won't get lost. This short walk points out some of the area's details and historic anecdotes (➤ 138–141).

1–2
The large entrance arch into **Misraħ il-Katidral** (Cathedral Square) was only knocked through in 1957, the original is to the right. To the left is the former **Governor's Palace**, now used as the Law Courts. Straight ahead is the **Cathedral** (➤ 141). It was elevated to cathedral status in 1861 but in size and grandeur is more akin to a superior parish church. As in the cathedrals of Valletta and Mdina, the nave pavement features beautiful inlaid marble tombstones. Marvel at the *trompe l'oeil* ceiling.

From the Cathedral, turn right into Triq il-Fosos (Fosse Street) and through a side entrance is the first of the four Citadel museums, the **Cathedral Museum**, with a modest collection of religious paintings, church decoration and old manuscripts.

2–3
Backtrack a few steps and turn right into Triq Bernardo de Opuo where you will find the charming **Folklore Museum**, made up of three early 16th-century houses with rare surviving Norman-style windows. This is the most popular of the Citadel museums, with a lovely setting and some curious bygones. High on the wall opposite, a plaque marks the house of Bernardo de Opuo. Rather than let his wife and two daughters be enslaved in the 1551 invasion, he killed them before fighting to his death against the Turks.

Continue along the street and at the end turn right, through the archway, into Triq il-Kwartier San Gwann which leads to the north **ramparts** and magnificent views across the north of the island. Follow these to your left, along

surviving sections of the older medieval citadel with views to the west across the island. Turn left back into Triq il-Kwartier.

On the right, behind a locked grille, is a small armoury exhibition. This building was originally the Citadel granary. Opposite is the **Natural History Museum**, with its collection of minerals and stuffed animals and birds. Follow the walls round and you are back in Cathedral Square.

3–4
Pass through the narrow entrance between the wall and the Chapter

The cathedral is more ornate inside than out

ramparts

TRIQ IL-KWARTIER
SAN GWANN

TRIQ
IL-FOSOS

Cathedral
Museum

2

ST JOHN
DEMI-BASTION

Ditch

Natural
History
Museum

3

TRIQ DE BERNARDO
DE OPUO

Folklore
Museum

Armoury

TRIQ IL-KWARTIER

Governor's
Palace

Cathedral
Square

TRIQ IL-FOSOS

Cathedral

craft
shops

ST MARTIN
DEMI-BASTION

1

Main
Gate

4

TRIQ BEB IL-IMDINA

Museum of
Archaeology

ST MICHAEL
BASTION

0   50 metres

0   50 yards

Places to Visit

Cathedral Museum, Folklore Museum, Museum of Archaeology, Natural History Museum (►141).

Hall, built in 1899. The gap in the wall was the original main gate, as noted by its Roman inscription. In front of you is the **Museum of Archaeology**, housed in the citadel's last surviving palace, the former Palazzo Bondi.

Turn right out of here and go along Triq Bieb l-Imdina which leads to a series of small craft shops located in rooms that were prison cells between 1880 and 1964. Come back this way and walk up the stairs beside the Museum of Archaeology on to the St Michael Bastion. From here you can look down over the town centre and east across the island. Return to Cathedral Square.

Taking a Break

Ta' Rikardo

+ 186 B3 **⊠** 4 Triq il-Fosos **☎** 21 555953
◉ Mon–Sat lunch only

Practicalities

GETTING ADVANCE INFORMATION

Websites

- Malta Tourist Office
  www.visitmalta.com
- www.searchmalta.com
- www.tourism.org.mt
- www.gozo.com

In the UK (also for the Republic of Ireland)
Malta Tourist Office
Malta House
36–38 Piccadilly
London W1J 0LD

☎ 020 7292 4900;
fax: 020 7734 1880;
email:
office.uk@visitmalta.com

BEFORE YOU GO

WHAT YOU NEED

- ● Required
- ○ Suggested
- ▲ Not required
- △ Not applicable

	UK	Germany	USA	Canada	Australia	Ireland	Netherlands	Spain
Passport/National Identity Card	●	●	●	●	●	●	●	▲
Visa	▲	▲	▲	▲	▲	▲	▲	▲
Onward or Round-Trip Ticket	●	●	●	●	●	○	●	▲
Health Inoculations (tetanus and polio)	▲	▲	▲	▲	▲	▲	▲	▲
Health Documentation (►176, Health)	▲	▲	▲	▲	▲	●	▲	▲
Travel Insurance	○	○	○	○	○	○	○	○
Driver's Licence (national)	●	●	●	●	●	●	●	●
Car Insurance Certificate	●	●	●	●	●	●	●	●
Car Registration Document	●	●	●	●	●	●	●	●

WHEN TO GO

Peak season   Off-season

JAN	FEB	MAR	APR	MAY	JUN	JUL	AUG	SEP	OCT	NOV	DEC
15°C	15°C	16°C	19°C	23°C	28°C	30°C	31°C	28°C	24°C	20°C	17°C

Very wet   Wet   Cloud   Sun   Sun/Showers

Temperatures are the **average daily maximum** for each month. Average daily minimum temperatures are 5° to 9°C lower. The best times of the year for **good weather** are May, June and early to mid-September, when it is warm and dry without being uncomfortably hot. July and August are scorching, with temperatures pushing up to the mid-30sC. On the coast **sea breezes** usually make life more bearable, though the **hot dry sirocco** can sweep in from North Africa and make things worse. **High winds** sometimes occur during spring and there is **heavy rainfall** often in October and between then and March **showers** are likely. Little rain falls in May, June and August and virtually none in July.

In the USA (also for
Canada)
Malta National
Tourist Office
300 Lanidex Plaza
Parsippany

NJ 07054
☎ 973/884-0899;
fax: 973/884-3425;
email:
office.us@visitmalta.com

GETTING THERE

By Air The national airline, **Air Malta** (tel: 21 690890), operates scheduled flights from
major European cities, and there are also charter flights. Gozo has no airport. Many
seats are sold by tour operators as part of a package holiday, but it is possible to get a
flight-only deal through travel agents or on the internet. For independent travellers, the
disadvantage of charter flights is that you are usually restricted to periods of 7 or 14 days.

There are no direct scheduled flights to Malta from the USA, Canada, Australia or New
Zealand. There are occasional US packages including a number of specialist archaeological
and New Age-oriented tours. If you want to travel independently, **Transatlantic** fly to a
European hub airport (for example London or Rome), and then on to Malta.

If you are travelling from Australia or New Zealand, enquire at your local embassy or
tourist office. The **cheapest route** may be via Southeast Asia, Russia or Egypt, but prices do
change. Depending on your other plans, a Round the World ticket may be the best option.

By Sea There are **ferry and catamaran services** from southern Italy and Sicily to Malta
(Valletta). Embarkation cards are to be filled in before passport control.

Travelling between Malta and Gozo Ferries from Malta to Gozo (Mġarr) depart from Ċirkewwa
(20-minute crossing) or Sa Maison (75 minutes). Services are frequent. In summer there
are also passenger-only hover-marine services from Sa Maison to Mġarr (25 minutes) and
from Sliema (30 minutes); some trips go via the island of Comino. For information on all
services, tel: 21 556114.

TIME

Malta is one hour ahead of Greenwich Mean Time (GMT+1), but from late
March, when clocks are put forward one hour, to late September, summer time
(GMT+2) operates.

CURRENCY AND FOREIGN EXCHANGE

Currency The monetary unit of Malta is the Maltese *lira* (plural: *liri*), which is abbreviated
to LM. It is sometimes confusingly referred to as the pound or the Maltese pound. The lira
is divided into 100 *cents* (c). Coins come in denominations of 1, 2, 5, 10, 25 and 50
cents and 1 lira, and notes come in 2, 5, 10 and 20 liri.

Credit cards Credit cards are accepted in the resorts and ATMs are common. Elsewhere
it's best to carry cash. Some petrol stations, even in built-up areas, only accept cash.

Exchange and travellers' cheques Exchange bureaux generally offer a better deal than
banks when charges are taken into account, but it often pays to shop around. Travellers'
cheques in sterling are widely accepted. Some establishments, typically those run by ex-
pats and with strong links to the UK, will also accept sterling currency, though you may
pay a slight premium for the service.

Practicalities 173

TIME DIFFERENCES

GMT	Malta	Germany	USA (New York)	Spain	Sydney
12 noon	→ 1 pm	→ 1 pm	← 7 am	→ 1 pm	→ 10 pm

WHEN YOU ARE THERE

CLOTHING SIZES

UK	Malta	USA	
36	46	36	
38	48	38	
40	50	40	Suits
42	52	42	
44	54	44	
46	56	46	
7	41	8	
7.5	42	8.5	
8.5	43	9.5	Shoes
9.5	44	10.5	
10.5	45	11.5	
11	46	12	
14.5	37	14.5	
15	38	15	
15.5	39/40	15.5	Shirts
16	41	16	
16.5	42	16.5	
17	43	17	
8	34	6	
10	36	8	
12	38	10	Dresses
14	40	12	
16	42	14	
18	44	16	
4.5	38	6	
5	38	6.5	
5.5	39	7	Shoes
6	39	7.5	
6.5	40	8	
7	41	8.5	

NATIONAL HOLIDAYS

1 Jan	New Year's Day
10 Feb	Feast of St Paul's Shipwreck
19 Mar	Feast of St Joseph
31 Mar	Freedom Day
Mar/Apr	Good Friday
1 May	Workers' Day
7 Jun	Sette Giugno (Commemoration of 7 June, 1919)
29 Jun	Feast of St Peter and St Paul
15 Aug	Feast of the Assumption
8 Sep	Victory Day
21 Sep	Independence Day
8 Dec	Feast of the Immaculate Conception
13 Dec	Republic Day
25 Dec	Christmas Day

OPENING HOURS

○ Shops	● Post Offices
● Offices	● Museums/Monuments
● Banks	● Pharmacies

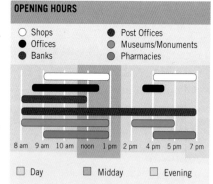

8 am 9 am 10 am noon 1 pm 2 pm 4 pm 5 pm 7 pm

☐ Day   ■ Midday   ☐ Evening

Shops Many shops in tourist areas stay open throughout the day. In Valletta shops close at 1 pm on Saturday, and except for a few in Buġibba, shops are closed on Sunday.

Offices Offices open around 8:30 am, but do not reopen for the afternoon during the height of summer.

Banks Banks open 8:30–12:45 in winter and also open on Friday 2:30–4 (4:30–6 in winter) and on Saturday 8–11:30 (8:30–noon in winter).

POLICE 191 (on Gozo: 21 562044)

FIRE 199 (on Gozo: 21 562044)

AMBULANCE 196

PERSONAL SAFETY

There is little to fear on Malta and Gozo as the crime rate is low and people are generally honest and courteous. The police (*pulizija*) wear blue uniforms and have a station in every town and village. Report any crime to them immediately.

Some precautions:

- Leave valuables in your hotel or apartment safe, never on the beach nor visible in a car.
- Don't make yourself an obvious target for bag snatchers or pickpockets.

Police assistance:

☎ **191** (on Gozo: 21 562044) from any phone

TELEPHONES

take a phonecard (*telecard*) available for LM2, LM3 or LM5 from Maltacom offices, post offices, banks and newsagents. The prefix 21 should be added to all numbers in Malta and Gozo, except for mobile phone numbers. There is no special prefix for calls from Gozo to Malta.

Malta's public telephone boxes are either green, red or transparent booths. Few phones accept coins, but most

International Dialling Codes

Dial 00 followed by	
UK:	44
USA/Canada.:	1
Republic of Ireland:	353
Australia:	61
Germany:	49

POST OFFICES

Normal post offices opening hours are Mon–Sat 7:45–1:30. Closed Sun. The post office at 305 Qormi Road, Qormi (tel: 21 224421) is open Mon–Sat 7:45–6:30. On Gozo the post office at 129 Republic Street, Victoria (tel: 21 556435) is open later.

ELECTRICITY

The power supply is 220/240 volts, 50 Hz. Sockets are the 3-square-hole type taking

square plugs with 3 square pins. Visitors from continental Europe should bring an adaptor. Visitors from the US will require a voltage transformer.

TIPS/GRATUITIES

Tipping is not expected for all services. As a general guide the following applies:

Restaurant waiters (service not included)	10%
Cafés/bars	Small change
Taxis	Discretion
Porters	50c
Chambermaids	5–10%
Cloakroom attendants	Small change
Toilet attendants	Small change

CONSULATES

UK	USA	Germany	Australia	New Zealand
21 233134/5/6	21 235960/5	21 336531	21 213382	21 435025
(High Commission)	(Embassy)	(Embassy)		

HEALTH

 Insurance Nationals of the UK and certain other countries staying less than 30 days get free medical treatment with the Maltese health service, but prescribed medicines must be paid for. Private medical insurance is advised for all.

 Dental Services Dental treatment must be paid for. If you need a dentist, enquire at your hotel or call directory enquiries (tel: 190 on Malta, 890 on Gozo). Private medical insurance covering dental treatment is advised for all visitors.

 Weather The Maltese islands bask in virtual year-round sunshine almost non-stop April to September. The sun is at its strongest in July and August, so wearing a sunhat and covering up the skin is highly recommended. No topless/nude sunbathing is allowed.

 Drugs On Malta, pharmacies, usually known as chemists, are recognisable by a neon green cross sign. They sell most international drugs and medicines over the counter or by prescription. They open normal shop hours, with a Sunday duty roster.

 Safe Water Tap water is quite safe, although not very tasty. Water from fountains should be avoided as it may not come directly from the mains supply. Bottled "table" water is widely available, at a reasonable cost, along with imported mineral water.

CONCESSIONS

Students/Youths Holders of an International Student Identity Card (ISIC) can take advantage of concessions for students, including reductions of between 15 and 40 per cent on transport, exhibitions, restaurants and shops, while entrance to museums is free.

Senior Citizens Malta is a popular destination for senior citizens as it offers low-cost, long-stay winter package holidays. However, apart from a reduction on some museum entrance fees, there are no specific discounts available.

TRAVELLING WITH A DISABILITY

Malta is not an easy destination for travellers with certain disabilities and facilities can only be found in the larger hotels and newer resorts. Unmade roads, thoughtless parking, steep kerbs and lack of ramps conspire to make life difficult for wheelchair users. The Maltese National Commission for Persons with Disabilities should be able to help (tel: 21 245952; www.knpd.org)

CHILDREN

Most hotels and restaurants are geared towards families and the Maltese are very tolerant of children. However, outside hotels and resorts there are few, if any, facilities such as high-chairs or baby-changing facilities.

TOILETS

Use the toilets that are provided in cafés or hotels as public toilets are rare and to be avoided if possible.

CUSTOMS

The import of wildlife souvenirs sourced from rare or endangered species may be either illegal or require a special permit. Before buying, check your home country's customs regulations.

Maltese (or Malti) and English are the official languages of Malta and Gozo. Almost everyone speaks English but a knowledge of basic Maltese pronunciation is helpful, especially for reading place names which often do not sound at all how they look. The letters which cause most confusion are: ċ – ch (as in church); ġ – j: għ – silent; h – silent, except at the end of a word when it is aspirated; ħ – h; j – y; m – m, except if the initial M is followed by a consonant, when it becomes im (Mdina is therefore imDEEnah); q – silent, x – sh; ż – tz; z – z. For those who feel tempted to give Maltese a go, here are some basic words and phrases.

GREETINGS AND COMMON WORDS

Yes **Iva**
No **Le**
Please **Jekk jogħġbok**
Thank you **Grazzi**
Hello **Merħba**
Goodbye **Saħħa**
Good morning **Bonġu**
Good evening **Bonswa**
How are you? **Kif int?**
Sorry **Jiddispjaċini**
Excuse me **Skużi**
My name is... **Jisimni...**
Do you speak English? **Titkellem bl-Ingliz?**
I don't understand **Ma nifimx**
How much? **Kemm?**

EMERGENCY!

Help! **Ajjut!**
Stop! **Ieqaf!**
Stop that thief! **Ieqaf halliel!**
Police! **Pulizija**
Fire! **Nar!**
I've lost my purse/wallet **Tlift il-wallet**
My passport has been stolen **Insteeraqli il-passaport**
Could you call me a doctor? **Qibgħad ghat-tabib?**

DIRECTIONS AND TRAVELLING

Airport **Ajruplan**
Beach **Plajja**
Bus **Karozza tal-linja**
Bus station **Stazzjon tal karozza tal-linja**
Car **Karozza**
Cave **Għar**
Church **Knisja**
Cliff **Rdum**
Hospital **Sptar**
Market **Suq**
Museum **Mużew**

Sandy bay **Ramla**
Square **Pjazza**
Street **Triq**
Taxi rank **Taxi**
Ticket **Biljett**
  Return **Bir-ritorn**
  Single **Singlu**
Non-smoking **Tpejjipx**
Reserved **Riservat**
Seat **Seat/post**
Station **Stazzjon tal**
Timetable **Orarju**
Left **Xellug**
Right **Lemin**
Straight on **Dritt il-quddiem**
Where is...? **Fejn hu...?**
My car has broken down **Waqfitli l-karroza**
My car has a puncture **Il-karroza tieghi għanda puncture**

MONEY

American dollar **Dollaru Amerikan**
Bank **Bank**
Banknote **Karta tal-flus**
Cash desk **Cash**
Cashier **Kaxxier**
Cheque **Cheque**
Coin **Munita**
Commission charge **Senserija**
Credit card **Karta ta'kredtu**
Exchange office **Uffiċju tal-kambju**
Exchange rate **Rata tal-kambju**
Foreign currency **Flus barranin**
Foreign exchange **Uffiċju tal-kambju**
Post office **Posta**
Pound Sterling **Lira sterlina**

ACCOMMODATION

Air-conditioning **Kundizzjunata**
Balcony **Gallarija**
Bathroom **Kamra tal banju**
Chambermaid **Kamriera**
Hot water **Ilma sħun**
Hotel **Lukanda**

Useful words and phrases 177

Key **Ċiavetta**
Lift **Lift**
Reservation **Riserva**
Room **Kamra**
...single **singlu**
...double **doppja**
...one/two nights **lejl/żweġ iljieli**
...per person **kull persona**
...per room **kull kamra**
Room service **Servizz fil-kamra**
Shower **Doċċa**
Telephone **Telefon**
Towel **Xugaman**
Water **Ilma**

RESTAURANT

I'd like to book a table **Nixtieq nibb-bukja mejda**
A table for two please **Mejdaghal tnejn jekk jogħġbok**
Where are the toilets please? **Fejn huma it-toilets, jekk jogħġbok?**
That was very good (of food/drink) **Tajjeb ħafna**
Beer **Birra**
Bill **Kont**
Bread **Hobż**
Breakfast **L-ewwel ikla tal-jum**
Café **Café**
Coffee **Kafe**
Dessert **Deserta**
Dinner **Jantar**
Drink **Xorb**
Ice **Sliġ**
Lunch **Kolazjonn**
Main course **Ikla**
Menu **Menu**
Milk **Halib**
Pepper **Bzar**
Restaurant **Restorant**
Salt **Melħ**
Set menu **Menu fiss**
Table **Mejda**
Waiter **Waiter**
Water **Ilma**
Wine **Inbid**
Wine list **Lista ta'l-inbid**

DAYS

Today **Illum**
Tomorrow **Għada**
Yesterday **Il-bierah**
Tonight **Il-lejla**
Last night **Il-lejli-għadda**
In the morning **Fil-għodu**
In the afternoon **Wara nofs in-nhar**
In the evening **Fil-għaxija**
Later **Iktar tard**
This week **Din il-gimgħa**
Next week **Il-gimgħa D-dieħla**

Monday **It-tnejn**
Tuesday **It-tlieta**
Wednesday **L-erbgħa**
Thursday **Il-ħamis**
Friday **Il-gimgħa**
Saturday **Is-sibt**
Sunday **Il-ħadd**

PLACE PRONOUCIATION GUIDE

Birżebbuga	beer-zee-booja
Borġ in-Nadur	borjin nah-DOOR
Buġibba	buj-ibba
Ġgantija	j'GAHN-tee-yah
Għar Dalam	ahr DAH-lam
Għar Ħassan	ahr hahs-SAHN
Għar Lapsi	ahr LAHP see
Għarb	ahrb
Ħaġar Qim	hajar-eem
Hypogeum	hi-po-gee-um
Marsamxett	mar-sam-schett
Marsaxlokk	marsa-schlok
Mdina	im-deenah
Mġarr	im-jar
Naxxar	nash-shar
Qala	ala
Qawra	owwra
Qormi	or-me
Siġġiewi	SEEJ-jee-eh-wee
Tarxien	tar-sheen
Xaghra	shar-rur
Xlendi	shlen-dee
Żebbuġ	ZEHB-booj
Żejtun	ZAY-toon

NUMBERS

0 xejn	6 sitta	12 tnax	18 tmintax
1 wiehed	7 sebgħa	13 tlett ax	19 dsatax
2 tnejn	8 tmienja	14 erbatax	20 għoxrin
3 tileta	9 disgħa	15 ħmistax	30 tletin
4 erbgħa	10 għaxra	16 sittax	40 erbgħin
5 ħamsa	11 ħdax	17 sbatax	50 ħamsin

Atlas

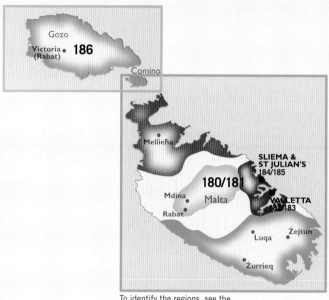

Gozo
Victoria
(Rabat) • **186**

Comino

Mellieħa

SLIEMA &
ST JULIAN'S
184/185

180/181

Mdina
Rabat   Malta

VALLETTA
182/183

Luqa   Żejtun

Żurrieq

To identify the regions, see the
map on the inside of the front cover

Regional Maps

▬▬ Major route			□	Town
░░░ Main road			○○	Village
── Other road			▣	Featured place of interest
─ ─ Ferry route			■	Place of interest
□ City			✈	Airport

180/181 — 0   1   2   3 km / 0   2   3 miles

186 — 0   1   2   3 km / 0   1   2 miles

City Plans

░░░ City wall		▒ Park
─ ─ Ferry route		▣ Featured place of interest
▤ Important building		

182/183 — 0   100   200 metres / 0   100   200 yards

184/185 — 0   100   200 metres / 0   100   200 yards

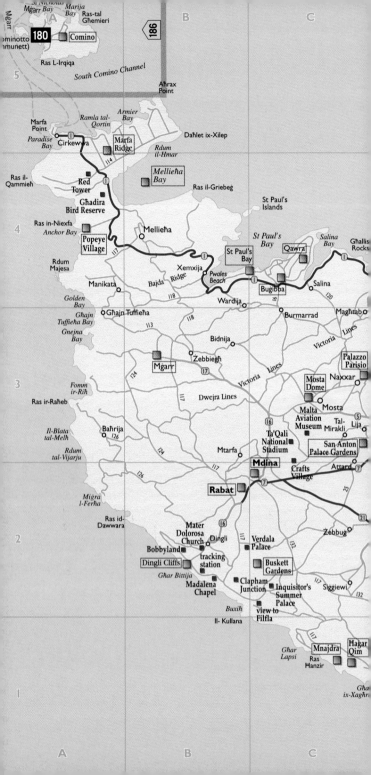

D   E   F

5

4

3

2

1

Qalet Marku

Ras il-Qrejten

Baħar iċ-Cagħaq (White Rocks)

Baħar iċ-Cagħaq

Ras L-Irqieqa

Madliena

Pembroke

Paceville

Għargħur

Swieqi

Spinola Bay

St Julian's Bay

127

St Julian's

Sliema

L-Iklin

San Gwann

128

Dragut Point

Marsamxett Harbour

St Elmo's Point

Manoel Island

Balzan

Birkirkara

Ta'xbiex

VALLETTA

Grand Harbour

20

19

Msida

Pietà

22

Floriana

Kalkara

Fort Ricasoli

Santa Venera

Ħamrun

Marsa

Marsa Creek

Senglea

Vittoriosa (Birgu)

Xgħajra

Ras il-Gebel

Blata l-Bajda

Qormi

Marsa Racecourse

Marsa Sports Club

9

Paola

Cospicua

24

Żabbar

Sala Rock

Għar id-Duħħa

8

Ħal Saflieni Hypogeum

Tarxien Temples

23

Marsaskala

Zonqor Point

Marsaskala Bay

152

Luqa

9

Santa Lucija

Tarxien

26

Żejtun

134

Gżira Point

Mignuna Point

St Thomas' Bay

134

Malta International Airport

132

136

9

Gudja

Għaxaq

28

29

30

137

Mqabba

31

Kirkop

Qrendi

139

Safi

Żurrieq

117

Ras -il Bajjada

Blue Grotto

Ghar Dalam Cave and Museum

Marsaxlokk

Delimara Power Station

Delimara Peninsula

Peter's Pool

Tumbrell Point

Birżebbuġa

St George's Bay

Pretty Bay

Marsaxlokk Bay

Delimara Point

117

Kalafrana

Malta Freeport

142

Ħal-Far

Għar Ħasan

D   E   F

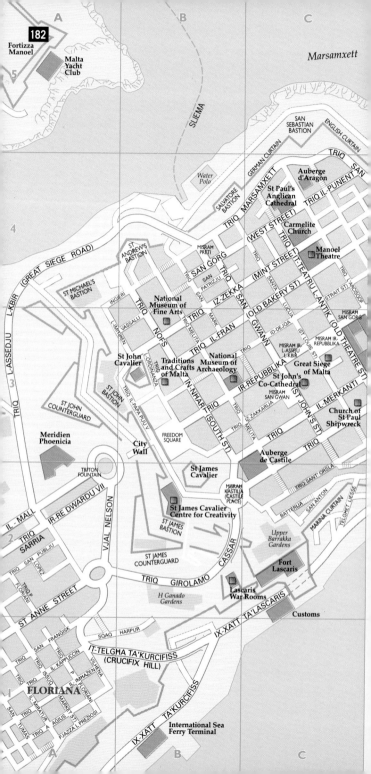

Fortizza
Manoel

Malta
Yacht
Club

Marsamxett

FORTIZZA MANOEL

SLIEMA

SAN
SEBASTIAN
BASTION

ENGLISH CURTAIN

Water
Polo

GERMAN CURTAIN

SALVATORE
BASTION

TRIQ IL-MARSAMXETT

Auberge
d'Aragon

TRIQ SAN

TRIQ IL-PUNENT

St Paul's
Anglican
Cathedral

(WEST STREET)

Carmelite
Church

Manoel
Theatre

ST ANDREW'S
BASTION

MISRAH
PRETI

SAN GORG

TRIQ SAN PATRIZJU

(MINT STREET)

IT-TEATRU L-ANTIK (OLD THEATRE ST)

TRIQ MARCISSO

STRAIT ST

ST MICHAEL'S
BASTION

INGERI

TRIQ SAN MARK

IZ-ZEKKA

TRIQ SANTA
LUCIJA

TRIQ ID-DEJQA

MISRAH
SAN GORG

TRIQ NOFS IN-NHAR (GREAT SIEGE ROAD)

TRIQ L-ASSEDJU L-KBIR

L'MPEREN

L.VASSALLI

TRIQ MELITA

SAN GWANN

(OLD BAKERY ST)

ID-DEJQA

ST LOUIS ST

MISRAH
IR-REPUBBLIKA

National
Museum of
Fine Arts

TRIQ IL-FRAN

MISRAH IR-
LASSEIU
L-KBIR

Great Siege
of Malta

St John
Cavalier

ST JOHN
BASTION

TRIQ IL-PAPA PIJU V

Traditions
and Crafts
of Malta

TRIQ IL-KORDINANZA

IN-NHAR (SOUTH ST)

National
Museum of
Archaeology

TRIQ IR-REPUBBLIKA

St John's
Co-Cathedral

MISRAH
SAN GWAN

TRIQ IZ-ZAKKARIJA

TRIQ ST JOHN'S ST

IL-MERKANTI

Church
of St Paul
Shipwreck

ST JOHN
COUNTERGUARD

Meridien
Phoenicia

TRIQ MELITA

TRITON
FOUNTAIN

City
Wall

FREEDOM
SQUARE

TRIQ

Auberge
de Castile

IL-MALL

IR-RE DWARDU VII

VJAL NELSON

St James
Cavalier

St James Cavalier
Centre for Creativity

MISRAH
(KASTILJA
(CASTLE
PLACE)

TRIQ SANT ORSLA

SAN ANTON

BATTERIJA

MARINA CURTAIN

TELGHET L'ESSE

TRIQ
SARRIA

ST JAMES
BASTION

Upper
Barrakka
Gardens

TRIQ SAN
PUBLIJU

TRIQ SAN
LOPE

TRIQ
FLORIANI

ST JAMES
COUNTERGUARD

CASSAR

Fort
Lascaris

ST ANNE STREET

TRIQ GIROLAMO

H Ganado
Gardens

Lascaris
War Rooms

IX-XATT TA'LASCARIS

Customs

SOAQ   HARPUR

IT-TELGHA TA'KURCIFISS
(CRUCIFIX HILL)

TRIQ SAN
FRANGISK

TRIQ
OSSUO

IL-KAPPUCCIN

TRIQ
FLORIANI

IL-MHAZENI

FLORIANA

TRIQ
MIRATUR

TRIQ A
AGIUS

TRIQ
TUMAS

PIAZZA L'PREZIOSI

IX-XATT TA'KURCIFISS

International Sea
Ferry Terminal

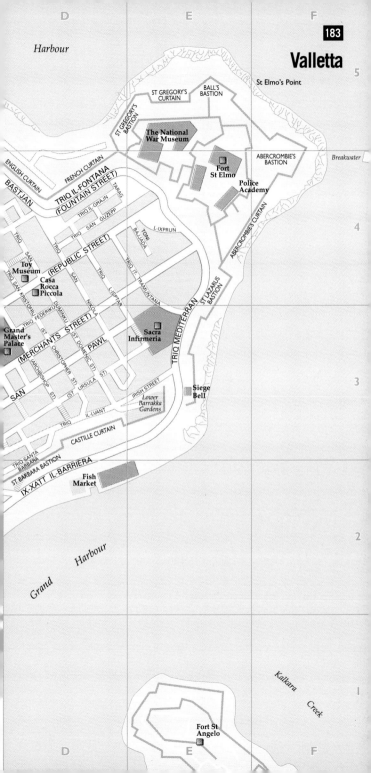

Valletta

Harbour

St Elmo's Point

ST GREGORY'S
CURTAIN

BALL'S
BASTION

ST GREGORY'S BASTION

The National
War Museum

Fort
St Elmo

ABERCROMBIE'S
BASTION

Breakwater

Police
Academy

ENGLISH CURTAIN

FRENCH CURTAIN

TRIQ IL-FONTANA
(FOUNTAIN STREET)

BASTJAN

TRIQ IL-GHAJN

TARAG

TRIQ SAN GUZEPP

L-IXPRUN

TRIQ

REPUBLIC STREET

TONI
BAJADA

TRIQ SAN

ABERCROMBIE'S CURTAIN

Toy
Museum

TRIQ SAN KRISTOFRU

TRIQ SAN

TRIQ IL-TRAMUNTANA

Casa
Rocca
Piccola

NIKOLA

L-ISPTAR

TRIQ FEDERIKU

DUMINKU

Grand
Master's
Palace

(MERCHANTS STREET)

CHRISTOPHER ST

IST DOMENC ST

Sacra
Infirmeria

ST LAZARUS BASTION

PAWL

TRIQ MEDITERRAN

ARCHBISHOP ST)

IST URSULA ST

SAN

IRISH STREET

Siege
Bell

IL-LVANT

*Lower
Barrakka
Gardens*

TRIQ

CASTILLE CURTAIN

TRIQ SANTA
BARBARA

ST BARBARA BASTION

IX-XATT IL-BARRIERA

Fish
Market

Grand

Harbour

*Kalkara
Creek*

Fort St
Angelo

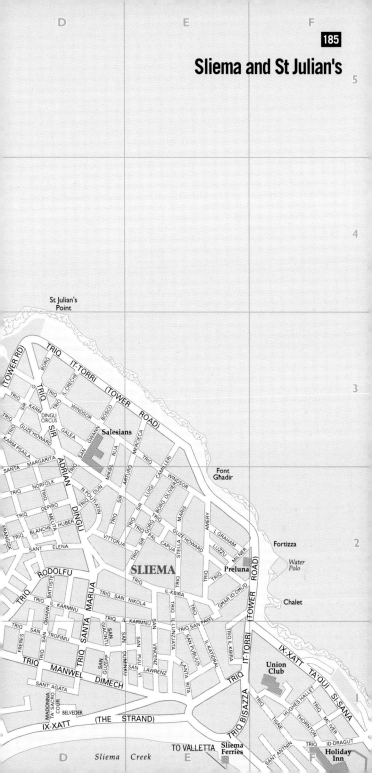

Sliema and St Julian's

St Julian's
Point

TRIQ IT-TORRI (TOWER ROAD)

(TOWER RD)

TRIQ

BORG

IL-CRECHE

WINDSOR

BOSCO

MERCIECA

Salesians

TRIQ

SIR

KARM

DINGLI
CIRCUS

GUZE HOWARD

GALEA

SAN GWANN

MIKIEL

RUA

ARTURO

CAMILLERI

WINDSOR

KARM PSAILA

TRIQ

SANTA
MARGARITA

SIR

ADRIAN

TRIQ

N POLITATIN

SIR

LUIGI

BORG OLIVIER

MARIS

AMERY

L GRAHAM

Font
Ghadir

TRIQ

NORFOLK

DEPIRO

DINGLI

SIR
GORG

SIR

GUZE-HOWARD

LUZZU

MILNER

Fortizza

FRANGISK

TRIQ

BLANCHE

MELITA

HUBER

TRIQ

PAL

CAPUA

STELLA

Water
Polo

SANT ELENA

VITTORJA

TRIQ

TRIQ

SLIEMA

IL-KBIRA

GMAR ID-DHUD

Preluna

Chalet

RODOLFU

BATTISTE

IL-KARMNU

TRIQ

TRIQ SAN NIKOLA

TRIQ

TRIQ SAN PAWL

IL-KBIRA

IT-TORRI (TOWER ROAD)

IX-XATT TA'QUI SI.SANA

TRIQ

SAN

TRIQ

SANTA
MARIJA

IL-KARMNU

TRIQ

SAN

VINCENZ

SAN PUBLIUS

TRIQ IL-KATIDRAL

SAN

GWANN

SAN
TROFIMU

GIADU

SAN

SAN
GUZEPP

PIJU

DUMINKU

SAN
LAWRENZ

SANTA
RITA

**Union
Club**

TRIQ

FRERES

TRIQ

MANWEL

DIMECH

SANT' AGATA

MADONNA
TA' SACRO
COUR

BELVEDER

HUGHES HALLET

TRIQ

TIGNE

THORNTON

MC IVER

IX-XATT

(THE STRAND)

TRIQ BISAZZA

SANT ANTNIN

TRIQ

ID-DRAGUT

**Holiday
Inn**

Sliema Creek

TO VALLETTA

**Sliema
Ferries**

D   E   F

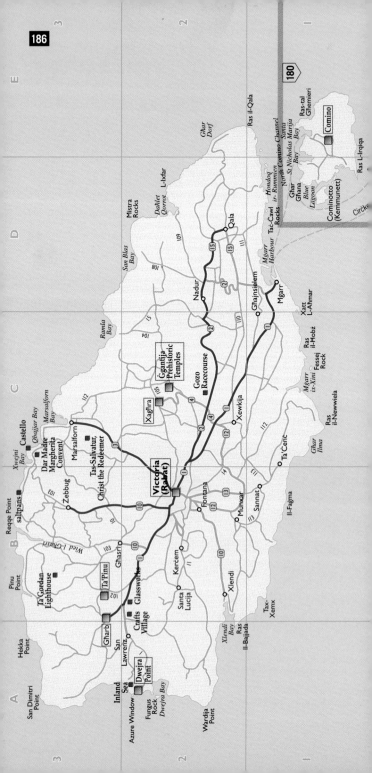

180

San Dimitri Point

Hekka Point

Pinu Point

Ta'Gordan Lighthouse

Reqqe Point
saltpans

Xwejni Bay
Castello

Qbajjar Bay

Marsalforn Bay

Dar Madre Margherita Convent

Marsalforn

Tas-Salvatur, Christ the Redeemer

Zebbug

Wied l-Ghasri

Ghasri

Ta'Pinu

Glassworks

Crafts Village

Gharb

San Lawrenz

Dwejra Point

Inland Sea

Azure Window

Fungus Rock
Dwejra Bay

Wardija Point

Kercem

Santa Lucija

Xlendi
Bay
Ras
Il-Bajjada

Tax-Xemx

Xlendi

San Blas Bay

Ramla Bay

Ghar Dorf

Dahlet Qorrot
L-Ixfar

Mistra Rocks

Nadur

Gozo Racecourse

Ġgantija Prehistoric Temples

Xaghra

Victoria (Rabat)

Fontana

Munxar

Sannat

Ta'Cenc

Ghar Ilma

Il-Fagma

Il-Newwiela

Ras Il-Newwiela

Xewkija

Qala

Għajnsielem

Mġarr

Mġarr Harbour

Xatt L-Ahmar

Ras il-Hobz

Fessej Rock

Mġarr ix-Xini

Ras il-Qala

North Comino Channel

Hondoq ir-Rummien

Tac-Cawl Rocks

Ghar Sta Marija

Santa Marija Bay

Ghana Bay

Blue Lagoon

Cominotto (Kemmunett)

Comino

Ras-tal Ghemieri

Ras L-Irqiqa

Circke

Index

Picture credits

Abbreviations for terms appearing below: (t) top; (b) bottom; (l) left; (r) right; (c) centre.

The Automobile Association wishes to thank the following photo libraries and photographers for their assistance in the preparation of this book.

Front and Back Cover: (t) and (ct) AA Photo Library/Philip Enticknap; (cb) VISIT MALTA; (b) AA Photo Library/Alex Kouprianoff; Spine: AA Photo Library/Wyn Voysey.

AKG, LONDON 62, 86/87; CORBIS (UK) LTD 63 (Araldo de Luca), 168 (Lawson Wood); MARY EVANS PICTURE LIBRARY 10/11; RONALD GRANT ARCHIVE 25, 26cl; HULTON GETTY 11t, 12t, 12b, 18; PAUL MURPHY 19t, 20t, 24t, 26cr, 30, 59b, 66, 84c, 167; THE ART ARCHIVE 87 (Dagli Orti [A]), 88t (National Museum, La Valletta, Malta/Dagli Orti [A]); THE TRAVEL LIBRARY 50, 102cr, 108/109, 137b, 142/143, 165, 169; VISIT MALTA 2iv, 3iii, 3iv, 6, 21t, 22t, 22b, 45c, 49, 81, 102cl, 133, 136t, 139t, 153, 162.

The remaining photographs are held in the Association's own photo library (AA PHOTO LIBRARY and were taken by ALEX KOUPRIANOFF, with the exception of the following: PHILIP ENTICKNAP 3i, 7, 8t, 13, 14t, 14/15, 23c, 23b, 24c, 45t, 53, 56, 57, 83b, 89t, 90, 92, 93t, 95c, 95b, 99, 101t, 102b, 107c, 107b, 117b, 134, 160; WYN VOYSEY 93b, 103b, 154, 159, 163, 175t, 175br.

Questionnaire

Dear Traveller

Your comments, opinions and recommendations are very important to us. So please help us to improve our travel guides by taking a few minutes to complete this simple questionnaire.

You do not need a stamp (unless posted outside the UK). If you do not want to remove this page from your guide, then photocopy it or write your answers on a plain sheet of paper.

Send to: The Editor, Spiral Guides, AA World Travel Guides, FREEPOST SCE 4598, Basingstoke RG21 4GY.

Your recommendations...

We always encourage readers' recommendations for restaurants, night-life or shopping – if your recommendation is used in the next edition of the guide, we will send you a FREE AA Spiral Guide of your choice. Please state below the establishment name, location and your reasons for recommending it.

_____

_____

_____

_____

_____

Please send me AA Spiral _____

(see list of titles inside the back cover)

About this guide...

Which title did you buy?

_____ **AA Spiral**

Where did you buy it? _____

When? m m / y y

Why did you choose an AA Spiral Guide? _____

_____

_____

_____

Did this guide meet your expectations?

Exceeded ☐   Met all ☐   Met most ☐   Fell below ☐

Please give your reasons _____

_____

_____

_____

_____

continued on next page...

continued on next page...

Were there any aspects of this guide that you particularly liked?

_____
_____
_____
_____
_____

Is there anything we could have done better?

_____
_____
_____
_____
_____
_____

About you...

Name (Mr/Mrs/Ms) _____

Address _____

_____

_____ **Postcode** _____

Daytime tel nos _____

Which age group are you in?

Under 25 ☐   25–34 ☐   35–44 ☐   45–54 ☐   55–64 ☐   65+ ☐

How many trips do you make a year?

Less than one ☐   One ☐   Two ☐   Three or more ☐

Are you an AA member? Yes ☐   No ☐

About your trip...

When did you book? mm / y y   **When did you travel?** mm / y y

How long did you stay? _____

Was it for business or leisure? _____

Did you buy any other travel guides for your trip? ☐ Yes ☐ No

If yes, which ones? _____

_____

Thank you for taking the time to complete this questionnaire. Please send it to us as soon as possible, and remember, you do not need a stamp (unless posted outside the UK).

We may use information we hold about you to write or telephone you about other products and services offered by us and our carefully selected partners. Information may be disclosed to other companies in the Centrica group (including those using the British Gas, Scottish Gas, goldfish, One-Tel and AA brands) but we can assure you that we will not disclose it to third parties.

Please tick the box if you do not wish to receive details of other products and services from the AA

☐